Unlovable

SHAWN SPENCER

Copyright © 2022 Shawn Spencer.

All rights reserved. No part of this book may be reproduced, stored, or transmitted by any means—whether auditory, graphic, mechanical, or electronic—without written permission of both publisher and author, except in the case of brief excerpts used in critical articles and reviews. Unauthorized reproduction of any part of this work is illegal and is punishable by law.

ISBN: 979-8-88640-412-8 (sc)
ISBN: 979-8-88640-413-5 (hc)
ISBN: 979-8-88640-414-2 (e)

Because of the dynamic nature of the Internet, any web addresses or links contained in this book may have changed since publication and may no longer be valid. The views expressed in this work are solely those of the author and do not necessarily reflect the views of the publisher, and the publisher hereby disclaims any responsibility for them.

One Galleria Blvd., Suite 1900, Metairie, LA 70001
1-888-421-2397

CONTENTS

Chapter 1　Introduction to Shawn 1
Chapter 2　Coming to America 17
Chapter 3　Leaving Me Now 40
Chapter 4　New Beginnings 72
Chapter 5　The Bandwagon 119
Chapter 6　On My Own Again 129
Chapter 7　New Beginnings 140
Chapter 8　Melvina's Story 205
Chapter 9　Brothers' Bonds 213
Chapter 10　Home Running 217

Chapter 1

INTRODUCTION TO SHAWN

No time in my life had ever been good until at the age of ten, except for when I lived with my grandmother in a West African country called Liberia. You see, my parents had me at a young age; and when my mother's father found out that my mom was pregnant with me, he threw her out when he discovered that my dad was the one she claimed was the father. My grandfather, being a high-ranking military man, went to my dad and told him to deny the baby and get on with his life. And if my father was to agree to this proposal, my granddad would not go and report him to my dad's eldest brother, whom they called Mr. Spencer, who was also my grandfather's best friend, with whom my dad lived, and who treated him more like a servant than a family member because of the wife of my dad's brother.

When my father was about ten years old, his father died. My grandfather was a wealthy guy, but he had over fifty children and was married to thirteen women, with my dad's mom being the thirteenth wife, who bore eleven children. When he was alive, my grandfather was big on education, so all the elder children, like my father's eldest brother and the eldest child from the other women, were put through school. They were supposed to take care of their younger siblings and their mothers. Mr. Spencer was so academically inclined that he got a scholarship but never told his father. During school breaks when he came home, his father would give him tuition money for the next year, which he took and used to pay the tuition of his friends who needed it. He was a great guy. And after he graduated, he had a job with Citibank in Nigeria as a young vice president. Since my dad was his favorite younger brother, he took care of him and treated him well until he got married. His wife got him to only take care of her family, so when my dad was in the house, he was treated more like a servant. It's funny how life turns out. Even my dad's other brother Francis, who was older and a man, could not even shower in their house; he had to use a hose out back.

So it was while living with his brother that my dad met my mom. Because my mom's dad and Mr. Spencer were best friends, their families were close, so my dad was the only boy there when my mom's dad would come into the compound. My dad would tell me how he would go visit, and my mom's dad would talk his head off for hours before he would tell him, "The girls are in the back. You should go see," which was the only reason he was there in the first place.

After the visits, my dad would head back, at which time my mom's dad would give him cab fare to get home, but he kept the money and walked so he could have money for school because, even though Mr. Spencer made a lot of money, my father had to earn it himself. Mr. Spencer and my mom's dad were pretty wealthy guys; to explain it using today's term, it would be like Colin Powell and Bill Gates being friends, but with all that wealth, they never helped the people close to them.

Anyway, when my dad refused my grandfather's offer, my mom's dad went to his friend Mr. Spencer and told him about the pregnancy. Mr. Spencer kicked my dad out of the house. So at twenty-one, my dad—still in school—had to find a place for his pregnant girlfriend. He was able to ask a friend to let my mother crash on the floor, while he had no place to go. So he went to the marketplace and waited for everyone to leave, and then he would sleep on one of the tables until morning.

After a few weeks of this, he decided to leave and pay for a correspondence course from England with the money he had. He took the test, passed it, and was able to get a job earning sixty dollars a week, which was real good money at that time and today would probably be like a thousand. So with that money, he got an apartment with some furniture, and he went to get my mother, putting her there. He applied for another job earning three hundred dollars a week, which he saved to put both of them through school in America. He planned to tell her about this after she gave birth, and he was not going to wait long.

Lopu started yelling at the top of her voice; the pain was too much. The doctors told her to push, but she refused; she said she was not going to give birth until my dad was there, but they told her that I would soon be coming. "No!" she yelled "Frank! Frank!"

My dad was out of breath, trying figure out where he should go, so he started running when he heard a nurse ask him, "Are you Frank?"

"Yes," my dad replied, turning around.

"Well, come on," the nurse said, grabbing and pulling on him.

As they ran through the halls, he could hear my mom yelling. "Lopu," he said, calling out to her. "I'm coming! Hold on!" He ran in the room, reaching out his hands and touching her, and then he saw something he never wanted to see again as I was pulled out, screaming, and given to him. But he just stood there in shock, so they put me in my mother's arms, and I think she loved me at that point because she was happy.

My grandfather I was talking about was not my biological grandfather, but he was the second husband of my mother's mother. He was in the military as well, but he was only sergeant first class, not an officer like my biological grandfather, whom I only saw once anyway, so I really did not even know him, and I did not care to. So my grandfather, whose name I cannot pronounce until this day, held he was almost seven feet tall and over 280 pounds. I would remember later, as I got older, how my hand would disappear inside his, and when he picked me up to put me on his shoulder, it scared me because he did it so fast that I would cry. He would say, "My grandson doesn't love me," but I really loved him and thought he must be strongest guy in the world.

As the nurse tried to get me out of my grandfather's hand, he refused to let me go because my grandmother, who was called Ma Korto, had not yet arrived, and he wanted her to see me first. He only relented when the nurse informed him that she would be right back with me.

While they waited for my return, my dad came out of his daze and started speaking. "I have never seen anything like that before," he said as he sat down.

It had almost been an hour when my grandmother arrived, and a nurse brought a baby for my grandmother to see. My grandfather, being a military man and always alert, said, "That's not my grandson."

The nurse started to argue with him, saying, "Sir, this is your baby."

"I know my grandson. His my first one, and I held her longer than anyone, and that's not him," my grandfather argued back. Another nurse walked in with me in her arms, and immediately, my grandfather stood up. "That's him. That's my grandson."

"Yes," the nurse replied. "Sorry about that." The nurse placed me in my grandmother's arms, and I would remain with her from here on out.

After leaving the hospital, my mother, my grandmother, and my dad, along with me, all went home together, at which time my dad informed my mother that he was sending her to America for her studies. She started screaming, which surprised me, causing me to start crying. "Are you serious? How? I mean why?" She kept mumbling her words as she tried to understand how he had been able to do this in such a short period.

For most people, coming to America was only a dream; and when people spoke of it, they would say, "Everyone is rich, there is no trash, there's no suffering, and it's all free in America." Obviously, most of the people who spread that crap had never been to America, and the ones who did make it there only wanted to go back home because they complained that all they did was work and pay bills and there was no time for anything else. "At least back home, you saw what you are working for. Even with all of that, America is still better than most places in the world. It may not be heaven, but it's up there."

My father pulled out the plane ticket to show her that it was real, and she would be leaving in a week. Before he had even bought the tickets, he told a few of his friends his plans, and all of them told him he was crazy to be sending a woman instead of going himself. "To come to

America is like winning the lottery, so why would you give the winning ticket to someone else instead of cashing it in yourself?" But being the man he was, my dad never went back on his word, and so he got ready to send her. Besides, he planned on marrying my mother; she was his first love, the love of his life, so no one could change his mind.

On the day of her departure, my father had borrowed his boss's car to see his best girl off, but she had plans of her own. She had also gotten her boss's car, but the only different thing was her boss was driving. When I, my grandma, and my dad got in one car, she got into the other car with her boss, at which time my grandmother asked her why she was not riding with us but got no reply. My dad told my grandma not to worry about it. And with that, they sat silently on their way to the airport, not that my dad and grandmother could communicate anyway because she did not speak English, only Lurma, her native tongue, and my mother had to translate everything they said. My grandmother was really fond of my dad; she thought he was the best and could do no wrong in her eyes.

We finally arrived at the airport, and we went inside to see her off. In those days, you could walk all the way through the airport to the gate with the traveling person, so my dad pulled my mom to the side to talk to her privately. "I know where you were last night. I know the hotel, I know with whom you were, and I even know what you ate for breakfast."

My mother started to cry; she looked at the tickets in my dad's hands as if she wanted to grab it and run because she just knew there was no way in hell he was sending her now. So she must have been thinking, *Why did he bring me here anyway?* My father handed her the ticket, told her he would see her in a month, and watched as she went down to the tarmac. And just before she got on the plane, he saw her kissing her boss and got on the plane.

The car ride back home was even quieter as my dad cried the whole way back, and I think my grandmother understood what had happened as well. She held me close to her, singing some songs, at which time I fell asleep.

Early the next morning, my grandmother woke up and packed her bags, as well as mine, and we left my dad to head back to the country of my grandmother. Even though she was illiterate, she was a businesswoman, and she ran her own market, which was mostly for the tourists who visited and was situated next to a bus stop, where travelers could stop and buy things for the long trips they were about to embark on. Besides the market, my grandmother also rented out rooms in her house to students, young couples, or anyone needing a place to rent, but it was usually medical students because we lived right next to a big hospital where a lot of them studied and worked at before going to America. Even though she could not read or write, my grandmother could count, and she knew money, and no one could cheat her out of it.

Unfortunately for my grandmother, she had become a mother all over again by taking me, and I would become a burden whom she would love regardless. I was a sick child, and not too long after being with her, my whole body turned yellow, including my eyes, and she ran me to the hospital where I would stay for two. She and my grandfather stayed with me the whole time. I started remembering being in the hospital because it would happen repeatedly.

It was around this time when my grandmother and grandfather separated only because I don't remember seeing as much except those days—more like months—I was in the hospital, but what I do remember was my uncle Flomoson, who lived with us, was abusive toward my grandmother every time he got drunk. Well, he would turn on his poor wife first, and when my grandmother tried to stop him, he would turn it on her. Man, I hated him, and even at that age, I hated him, and I wanted to kill him. I never hated anyone more than I hated him, and since then, there's been no one I hated more. You see, my grandmother was everything to me; she was my father, my mother, my Christmas, and everything that's good in this world.

As I got older, my grandmother pushed education on me, so I started school at the age of three. Unlike in America where you had to be five to get to kindergarten, they started you in school as soon as you can talk, and I learned my alphabets, as well as my time tables, in the first grade; there was no kindergarten. And if you did not pass your test, you wouldn't get automatically transferred to the next grade; you'd repeat it all over. I was in class with some older kids, and before long, I was in the second grade. By the age of four, I was in the third grade. I was a very good student, and my grandmother was proud of that fact.

When I learned to speak English, she was even prouder because I would go to the market with her to sell things to the tourists who spoke English, and all the markets were run by people who did not speak the language. So being as cute as I was, I would talk to the tourist, see what they wanted, go back to my grandmother, get the products to the tourist, and give her the money.

It was while I was doing this that I heard someone whom I didn't know call my name. I stood there until my grandmother told me, "That's your father," at which time I cried and ran to him. He picked me up and spun me around, and the way he called my name was better than I had heard anyone call me. Hugging him tight, he carried me to the car and helped my grandmother pack up, and we headed home. He gave me all the toys and new clothes he had bought, which no other kid in the village had or had ever seen, and kids I had never known before suddenly knew my name and wanted to be my friend. Of course, my dad bought gifts for my grandmother as well, like a radio with a neon light on the top, and he would give her money. Everywhere he went, I went, and people follow. You see, for most people in the village, to be able to travel to America or to live there was a huge accomplishment, so he was a sort of hero to them. And I, being his son, was automatically better than most of them. I know it's crazy, but that's how it is.

So for the next few days, I tailed my dad everywhere, always sitting on his lap or holding on to his hand. My father, being a young man at the time, was crazy about women. He had this toy on his key chain of a man and woman having sex as you moved them up and down, and he tried to shield it from my eyes as he showed it to other people, but I really did not care about that. I was just fixated on him the whole time, so nothing else really mattered to me.

After three days of wonderful bliss with my father, he was gone, and I cried that whole day and refused to eat. My dear grandmother told me it would be okay and that he would be back, but that did nothing for me. She even made my favorite meal, but I did not eat. She was worried, especially with me being sick as I had been, so as we were lying down for the night, she told me, "If you keep crying and your tears get on the pillow, you will go blind." I did not care, but after thinking about it, I made an effort to stop and finally cried myself to sleep.

Waking up the next day, I was sad all over, but I would try to remember my dad's voice, especially the way he called my name. It was not too long before I was back in the hospital, and my grandmother was by my bedside, crying and praying. These were the only times I would see my grandfather; he would come mostly at night with my favorite soda, the orange Fanta. It gave my grandmother a chance to stretch her legs and go home, get some sleep, and pick up some new clothes for herself and for me; and when she got back, she always had something new for me. So it was not too long that I was released to go home, and my grandmother would tell me, "Your daddy is coming. Just get better." But I never saw him anytime I was in the hospital, but as she promised, he would surprise me with a visit every now and again.

As time went, I was in and out of the hospital, and my grandmother had to make trips to pick up supplies for her market, so she got me a babysitter —some girl who was around nineteen years old, I'm guessing. Being sick as I was, my grandmother wanted someone who would pay full attention to me, and this girl did just that.

On the first day she was to watch me, she played with me outside, and then she brought me in the house, where we played hide-and-seek, and that was when things changed. She was supposed to hide while I sought her out, but she called out to me to come in the room where she was, so I ran in the room to tell her she was playing the game all wrong. I saw her completely naked, sitting on the bed, and she told me to get on top of her. Then she took off my clothes and instructed me to play with her breast and suck on it, which I did. She made me put my hand inside her, and I did, but I did not like that too much; it felt funny to me. But that was nothing compared with her placing my head between her legs and holding it there for a while, and no matter how hard I tried, I could not move; it was as if I was suffocating. I was okay with just about everything until she did that. When she finally let me up, I gasped for air and still thought nothing was wrong with what just happened. I had heard my elder cousins talking about their sexual escapades, and I figured this girl was doing me a favor and was making me a man. And when she told me not to tell my grandmother, I promised her I wouldn't, but my elder cousins whom I looked up to, especially the one we used to call Big Boy, were a different story, and I could not wait to share this with him.

My grandmother returned from her trip the next day, and before she arrived, my cousin and some of his friends took me swimming at a place that was secluded; it had a waterfall, and like most places in Liberia, there were fruit trees of every kind. It was really beautiful. Since I did not know how to swim, my cousin told me to wait in the shallow part of the water, and they left me. They went diving for crabs, lobsters, and other fish they had the traps for, and sometimes they just dived without the trap.

As they went up and down, showing off their catches, a big fish splashed by me, and I saw the fins. All I remember thinking was that I was going to catch that fish for my grandmother. *She is going to be so proud of me, and she's going to put it in a soup.* With that, I jumped after the fish; and before I knew it, I was under the water. I could no longer see the fish, just water and a tree with roots that ran in all directions. I did not panic or anything, so I started thinking how I could get back to the top of the water. I tried to grab the tree and climb it to the top because I tried swimming and flapping my arms and got nowhere.

I must have been down there a long time because, at this time, my cousin was freaking out, looking for me. He knew if anything was to happen to me, he could never go home again. My grandmother was really protective of me because of all the ailment I suffered growing up. I even remember a time when my cousin had taken me out with him, and on the way home, I was tired, and he put me on his shoulders. When my grandmother saw me on his shoulders and not walking, she came running out to meet us asking, "What's wrong? Is he sick?" When she saw I was fine, she scolded him. "Don't ever do that again." So under those conditions, he could not let anything happen to me. Plus, he treated me more like a little brother than his cousin.

Finally, after being underwater for a while, my poor cousin was losing his mind trying to find me. He and his friends looked everywhere; all of a sudden, in all this dark, murky water, two arms pulled me out, and it was then I took a deep breath. But while I was underwater, I was fine, and I was not fighting for air or anything. After a good tongue-lashing, my cousin hugged me and asked me, "What happened? Why didn't you stay where I told you?" I proceeded to tell him about the fish and how big it was. Then he told me a story I would hear about over and over again. Thank god I was alive to hear it.

My cousin told me about a female water spirit they called Mommy Water. She fools people and causes them to drown, and if you ever see a comb laid out by the water or a body of water, never pick it up because, if you do, she will come to you in your dreams to retrieve it, but you can never give it to her. To protect it, you have to keep it in a bi???, and she will give you all the treasures you ask for. But the day you do give the comb back, she will destroy and kill you. After that story, I was scared, straight and ready to go. I never got a chance to tell him about my babysitter and what we did.

As we neared the house, I saw a car outside, and someone was getting out of it. I knew my grandmother was home, so I ran to meet her. And when she saw me coming, she ran to meet me halfway, picked me up, and hugged me for a good while before letting me go. We helped her with her bags, carrying them in the house.

I hated going into that house anytime the lights were not on because in the hallway, for some strange reason, there was a picture of this ugly white lady. The eyes of the picture followed you wherever you went, and it always crept me out. I never knew who she was until sometime later. I learned it was Queen Elizabeth. This bitch still looks the same. Was she born old? Anyhow, I could not figure out why that picture was there. As far as I know, Liberia was not an English colony. But those damn missionary brought the philosophy that white people were gods or some better forms of humans; the natives buying that bullshit is my only reasoning for the picture. This particular time, however, I did not let the picture bother me. Now my grandmother was home, and I knew she brought me a treat as she had always done.

When she had a chance to sit and tell us about how her trip went, she then inquired about how we were, what happened while she was gone, and what we had been up to. I knew better than to tell her about my fishing trip, so I gave the usual "nothing" answer for selfish reasons. I looked up to my elder cousin and wanted to hang around with him more, especially with my grandmother being so overprotective of me because of my health, which made me even more eager to prove to them I was still tough. Also, if my grandmother found out what really happened, she could not take her usual trip to resupply her store.

While I was still talking, my cousin brought up the crabs, lobsters, and other things they had caught, and he proceeded to regale her of how we came about them and how I fearlessly grabbed one of the lobsters as it tried to make its escape. My grandmother congratulated me and said how proud she was of her brave "husband," which was the title she gave me because she said I was always taking care of her.

My grandmother woke up and found me sitting up and feeling sick. I was freezing, and I felt so miserable; she did not know what to do. She woke my cousin up, telling him to start a fire, which he promptly went to do. She wrapped me in a blanket and held me as I floated in and out of consciousness.

As she held me, I saw a dark figure on the ceiling that would move its eyes and its mouth but said nothing. Now this would not be a big deal usually, but there was nothing that threw that shadow. I had seen this figure many times before, and I had informed my grandmother and my cousin; however, they could never see what I was trying to show them, and they thought I was just trying to play a game on them. I was never into that as a child as I am now. I had always seen the figure before. And it was always right before I got seriously sick and throughout my ailments. It was always only in my house that I saw it and no other time. It would come out, and I knew I was about to be really sick or something bad was going to happen.

For instance, there was a cousin of mine who was always very sickly as I always was. He had sickle cell anemia, which is a very serious, lethal, and life-threatening medical condition; and outside of the pain, you have many other issues like the damaging of major organs in your body due to lack of oxygen in your blood. The deformity of the hemoglobin produces deformed red blood cells that last for only three days before being destroyed. When a normal blood cell is usually lost for sixty days, so do to the rapid destruction of the red blood cells; the body has to work even harder to keep up the production of the red blood cells but cannot.

Anyway, as my cousin and his mom came to visit one night, he and I had to sleep in the same room. I was four at the time, and he was six. As he and I lay down, he became very ill, so I got out of bed and walked over to my grandmother's room, where she was talking to my aunt. I told them they needed to start praying for my cousin because he was about to die, which immediately got me their undivided attention. My grandmother scolded me, telling me never to say anything like that again. I asked her why not, and she told me it was not nice. But I told her it was true while we walked back toward my room. My aunt was ahead of us naturally, and she entered first. Seeing her son dead, she began to cry; so instantly, my grandmother turned me around and brought me back to her room to interrogate me about where I got the information about my cousin. That was the first time I explained to her about the shadow on the ceiling, which I had tried showing her, but she never saw it.

She kept me in her room and tried to distract me from what was going on in the house, making sure I did not see my cousin's body. She forgot to close the bedroom door, and I saw them take him out wrapped in my bedsheet. As they walked by, my grandmother realized her error, thus shutting the door as quickly as she could.

My cousin had started the fire and returned. My grandmother handed me to my cousin and told him to take me and warm me up in front of the fire. "Okay," he replied as we walked out toward the fireplace. A few moments later, my grandmother joined us and gave me a drink of some herbal medication before taking me from my cousin's arm and holding and cradling me in her arms as we sat in front of the fire.

We were there for over an hour and a half, but I was still trembling from the cold; it seemed as though I was getting colder. She took my temperature, and it was 103 degrees; that was when my grandmother gave me back to my cousin, and she went to pack us a bag for the hospital. My cousin was trying his best to cheer me up, so he sang and told me stories and a list of other things, but none of it worked. I was still drifting in and out. So as she finished packing up everything, she instructed my cousin to come on, and he got up with me in his arm and followed her out the door.

The hospital was a fifteen-minute walk from our house. Since we had no car, we headed up the hill; the only vehicle at the house was my uncle's motorcycle, but he was useless anyway. I remember that night because the moon was full and huge that you could see every star, and our path was lit up because of the show in the heavens; it was beautiful. We had electricity; sometimes it would work, but most times, the power was out, but it was not something we relied on anyway because the night sky was always lit, not like America, where you never see the sky or stars because of electricity or smog and pollution. In Liberia, there was none of that.

We arrived at the hospital, and we were checked in. The nurse was very friendly, and when she saw me, she said, "Again, your baby," as she always saw me more in the hospital than out of it. I shook my head slowly. I was very weak at this point. They started an IV, drew some blood from me, and gave me some medications, which made me even drowsier.

Upon completion of all the blood tests, the doctors got the results and explained it to my grandmother in the best that they could, but she really did not understand. My cousin and the nurse who checked me in explained to her I needed blood, but since there was no such thing as a Red Cross blood bank there, they would have to resort to getting it from a family member whose blood was compatible. Of course, when she heard this, my grandmother promptly offered herself as did my cousin. And after they both were tested, it turned out that my grandmother's blood was compatible to mine, so they put her on a bed next to me and started an IV on her, connecting it to mine. They began the transfusion, at which point the medication put me to sleep.

When I woke up the next morning, my grandmother was curled up in the bed next to me. I figured that they had admitted me after my transfusion. As I looked around, I saw other children with their parents lying next to them in their beds, so I lay back down next to her. As soon as I did, a lady with a huge cart with wheels stopped at my bed and waved at me. I waved back, and she placed a tray of food on my table, waved goodbye, proceeded to the next bed, and repeated the same process.

The doctors walked in shortly after the lady with the cart of food left, and one of the younger doctors woke my grandmother up to fill her in on my condition. Since my cousin was already gone, they had to find someone else to translate, so they got the nurse from the previous night to do so. The doctor gave me a fake little smile and looked down as he began to speak very softly to the point that the nurse asked him to speak up as she could not hear him. Even though I was only four at this point, I knew whatever he had to say was not because I had been in front of many doctors, and I knew my grandmother felt the same as I thought I saw a tear about to appear in her eyes. The doctor finally picked his voice up, and I heard him say, "Your grandson will not be alive much longer. It will be a miracle if he lives past the age of five." She began to cry, and for some reason, I held her hand and told her not to cry because I was not going to die. She looked at me and smiled but continued sobbing. The younger doctor smiled at me, gave me a hug, and gave my grandmother one before they left. My grandmother stood up, told me she would be right back, and disappeared out of the room. I knew she was leaving because she did not want me to see her crying.

After being in the hospital for a few more months, I was released again, and we left to go back home. I knew it had been a while since my grandmother had gone out of town to buy supplies for the market, so she sent someone else because she was still worried about what the doctors had told her not too long ago, and she was even more protective. She told me she had word to my father about me being in the hospital, so I was surprised he never showed up there, but she assured me that he would be there not too long from now.

My grandmother and I woke up a little later than usual, so she fixed me some breakfast and gave me my medication, which I hated because one of them had a taste that made you gag to the point of throwing up. Now I was not a difficult child and would usually take my medications with no problems, but this particular one I could not do.

While trying to give me my medication, I heard my name being called; and with the way it was said, I knew it could be my dad. So I got up and turned around, and there he was standing there. Then he got on his knees, clapped his hand, and opened it as I ran and jumped in his arm, almost knocking him down. He picked, hugged, and gave me a kiss before walking over to my grandmother, giving her a hug as well.

I was happy the next few days just hanging out with my dad. I talked to him about everything that was going on, including the time I had gone swimming with my cousin and almost drowned. I also told him about the fish I saw, how I was underwater for such a long time, and the water spirit my cousin told me about. That was when my dad told me about an experience he had as a kid.

One day, as he and his mother were going into the country, they came to a river that washed down the bridge due to a rainstorm that had come through the night before. His mother had to put him on her back because, if he was to cross just holding his mother's hand, he would be washed down the river for sure. As they tried to start walking across the river, the water got stronger, and my dad and his mom had to slow their pace. The slower she went, the more my dad would go down on her back, trying to reach the river. So his mom spanked his behind and told him to be still, but my dad paid no attention; he still kept trying to reach the river, and that was when his mom spanked him and asked him what he was doing. So my dad proceeded to tell her that there was a lady at the bottom of the river who was smiling at him and that on top of the water was a beautiful plate encrusted in jewelry, and on the plate was a bejeweled comb. He also informed his mom that the beautiful lady at the bottom of the plate was telling him to come into the water.

After hearing his story, my dad's mom looked around frantically, asking him where these things he saw were; but even after he showed her, she still was not able to see it. So after they were out of the water, they headed straight to medicine man or a witch doctor as it is called in America. When they arrived, the doctor asked them how they were and what he could do for them. My dad's mom told him about the things my dad saw, and the doctor asked if she could see them as well, to which she replied no. The doctor then walked over to my dad and studied him for a minute before telling his mom, "Your son can see, so we have to close his eyes to keep him from seeing those things again." Interpreting what the doctor said, my dad was born with a spiritual sight, which basically meant that he could see into the spiritual world; thus he could see spirits and things invisible to us. The doctor had to do something so he could not find or see things that would try to lure him to his death or to do things for them because he was a child and could have been easily fooled.

Upon explaining all these things to my dad and his mom, the doctor performed a ceremony that closed his spiritual eyes for good. However, my dad is still able to interpret dreams and a few other things I really don't understand.

When he finished his story, I was a little scared; and before he told me his story, I was a little skeptical of my cousin's tale until now.

Chapter 2

COMING TO AMERICA

I was now five years old, and I was still going in and out of the hospital. My last started when I went to urinate, and nothing but blood came out, which scared me so bad that I did not even finish with my urinating and began running straight to my grandmother to tell her what had just happened. That was when she told me, with a startled look on her face, to come and show it to her, so we walked back into the bathroom, where I urinated again. The water turned dark with nothing but blood coming out of me. I think my grandmother was a lot more shocked and scared than I was. She hustled me out of the bathroom, and once again, we headed to the hospital.

I spent another three months in the hospital before I was released, but on my last day, right before we went home, my grandmother was packing up all our things when she stopped and told me that my mother was coming to get me to bring me to America. I had never seen my mom, nor did I know anything about her. As a matter of fact, I had always thought my grandmother was my mother. I mean, she had always been there, so I never longed for a mother or anything like that because my grandmother had been everything to me and more.

It had been a week since my grandmother and I had been home from the hospital when we received a visitor; it was my uncle George.

I knew who he was because he would come to visit my grandmother and me when my mom would send us packages with food, clothes, and money; he was always the one who delivered them. And this time was no different except he came to bring me to Monrovia, the capital of Liberia, so I could stay there with my dad until my mom came to get me to bring me to New York.

It was late at night when we arrived at my dad's house. There were a lot of people just sitting at his house waiting for his return; for what particularly, I did not know. At that moment, my uncle George and I went to his house to wait for my dad to return to his.

I ate dinner with my uncle and his family before we caught a taxi to my dad's house again. When we got there, this time, he was home. A lot more people were sitting there still waiting to see him. My uncle George and I went inside and knocked on the door, which was opened by a young man who was older than me. My uncle George introduced him as my brother Samuel, which surprised me. Samuel hugged me, took by the hand, and led me into the house. That was when I heard my dad's voice say, "Samuel, who is it?" But Samuel said nothing as he led me to the room where my dad was. When he saw me, he yelled my name and walked over to me, picked me up, and hugged me before putting me back down. I was happy to be with my dad and happy to have met my brother; however, I did miss my grandmother dearly. My dad then asked my uncle how the trip was, and it took a while for my uncle to explain because he stuttered so badly that, most times, I could not understand what he was saying, so I would just shake my head in agreement with him.

When we woke up the next morning, it was raining really hard. I have always loved the sound of the rain on the roof. It reminded me of the times when my cousins and I ran naked in the rain.

My dad fixed us some breakfast before we got dressed and left to go get my mother from the airport. My dad had a houseboy who ironed our clothes, and we got ready to head out. We all piled into my dad's car, including the houseboy, and because my mother's plane would not be there until later, my dad brought us to his big brother's house, Mr. Spencer. When we went in the house, there were my cousins Ricky,

Thua, Lanzo, and Singma, along with their mom, Auntie Princess Spencer. I also met Edward, who was the eldest child from a previous marriage. We talked for a while, about what I don't really remember. It, however, became time for us to get to the airport, so we did just that.

At the airport, it was still raining hard when the airplane landed. We proceeded to the tarmac when we saw people start to descend from the plane and go to the various people or family members waiting for them. That was when my dad's houseboy pointed at one particular woman and asked me if she was my mother, to which I replied, "I don't know."

He said, "Well, she looks like you."

When she got closer to us, my dad said, "There she is." She was dressed in a blue denim outfit and had short curly hair; she was pretty and looked very youthful. She came over to me and gave me a kiss, asking me how I was. I really did not say much because, even though I had a mother because of the packages she would send me or the stories my grandmother told me about her, I never really put too much thought into it as I've always thought my grandmother was all of those things to me. With all the introductions complete, we piled up in the car one more time and headed back to my dad's house.

That night, I started thinking about all the times my dad had visited me and how, every time before he left, I would beg him to take me to go live with him. He had always given me excuses about how he lived alone and how he was too busy, that there would be no one at the house to take care of me. So I started thinking, *If all of those things were true, why was my brother living with him?* I mean, his mom, with whom he lived, was educated and had a job that could support them both. On the other hand, my grandmother was older and uneducated and had to struggle to take care of us. Thinking about that made me a little bitter, but I just accepted it and lay down to sleep.

In the morning, my mother and I went to the U.S. Embassy to try to get a visa for travel. We went from office to office the whole day, and my mom was frustrated because we did not accomplish anything. We did not achieve a whole lot that week either, which frustrated my mom even more. She only had a few more days before she had to return to work. That was when my dad took my passport, went to the embassy, and got the visa. My father had always been able to get visas, and he helped a lot of people achieve their dreams of coming to the United States since he knew everybody who had anything to do with visas. So that day, my dad walked into the office of the man who issued visas and got him to order a blank passport, in which he put my visa.

The night I had arrived at my dad's house, there were a lot of people sitting outside waiting for him for that very reason, which I found out later; and those people, including some new ones, would show up every day while I was there to wait for him to get home. It was for this very reason that my father almost lost his life.

There was a guy who wanted to travel to America immediately, so someone told this guy about my dad and how he would help anyone who came to him. Now remember that my dad was born with the ability to see into the spirit world, and even though his spiritual eyes were closed, my dad could interpret dreams, along with some other things. Well, you are about to see what I mean.

Early the next morning, the guy who needed my dad's help with the visa showed up. After he explained to my father why he wanted to go and how he wanted to depart, my father refused to help him. This kind of threw the guy back because my dad would help anybody else. Whether they had the money to pay for it or not made no difference to my dad, and that was what the gentleman had been told before. The guy asked my dad if he could lend him a necktie for tomorrow as he was going to the U.S. Embassy to try to get a visa on his own. With that, my dad got up, went through his closet, and gave the guy a necktie, telling him he could keep that. The man thanked my dad and got up; before he left, he told my dad to reconsider and that he was willing to pay him double his fee, which my dad turned down.

When he woke up the next morning, my dad felt horrible; his throat hurt, and he could hardly talk. Having a lot of appointments, he decided to go on with his day; but when he tried to get up, he felt pain as he turned his neck. So he walked into the bathroom, and that was when he saw that his neck was seriously swollen. My dad could hardly believe what he was looking at. So immediately, he knew this was not flu, cold, or anything like that.

While he took a shower and got dressed, my dad instructed my brother Samuel to fix him a cup of tea with lime, hoping it would make his throat feel better. After his shower, he was in more pain than when he first woke up. He then went to drink the tea, and my dad found out that he was not able to even swallow anything, including his own spit. That was when he knew it was serious and that he would have to pay a visit to the hospital, which was one place my dad would not go unless he was unconscious; that was the way anyone was going to take him.

He had most of the day trying to take care of the things he needed, as well as taking in people to get their visas, but the pain in his neck was throbbing very hard at this point, so much so that he had to cancel his appointments.

My brother Samuel, expecting my dad by now because he had called, heard someone at the door. He thought it was my dad, but he was disappointed when saw it was the guy my dad had refused to help. The guy asked my brother Samuel if it was okay for him to come in and wait for my dad, but Samuel told him no because my dad was not home and because he could not to let anyone in the house while he was away, which was a lie Samuel had concocted—for what reason, who knows? People always came to wait for my dad, especially women. With that, the guy tried several other things to try to get my brother let him in the house, but Samuel smelled a rat and told him no again. Then he told the guy he had to go to the store and that he could come back when my dad got home, so the man turned and finally left.

With his neck throbbing and hurting now to the point that he could no longer bear it, my dad walked into Mr. Spencer's office because they had a lunch appointment. As he sat down, Mr. Spencer looked at my dad's neck, which was three times more swollen now than it was earlier. Mr. Spencer asked my dad what happened to him. When he started talking, my dad realized his voice was almost completely gone at this time. So Mr. Spencer told him about a bishop he knew who could help him; he told my dad to take some time and go see him. Not being a very religious person, my dad had his reservations.

Even though the pain continued to get worse and he wanted to lie down, he decided to seek out this bishop and follow his brother's advice. In so much pain now that he could not even drive, my dad took a taxi to the bishop's church. When he arrived, he saw it was an all-white building that, of course, looked like a church. Now he realized he had passed by this place on many occasions but never really paid attention to it. As he got out of the taxi, he saw a lot of activities going on, with people coming and going. My dad thought that the church was heavily packed for a weekday, so he went up to a secretary, asking her if the bishop was in, to which she replied yes. Then he told her that he was here to see him; she instructed him to sit and wait, and my dad did just that.

The bishop was a really popular guy. He had grown up a Muslim, but at the age of twenty-three, he said he got a calling from God; and with that, he had to go into the wilderness to fast and pray so that God could talk to him and instruct him on what he was to do to carry out his works. Often spending thirteen days and nights in the wilderness, the bishop's mother thought he had lost his mind, so she cried every day and tried to get him committed. But after he was done with his fasting and praying, he returned to civilizations. He began to prophesy and to perform other wonders, so he got a lot of notoriety and was called over by presidents and other leaders of many African nations to pray for their countries. He also started churches in many countries, including in the United States.

So finally, after about thirty minutes, the bishop—whose name was Alpha Bunde—came out of his office and immediately saw my dad and asked, "Are you Spencer?" My father answered yes. "I thought so. You look just like your brother." It was true because my father and all his siblings looked just alike. The bishop told my dad to follow him to his office, and as my dad did, he studied the bishop and was not too impressed about him. I guess because he expected a whole lot different, and this was not how he had pictured this powerful guy he had heard of. The bishop was a slender gentleman in a white robe that reached down over his feet, his face was clean-shaven, he had a low haircut with his hair slicked back, and he had dark skin.

They reached the bishop's office, and he offered my dad a seat while he walked around to sit behind a huge oak desk with pictures on it and notepads, along with normal office things. The office was huge and nicely decorated with certificates of his achievements, as well as pictures of him and different dignitaries he had met. Before my dad could open his mouth to try to explain why he was there, the bishop told him it was okay, and he knew my dad could not talk, so he started to tell my dad why his throat was swollen and why he could not speak.

The bishop told him he had lent an article of clothing to someone who was upset with him, so the person had brought it to a witch doctor to put a spell on it. The witch doctor had taken it and stretched it over a candle so it would slowly burn through. On the third day, when the candle had burned all the way through, it would kill my father. The guy, however, after seeing my dad still moving around after the second day, returned to the witch doctor to speed up the process. He was told to go back to retrieve another article of clothing. And that was what he tried to do when he went back to my dad's house and persuaded my brother to let him come in. My brother refused to let him in for whatever reason, and that was uncommon because people always came into the house to wait for my dad to ask for help in different matters. My brother did not know that this guy meant harm to my dad. Hell, nobody knew, so it could have only been God who told my brother to not let that gentleman in the house.

When the bishop had finished telling my dad all of these things, he gave my dad a bottle of oil and three different passages from the book of Psalms in the Bible. He explained to my dad that he had to rub the oil on his neck while reading all three psalms for three days, and all would be well. My dad took the oil and the three psalms and left, and as he headed home, he thought, *Is that guy crazy? How the hell is rubbing some oil and reading psalms going to help him?* So he put them in his pocket and forgot about them for a whole day.

It was past three in the morning, and my dad could not sleep. His pain level had jumped to a thousand, and not having any other alternative, he remembered the oil and the passages from Psalms. So he thought, *What the hell, I might as well try it.* He rubbed the oil and read the three psalms. When he was done, he felt some relief, so he thought there must be something to this thing and that the bishop may not be full of hot air. My dad used the oil for the next three days and read the book of Psalms after the application of the oil. Before he knew it, the three days were up. That morning, he woke up pain-free, and he can talk. He said my brother's name, and Samuel, not hearing my dad's voice for the last few days, was very surprised to hear it said.

"Daddy, you can talk," he said, to which my dad replied yes.

When the three days were over, the guy who wanted to kill my dad stopped by to make sure he was dead but was surprised to witness my dad and Samuel out and about. My dad, seeing him, realized this was the guy he had lent an article of clothing to, so what the bishop had told him was making sense now because my dad had forgotten that he gave the guy a tie. The guy was almost not able to talk when my dad asked him what he needed. Without saying a word, the man turned and left, heading straight back to the witch doctor to tell him that the spell did not work. The witch doctor said there was a power protecting my dad, and for the spell to work, he would need to get something else that belonged to my father, but there was no way that would happen, so that was the end of it.

Not too long after his ordeal, my dad had received some surprising news. It turned out that the guy who had tried to kill my father had gotten in trouble because he had killed someone, and he was trying to get a visa to escape his crime. My father would help anyone, whether they were able to pay or not, but for some reason, he had a feeling, some sort of intuition, about this; thus he refused to help him.

My dad returned to the house. We were all waiting for him, and he had my passport with the visa in it, which he handed to my mother. She opened it and was surprised to see the visa and thought it was a fake, but it was not. So she asked my dad how he had gotten. She thought that the fact she was a United States citizen would make it easier for her to get it. "How did you get it?" she asked again.

My father just said, "I went to the embassy."

"If you could have gotten it so quick, why did you not tell me?" my mother said with frustration in her voice.

My dad told her, "You never asked me for help."

It was time for my mother and me to leave, so we went to go get my grandmother so she could see me before I left. We piled up in my dad's Honda Civic and headed to the airport. I remember sitting next to my grandmother, holding her hand as she held mine, not knowing this was going to be my last time seeing her for over twenty-plus years. She looked down at me and smiled. I could see her eyes starting to water up.

At the airport, my grandmother held me and told me not to forget about her, to be good, and that she would always be thinking and praying for me. I hugged her tightly, not wanting to leave her as my mom told me it was time to board the plane. I then also hugged my dad and brother before I got on the plane.

I had never been on a plane before, and it was huge with seats everywhere and a lot of people. We took our seats and buckled up. My seat was by the window, so I looked out, hoping to catch a last glimpse of my grandmother. It was just too dark, and the only thing I could see was the lights of the city. The pilot got on the radio to do the regular greetings and some other things that I was too excited to hear. When the pilot was done, I felt the plane come alive, and then we started moving slowly and then faster and faster before we took off. The plane had not been in the air for too long before some ladies came around to ask us what we wanted to eat and drink. Wow, was I surprised! I mean, being on the airplane was great in itself, but getting the chance to pick what I wanted to eat as well made it even better.

We had finished our meal, and it was about twenty hours before we would get to New York. It was at that instance that my mom told me she was married to some guy named David. She went on to ask me to change my name to David's last name, which was Haile. I declined, sending her into a rage. She asked why and said that this guy was her husband and that she had even changed her name to his. I just sat there surprised, not knowing what to do or say because I was scared, and my grandmother had never yelled at me or had ever gotten mad at me except the time she caught me play house with some girl by lying on top of her, but that had been only once. My mother then asked me what I wanted to call David. I could either call him Uncle David or Daddy.

Now after her blowing up on me, I wanted to give her the right answer. I said, "I will call him Dad." I think she was happy with my answer.

Almost all the lights on the plane were turned off as people were sleeping, and only a few lights were turned on for people who were reading. I had been moving in my seat. Finally, Mom asked if I needed to use the restroom, and I said yes. She told me where it was, which was another thing I just could not believe.

On my way to my seat from the bathroom, the plane began to rock side to side, and then it went down all of a sudden, which caused the passengers to scream. I was not scared only because I had no clue that we were in serious trouble. The captain came back over the speaker to tell everyone to buckle up and brace for a crash landing and that the storm hit one of the engines, taking it out. As we were descending, the plane rocked even more violently until we hit the ground. Actually, we crash-landed in a swamp. The stewardesses helped everyone off the plane, and then I saw buses and ambulance that had been called before our crash. We boarded the bus to get to the nearby hotel, where we were going to stay before another plane was to come to bring us to our destinations.

All of our food, drinks, and accommodation were all being paid for by the airline, so I don't need to tell you that all I ate was nothing but ice cream, and I kept throwing the cone away because I did not know it was edible until my mom asked me why. I explained my reason to her before she let me know I could eat it.

The next morning, we woke up to head over to the nearby airport, and the closer we got to the airport, the more anxious I began, thinking about how things would be and how beautiful it was going to be. I started telling myself I was going to get really rich and send my grandmother a lot of money, and then I would go get her to bring her to the United States, where I would build her a beautiful huge house. Finally, at the airport, we had to board the plane immediately because the hotel shuttle was running behind schedule. I was sitting next to the window again, and as the plane climbed higher, I tried looking out the window, hoping we would fly over by my grandmother so she could see me, but I was disappointed.

The flight was a very long one, especially when you had to sit the whole time except for an occasional bathroom break, so it was a relief when the pilot came over the intercom to let us know we were about to land in about thirty minutes, which really excited me because I was ready to move around and see my new home, as well as all the things I had heard about this place called the United States of America. As I leaned on the window with an eager mind, I started to see the lights of every building and of the vehicles driving below on the streets and the bridge; it looked so beautiful, breathtakingly wonderful. Then we touched down, and I quickly unfastened my seat belt. At the same time, my mother was awakened out of the slumber she had been in for the last few hours when the plane's tires hit the ground. I was amazed that anyone could sleep in a place where people were all around you and staring.

After we reached our gate, everyone on the plane seemed to have all been given an order at once because they got up and started to retrieve their bags above them in a place I thought was more like a drawer on a nightstand or a closet with no hangers. Watching people get off the plane was a nerve-racking experience, but finally, it was our turn, and I wasted no time and feverishly exited the plane so fast that my mother had to yell out at me to get my attention because of how far away I was from her.

It was great to finally be off that plane, but now we had to wait in another line, which really upset me because I was exhausted and ready for bed. So I asked my mother why we had to wait in another. She explained that this was a line for something called customs, where they made sure people did not bring things into the country they were not allowed to, which made no sense to me because my thought was *Why would anyone want to bring anything into a country that already had everything?* So I just accepted that reply and left it at that.

It was almost twelve midnight by the time we had gotten through the customs line; we had been in there for about forty minutes before we were through the large older white man whose belly was larger than any pregnant woman I saw, and I thought that this guy was having a lot of children because the buttons on his freshly ironed shirt looked as if they could not hold together any longer as his stomach hung over his pants, and his belt buckle was almost all covered except for a little glimmer reflected from the lights above us. He had the shiniest shoes I had ever seen. I could see different reflections on it; how, depending on the way that he moved, it would twinkle; and how his pants, with a perfect crease in the middle, stopped right above the shoe. I must have been seriously staring at this old guy, whose looks bewildered me, as I had never seen anyone quite like him before. It was just interesting to me. My mother nudged me forward to break my gaze from the older gentleman.

Once outside, we flagged down a taxi, which was not too hard because they were everywhere, but the one thing that blew me away was how cold it was outside, and the ground was covered with ice, so I asked my mom how it could be hot from where we just came from but be this brutally cold here. She told me about how the weather was called winter and that the white ice was called snow; she also told me that there was sunshine in Liberia all the time, so it was warm, but she said not to worry because the cold would eventually go away and that it would get warm here too. I was happy to hear because that; this cold was something I knew I could or would never learn to appreciate. At least it was warm in the cab. I was not dressed for the weather. One thing I learned about cars in the United States was they were all very silent, unlike the ones in Liberia, which were always beeping their horns. I had heard it so much that I started to think it was a mandatory part of driving.

The cab pulled up to a huge and very tall building filled with lights, and there were people entering and leaving out of it. I started to wonder who could possibly live in this building; it would probably be a president or a very rich man. I thought all of those people who were entering and leaving were there to pay respect to him, like they did with the president or a town chief in Liberia. Now imagine my surprise when the cabdriver said, "We are here," and told the price to my mom, which I did not hear because I could not believe this was going to be my home. And being only five years old and with the mind of a child, I started to think that all the stories I had heard about life in the United States was very true, especially the part about everyone being rich. So I immediately thought that I was rich and that this whole building belonged to us. The only thing that puzzled me, however, was why my mom would just leave the door open like that and give people the opportunity to come and go as they pleased. Then I remembered that my mom was married, so these people must have been there to see him. I mean, after all, people used to come by my dad's house to wait for him all the time. Plus, in Liberia, there was never a need to lock our doors whether we were home or not because no one would ever break in. I started to think my mother was a very important person to whom people see to show her their respect for whatever reason.

The cabdriver got out of the car, which took me out of my deep, focused thought because of the burst of cold air. We exited the cab as well to retrieve our luggage, which the driver had already gotten out of the trunk before walking us to our door. He waited for the elevator with us, put the bags on the elevator, and then held the door open for us before he followed us in. I had been on a few elevators back home, but I had never been up as high as we were going before coming to a stop on the top floor. When the elevator door opened, we walked down a long hallway, and then we came to a door, which my mom knocked on. It was opened by someone whom I assumed was her husband, David. At that time, the cabdriver put down our bags, we thanked him, and he left.

My mother and I then walked into the apartment, and David stepped aside to let us through before going and grabbing the bags. My mother made the introductions, and he shook my hands. David was a tall, slender guy with full facial hair and curly hair. He was dark with a cockeye. He never smiled; neither did I because, from the beginning, I felt there was something about him I did not like. After all, being only five, I had met a lot of people while working with my grandmother in her shop, and I had never had this foreboding feeling about anyone like I did with him. It was just an instinctive feeling, and before my first night in my new home, he would prove my instincts correct. I would come to rely on my instincts a lot, which I would need because my grandmother was not here to protect me anymore.

My mom led me around the apartment, giving me a tour. We started in the living room, which was huge, and it led into an open kitchen with a bar. In the living room was the biggest television I had ever seen, and above were

shelves with dolls all over it. One of the dolls was dressed in a bridal gown, and all the others were dressed in almost the exact white dress, which my mother told me were part of a bridal collection and were antiques; what that meant I had no clue, so I just shook my head in agreement. There were pictures of my mom all over the house, especially in the living room, but there was only one or two of David. She had some furniture that were floral and covered in plastic, and then there was a huge window, which was basically the length of the opposite wall. The walls also had African mask and art. The center table was all glass and had a male and female African statue.

She then led me down the hall, and the first door on the left was what she said was my bathroom. It was all white with two pictures that featured two white kids; the pretty one was smiling, and the other had a grunt look on his face. She then showed me the master bedroom, and since it was late, she showed me a bed in the couch, which was where I would be sleeping. I was fine with that because I like the big window and a big television, and that was when I thought my troubles began.

David came out of the back room, forcefully grabbed my mother by the arm, and removed her from the living room, asking her what took her so long to get back from her trip with me. I guess he must have figured that, if my dad was the only man she had ever truly loved and was her first love, something must have happened. But I slept in the room between both of them the whole time. Besides, my dad had so many women coming and going. He should have been nominated pimp of the year for over ten years in Liberia or Africa's man of the year or something. So when she called for my help, I ran straight to the room with the closest thing I could grab. As I was about to go through the door, David tried to close it, and we wrestled with the door for a while, with me putting my foot in the door until I heard my mom's voice. She told me it was okay. I did not stop, though, because at that point it reminded me of the abuse my uncle had given my grandmother, so I saw David as my uncle as well.

Now that I'm an adult and seeing that my grandmother and my mother are very petite women and David and my uncle are at least six feet, it makes me acknowledge the abuse even more seriously now. I had sworn I was going to kill both of them; unfortunately, my uncle drank himself to death, so I can't touch him. But David is still alive, and the day we run into each other, I don't give a fuck if he's on his crutches or on his deathbed. I will stomp whatever life is left in him. I will stomp out of him, and I'm willing to do the time. God have mercy on any of his children who will try to stop me, including my sister. Yeah, I know what you are thinking: let God handle it, right? But I'm not that patient. By the time you finish this book, you may just agree with me.

For the longest time, I used to wonder why, when my dad would come visit me, he would sit and talk with my uncle instead of killing him for what he was doing to my grandmother, so I asked him one day, and he told me he could not harm the man whose home his son and mother lived in because then he might harm me. That was his reasoning, and at the time, I thought it was bullshit. But I understand it a little more today as I am now a father, and I would pillage, burn, and kill an entire family if my wife or son was to ever be hurt—not killed, just hurt. So imagine what would I do if the other were to happen. May God forbid it.

I woke up early the next morning. I remember it because it was still dark outside, and there was a show called *Scooby-Doo*. Immediately after watching it, I did not like it, so I changed the channel and got up to go to the restroom. It was at that time when I felt a sharp pain in my back, and it was then that I turned around, and David had hit me with a cable. The pain was incredible, but he continued until I had blood dripping on the floor. Mom watched the whole thing, never saying a word. That was when I knew this guy could do whatever he wanted to do to me and that I was also in this new world. After the beating, I went back to my bed. I never cried. I was not going to give him the satisfaction of seeing my pain, and I continued to watch television.

That day, my mother had already taken me shopping because she told me, come Monday, I would have to start school. She told me something I think she would come to regret. "When you get to school, don't let anybody think they are better than you. If someone pushes you, make sure to push them so hard that they roll over twice. And if someone hits you, make sure you hit them so hard that they feel it for a week and they know not to ever mess with you again." I guess, back then, that was my mom's way of protecting me from the outside world because she could not protect me at home, which would be a process repeated through my life. But my mother would rule the day; she told me that because it would become a thorn in her side. I also think she would also kind of enjoy it, at least I think so now, and my reason for that is she had some foresight because my dad sent her to school in a racist town, Lansing, Michigan. She was an African with an accent and did not fit with the black Americans or the whites because they had their stupid ideas about Africans, and I'm sure it was frustrating for her and my dad. And being outnumbered and being adults, if they retaliated, the so-called law would be involved, but I would not have that problem.

Monday arrived, and my mom showed me how to catch the bus that would bring me to school, which was different from Liberia, where we walked everywhere. When I got to school, I had to stand up and introduce myself as did all the other kids at PS 38 because it was the beginning of the year. I was upset that I was only in the third grade because I was supposed to be a fifth or sixth grader, and I took a test that showed it to them and passed it, but because I was from Africa and they believed I was too young, they thought the test results must have been false. I was angry as was my mother, but the matter got nowhere, so I was put in the third grade.

So after my introduction to my new class, I got a lot of attention because of my accent, especially from the girls. Yes, I was crazy about girls then too. The teacher was even more inquisitive than the children were because, almost thirty minutes into the class, she was still asking me questions. But when the class finally started, she began to annoy me by telling me, "We are doing long division. It may be a bit advanced, so let me know if you need help." She put the first problem on the board and asked for a volunteer. I raised my hand, and as I held it up, it was no surprise when she would not pick me and kept looking around, but mine was the only hand up. She finally called on me, so I walked up to the blackboard and solved the problem. She was surprised it was right, so I guess to make sure it was not a fluke, she put two other problems up, which I solved and got a cheer from my classmates. After a week, my new teacher who doubted my intelligence was one of the people pushing for me to be promoted to a higher grade, but her efforts, as well as those of my mom, were denied. It was not surprising to me, and I would get used to people underestimating my capabilities.

The kids in my new school had all been very nice to me and had pitched in to help me learn the system like the combination to my locker, how it worked, and how to line up the numbers to open it. They would explain the foods that were unusual to me during breakfast and lunch, and those I had come to really like were hot dogs and fried pockets that had sausage and cheese with some other ingredients. The diet I had been used to was quite different. For instance, the first time my mom bought me a Whopper from Burger King, I hated it, and I thought it was the worst thing I had ever eaten. But the first time I had Chinese food, I came to love it because, in Liberia, we had something that was close to their fried rice, which we called *jollof* rice. *Jollof* rice is fried rice with meats, vegetables, and different seasonings, and all foods in Liberia are served with rice, so there's no need to tell you I love rice. Getting used to certain foods in America was a bit difficult, but at home, my mom always cooked our traditional foods, and she bought me a lot of hot dogs, which I would make for breakfast before school.

One food I did come to like outside of hot dogs was cold cereal, and my favorite was based on a cartoon character I liked named Mr. T Cereal. I would watch that cartoon every Saturday morning, along with *GI Joe* and *He-Man*. But the one series that scared me was called *The Muppet Show*. It was not all the characters that scared me, just the ugly-looking big monsters, and it was this that would get me in trouble.

You see, I was having breakfast with a few friends who had been helping me adjust to my school, and there was this big black kid in my class who was taller and bigger than everyone, including our teacher, and he would make some stupid remarks to me by calling me an African booty scratcher. I did not know what it meant, but I knew it was not a compliment. He would ask me some stupid questions, like if we sleep in trees because he saw it on a show called *Tarzan*, which I said was a stupid show because there was nothing realistic about it. I told him he was stupid. He was used to having authority because all the children were afraid of him, but I was not because of what my mother told me. In my mind, I had a "get out of jail free" card; so when I said that to him, the other children laughed, and it got around that the new African kid was not afraid of the class bully, and I got some new friends who cheered me on.

When we left the cafeteria after our meal, we went back to the class and finished the rest of our day, so I thought nothing of the situation with this bully. We had to line up at the door every day right before we were released to go home. So as I was in line, the kid I had an issue with earlier came along, hitting on the head all the kids who were with me and who had laughed at him, but I was not paying him any attention. When he got to me and slapped my head, without thinking, I retaliated as my mother had instructed. I punched him so hard that I broke his jaw, and the cracking of his jaw was so loud that it caught the attention of everyone in the class, including my teacher, who was shocked, especially as the kids around me yelled out; all of them were saying "oooh" like a rehearsed chorus. The boy grabbed his face, walked away from me, and sat down.

The teacher dismissed the other children but told me to sit on the opposite side of the room. "What happened? Why did you hit him?" the teacher screeched, and then she stopped a few of the students she just dismissed and asked them if they saw what had just occurred. Several of the kids at the same time started explaining what it was they thought had happened. I was told to wait in the classroom as she took the other boy to see the nurse.

As soon as she left, all my friends returned to the classroom to cheer me on and asked me how I did that. They told me, "Man, you're a crazy man," asking me if I was afraid and how come I was not afraid of him, but I just shook my head no. It was all I could think of. I was defending myself and my friends, at least that was the thought in my mind, and I was just doing what I was instructed to do. I knew my mother would understand, but David would use that as an excuse to beat me, as he had already done, with no provocation. This would be an easy excuse for him to beat me.

My teacher returned to the classroom with two other adults, one being the nurse and the other the principal. The nurse was there to tell me I had broken the other boy's jaw, so she feared I must have broken my hand in the process, but after a quick glance at my hand, the nurse was surprised to learn that I had not broken it. The principal started asking me about how the altercation started. I explained to him what they had already heard from my friends and the other classmates, and besides, the kid I had quarreled with had been in the principal's office more times than the school had been in business.

In the middle of my explanation, my mom walked into the room, asking me if I was okay. I nodded yes, and then she asked what took place. My teacher started to explain to her that this bigger and more opposing kid was picking on me and hit me, as well as a few of the other kids, and I retaliated, hitting him, thus breaking his jaw. My mom asked me, "Did he hit you first?"

And before I could say anything, one of my friends, who somehow was still in the room, answered for me, saying, "Yes, he hit Clhoe first, and he hit him really hard too. He also hit me and some of the other kids. And that was when Shawn hit him back." My mother thanked him for that as did the principal. So my mother asked me if I was okay, and I said yes. And that was when the principal let my mom know that the boy's jaw was broken and that we would have to sit down with the boy's parents to see about helping with his medical bills.

That must have been the straw that broke the camel's back because my mom had been calm until they said that. She asked them if they had lost their damn mind and why we should pay any damn thing when this bigger kid was a bully and had been known for picking on the smaller children in the class and only had gotten what he deserved. She told them, "You have already insulted us by thinking, because we are Africans, that we are dumber and less of a human being as you dumbass Americans when you put Shawn in a lower grade than where he was supposed to be even after he had passed the test." The principal asked her to calm down and said he understood her position. My mother told him he had no idea about her thoughts or what they had done to us. She got up, grabbed my hand, and told me we were leaving. My teacher followed us as we left, trying to calm my mother down, and she could barely keep up with my mom, and neither did I as she led me out of the building.

We had gotten home, and it was very late in the evening. I was very tired and not even hungry. I just took my bath and went to bed for the night. As I fell asleep, I was suddenly awakened by a flash of pain, and I immediately woke up to David hitting me. With this beating, I was not able to hold back my tears, and then he told me to get up and pick pain. I had no clue what that was, so he hit me, telling me to bend over, put one finger on the ground, and put one foot in the air and stay that way. Each time I lowered my leg, he would hit me, and he had me hold that position for hours until my whole body would tremble from the pain. After hours in that position, he finally told me to get to bed and that there better be no more calls from the school. I hated David and told myself that when I got older, I was going to kill him.

The next morning, when I got to school, I had become the most popular kid and had new friends. They asked if I used to fight lions while I was in Africa, which was why I got so strong. I just said yes, which impressed the crowd around me.

I started to feel really sick, and I was very cold. While in class, I laid my head down. My teacher told me to sit up, but I could not, and that was when she walked over to me and saw my bruises. Then she looked at me and saw that I was not acting like my usual self, and she felt my forehead, telling me, "Oh my goodness, Shawn, you are really hot. You may have a fever." And as I looked around the room, I saw my opponent whose jaw I had broken walking in a very solemn mood with his head hanging down, not held high, and making his usual wise cracks at different kids in the class. They stared directly at him now and even snickered at him as he walked by them. It seemed he had lost the respect from fear that he had on the class, and he did not even make eye contact with me. He also took a whole different route so he did not have to pass near my desk, and for some strange reason, I felt horrible for what I had done to him. I even think my teacher kind of appreciated the new change in him as he did not disturb the class, making her job easier, not that he could make any noise in the first place.

I had no more time to reminisce on what was going with him because I threw up everything I ate at that moment, but the only thing I had ingested that morning was orange juice, which caused my teacher and the other students to really get concerned. Everyone started asking about my well-being. My teacher calmed the class back down, instructing one of the students to be a monitor while she brought me to the office and called a janitor to clean up my mess. I cleaned off my desk and grabbed my things as my teacher held my hand, and that was when I noticed how young and very petite she was. Even though I was young, her hands was not that much bigger than mine, but she was pale, and she had freckles that matched her brown hair.

We finally got to the nurse's office, where I was told to sit. The nurse was a semiattractive older woman with blond hair and of medium built. She took my temperature, and she told my teacher it was 103 point something, which I thought was the largest number I had heard. The look on both of their faces changed and became that of worry and confusion. The questions started coming about when I started feeling sick and if I ate at home. I answered, "Yeah, I had food at home, but I did not eat because I was thinking they were talking about me that morning." So they went to call my mom and could not reach her. They called David too but did not hear from either one of them.

After four hours, two police officers were called, and I was brought to their precinct, where I was kept and offered all types of different treats, which I did not eat as I was not feeling great. I did not know while they were questioning me that, in America, parents can get in trouble for beating or mistreating their children, so I guess the officers were more curious of the fact that they could not get in touch with my mom or David, whom they called my dad, which I quickly corrected. Then they asked me about how he treated me, and I told them because I was told to respect my elders and authority.

It was late at night when my mom arrived at the police headquarters, and she was very loving to me, asking me how I was and how I felt.

I was ready to go, but we ended up staying even later because they brought her to a different room, where they questioned her for hours before finally letting us go but not before they told her not to go home without taking me to the hospital because of how high my fever was. So right after the police precinct, I was brought to the hospital, where we were for another four or five hours. Then we went to the pharmacy to get a cream for my skin because I had what was called chicken pox, about which I had no clue. All I knew was it itched, and I was covered in bumps all over my body.

It was after we left the pharmacy that my mom's attitude toward me changed. She went from being loving and caring to being angry. She told me I was nothing but a headache since I got in her life. She said I was ungrateful for telling those things to the officers. She told me I was just useless, and she did not even know why the hell she even brought me to live with them because I was just useless. The next time anyone asked me anything, she told me to keep my damn mouth shut. By the time she was done talking down on me, I felt a hundred times worse than I felt before. She had joined forces with David now, and I really felt alone and very useless.

At the house that night, I was turned on by both my mother and David as they joined forces. Now I didn't know if my mom did it to stop him from abusing her or if it was just because she hated me. Whatever it was did not matter because even my being sick did not stop them from beating me and making me pick pain, which made me feel even sicker than ever. I would be bedridden for the next week or so, hardly able to move. Then something happened the next day that would worsen my situation.

Early the next morning, we got a visit from a social worker who came to check on my well-being, so she went through the house checking every room and asking to see where I slept. She was told it was in the master bedroom with my mom, which of course was a lie. Every night, my mom went to work, and I don't know where the hell David went, and I really did not care. I was scared to death being by myself in a new place where I heard sirens every five minutes and would be so frightened until I cried myself to sleep. In the morning, I would get up, fix myself a hot dog, and leave for school and would repeat it almost every day. So after searching the house, the social worker asked to see what was in the refrigerator, which my mom kept stocked all the times with things I liked, especially traditional Liberian cuisine like cassava leaves and palm butter. If you were to ever try it, you would want it every day, trust me. My wife is American, and when she tried it, she learned how to cook it.

When the social worker was done, she said she would be back periodically to check on things. I don't have to tell you that, after she left, I did not get physical abuse but a tongue-lashing, which hurt me just as much. It was not physical but close, and the tone in my mother's voice and the look in her eyes were of pure hatred and disgust of me. She stated once again I was useless and was nothing but a burden, a headache, and she wished I were not here. My mom had become a whole different person.

As time went on, I got really sick from time to time and then more frequently because I was constantly afraid of the people I was living with. It was hard to be in the house with them because it had become them against me, and I was down, so I walked on eggshells and became very withdrawn. I only felt safe at school or anytime I was not at home. Because I was constantly being checked on by the social worker, when I came home one day, I found out we were moving to a whole new place. I guess David wanted to get away from the police looking for him, so we wound up in Texas, and it was not too long after our move that the abuse started all over again.

Chapter 3

LEAVING ME NOW

After the first six months of living in Texas, I got the reputation of being a tough guy when I beat up the neighborhood bully named Brian. Of course, I was the popular kid, but Texas was a lot different from New York. Racism here was in your face, and I remember being called a nigger for the first time. Back then, I did not know what it meant and had never heard the word, but when this white kid called me that, I knew it was no fucking term of endearment, so I proceeded to give him the beating of a lifetime. I took out all my pent-up rage and frustration on him. He had always said things to me, and I had just ignored it, but after I saw him messing with my girlfriend Barbra and then called me that name, I lost it. After beating him and while he was on the ground, I climbed up on one of the desks and was about to WWF his ass when our teacher grabbed me midair and swung me away from him before landing on him with both of my feet.

Of course, we were brought to the principal's office and asked what happened. I explained to the principal why the fight started and what he had called me, but the principal still told me that it was not how to handle things and that it was more appropriate to tell the teacher. I had stopped listening at that point, and of course, like all the other times, they called my mom. I really did not care at this point because I knew I was to be beaten anyway. I had done something to be considered worthy of the beating I would be receiving in a bit.

The principal was a balding older white gentleman, and the side of his head did not have any hair. He had salt-and-pepper hair and a forehead with furrows and a unibrow. I could see him turn, and he saw that I was not paying him any attention at all, which made him angry at me even more. But what could he do? He seemed defeated, so he just released us back to our classes.

The weirdest thing happened on the way to our class. My opponent, whom I was just assisting, stopped in the middle of the hallway to face me.

I turned to face him in a defensive motion because I thought he wanted to start the fight all over again, but he apologized to me for calling me what he had called me earlier—a nigger—and started to extend his hand away from his swollen eye and busted mouth to shake my hand. I was still in my defensive stance when we heard someone yell out in a loud voice, "No!" The voice started to come toward us. I and my opponent started to shake hands and were soon separated by a hand pulling both of us apart very quickly. It was the principal. He apologized shortly after, saying he thought we were about start another fight but soon realized we were trying to mend fences. He said he was very happy for us. But from where he has slanting and after the squabble we just had, it looked as if the fight was about to ignite all over again because I was still in a defensive stance, which I quickly fixed. The principal apologized to us, telling us he was happy to see us become friends, but he would still have to call our parents. He just discussed the situation as a mistake and told our parents how proud he was of us.

I came to find out that the kid's name was Brad. He was seven, just a year older than myself, and the word he called me was something he had heard from an elder cousin of his. When his parents found out that this was the word he had called me, they were shocked and apologized for their son, asking him where he heard this word from. Brad's father, Peter, asked his son in very loud, commanding, booming voice that also had a hint of embarrassment, especially with me sitting right across from him. I think it was that very reason he could not look me in the eye.

Brad sat there almost as an empty vessel as if whatever or whoever was controlling that body had been totally checked out. When I noticed, he had not even realized that Brad had not blinked or batted an eye until his father barked another order. Brad came back to life before he slowly turned to face his dad, and that was when I noticed how much Brad favored him.

Brad's father was a tall muscular guy with a dark tan from being in the sun. You could see the pulled upper part of his arm when he would pull up his sleeve. Brad's father had a buzzy military haircut and a tiny peanut head. He had piercing deep brown eyes as did Brad, but he had his mother's high cheekbone, as well as her complexion, which was a bit darker than his dad's. Brad had his mother's blond hair and small nose and mouth, as well as her bushy eyebrows, which looked better on her than on him because she was an attractive young woman in her mid- to late twenties or early thirties. And even though his father was about the same age as his mother, she looked a lot younger, while his dad looked as if life had been brutal to him.

Brad turned to face his father to answer his question about where he had learned to use such a word like nigger. Brad explained how he heard his favorite cousin, Lonnie, call somebody nigger. Then I heard Brad's father say under his breath, "I knew it." He said it so low that nobody else heard it. Brad's dad went on to tell him what this word meant and how people who are evil use it because they are too stupid and have a limited vocabulary. And as he went on explaining, I think Brad had an epiphany about the word. I myself did not even know its meaning until that day. Being so shocked about this word, Brad could not stop apologizing that day and the next few weeks. And let me tell you, he and I remained the best of friends.

It was around our seventh month in Texas when I found out that my mom would be having a baby girl soon and would need me to help her out because David would be out of town a lot, which I was happy to hear because the abuse I suffered would decrease. Also around this time, while I was just hanging out at the basketball court, just sitting there with no ball but just wanting to be out of the hell I called my life, I saw a young white guy who was very athletically built. He came on the court to shoot basketball, and it was very cold outside that day. When he started shooting hoops, he had seen me and acknowledged my presence as I did his, though neither one of us said a word. He dribbled the ball a bit and made all the baskets he attempted, and it was after about twenty minutes that he spoke to me, asking why I was out so late. It was not too late but just dark out; it was only five o'clock. I just shrugged as he asked me if I was cold. I noticed that it had gotten a lot colder, and I was starting to shiver. I nodded yes, and he removed his hooded sweatshirt to give it to me, and I immediately put it on. I saw he only had on some shorts and a T-shirt in this cold environment. He proceeded to show me how to shoot hoops, and he explained it so well that I was able to actually make the shots for the first time ever.

The guy had told me his name, but it has been so long ago that I cannot remember it, but he was a white guy between thirty and forty years old with black hair, brown eyes, and an athletic built. He was clean-shaven, and his hair was cut neatly and low with no sideburns. So after an hour of shooting hoops and talking, he asked me where lived, if I had brothers and sisters, and who my parents were. I answered him, and in turn, I asked him if he was married. He said yes but had no children. He worked in computers, and his wife stayed home.

When he and I were done with hoops, we both were thirsty and hungry, and he invited me to his house for a drink and food, to which I agreed. Looking back on things now, I realized children were abducted and killed. I had no knowledge of these things because I never heard of them in Liberia. Hell, we never locked our doors, and complete strangers would invite you to eat with them, and it was rude to turn down an invitation like that, so I thought the great United States would be the same way.

He led me upstairs to his apartment, and upon entering, I was hit with wonderful smells of food being prepared and the great smell of potpourri. He introduced me to his wife, whose name also escaped me, but she was very pretty with a slender build. She was wearing a blue floral dress that reached all the way down to her feet. I thought it was a great color of red and blue, which were good colors on her. The house was nicely decorated, and it was cozy, where you felt an immediate sense of home, ease, and comfort. It was decorated like one of those in *Country Living* magazines, and the statues and pictures were perfectly placed. This place should have been in a magazine. She invited me to sit with her as he went in the back to shower.

While I sat on the couch, it seemed that an invisible arm wrapped around me and held me in a loving, soft embrace. The wife returned with some chocolate chip cookies, which she said she had just baked, and offered me some. I took the cookie and could not believe that it was possible for people to bake these. I thought the only ones that were available were Chips Ahoy! you bought at the store. When I took my first bite, it was warm and almost like butter, and it melted in my mouth with no real need to chew. Hell, these were better than any damn Chips Ahoy! cookie in a funky store. They did these cookies injustice by comparing them with those or even calling them chocolate chip cookies. I never wanted another store-bought cookie after that; all I wanted were baked cookies. After taking a few more, I did not want to be greedy, but she told me to help myself and take all I wanted. She even packed me some to take home, and I was forever indebted. I know simple things please children; that's because, as adults, we lose sight of those things through no fault of our own.

I was asked if I wanted her to read me a book. I said yes, of course; no one had ever offered to read me a book, so she got up to retrieve a book she said was her favorite as a little girl. She returned and read me the title first, which was *The Velveteen Rabbit*. She began to read it to me. Now I don't remember the whole story, but I know it's about a toy rabbit, a velveteen, that wanted to become a real rabbit through the love of his owner. While she read the book, she cradled me in her arms for a long time. I had not felt this safe and secure, but I knew it was going to be short-lived. I mean, after all, I could not stay here forever. I would have to return home soon, but there was no need to rush because I only lived a few buildings over.

I must have fallen asleep during the reading because the next thing I remembered was a soft, sweet voice calling and asking me if I wanted to eat. I replied yes, thinking I must be dreaming. I went back to sleep because I knew no one in my house would be that caring to wake me up asking me if I was ready for a meal. At home, when and if I was woken up, it was by a loud yell or pain, unless I got up by myself. But then I remembered that I was not home, which had definitely woken me up. I saw a beautifully set table with a place for me, and that was not the norm in my house. I was not allowed to eat or drink from any of the dishes in my house or to even sit at the table. Nope. At home, they had purchased some plastic spoons, plates, and cups for me to use. They were for no one else but me because, from what I understood, I was disgusting. And for that, I was not to touch any of the dishes, and I usually ate sitting on the floor or in my room. So you can imagine my surprise when I was told to come sit at the beautifully set table. The plates were blue with a floral pattern and little birds drawn over them. The spoons, knives, and forks were of different sizes. Then there were two plates; one was of regular size, and the other was what I came to know was a saucer. I also learned the smaller fork was for something called a salad, and when they started to bring in all the food from the kitchen, the thing called a salad was nothing but a bunch of uncooked vegetables, and it was eaten with some creamy thing called salad dressing, which was poured on top of the salad. There were two of them sitting right in front of me on the dinner table, and I found out that Susan liked the one that was called a Thousand Island, and Ron liked the one called ranch.

The names Susan and Ron are what I will be calling my new friends because this happened to me when I was about six years old. I am now forty years old, and I don't remember. I do wish, though, I could remember their names so I could find them to explain to them the story I am telling you now, how important their love and friendship was to me and how it made my life a lot better, and how eager I was every day to come to their home. They never turned me away and were always very welcoming to me.

Anyway, back to the story. Susan brought out all the food, and it all was wonderful. As I looked around at all the food, it was a table set for a king or a president. Susan and Ron treated me as if I were their child. As I picked up the spoon, I saw letters on it, so I asked why there were all the same letters written on all the utensils. They explained it was put there to represent their name and that they received these as a wedding present. Now I have heard of people getting married, and of course, I had already known that one day it would be my turn, but I did not know people gave you free stuff when you got married. So in my six-year-old mind, I said I was going to tell people to give me millions of dollars, cars, houses, and other things. I would give some to my grandmother, but of course, that's not how things work unless your family and friends are all very wealthy.

My next question for Susan and Ron was how it was possible for the forks and spoons to get so shiny because I had never seen others shining like that. So Susan told me that they were made of pure sterling silver. "So is that the same thing the plates are made of?" I asked. Of course, she let me know they were china, which I immediately thought was the country, but I was corrected by Ron. I said okay, and we began to pray, and then we ate.

I had not felt that cared for and loved since I had left my grandmother's side. We began to eat by Ron opening up the dishes to reveal what each one held, and I was able to see that there was some rice, which I was happy about. Then in another bowl was a sauce with some crabs inside. The sauce made me extremely happy because, in Liberia, every meal we eat consists of rice with some sort of stew, soup, or sauce. And if you are Liberian and you eat a hamburger, ribs, or something else but no rice and someone asks you if you have eaten, all Liberians will tell you no because they are used to eating rice the whole day. Susan then informed me that when we had first came in the door, she had just started cooking. Then after talking and finding out I was Liberian, she took the chicken out and decided to cook something I would be more accustomed to, which was why she had asked me what tribe I was from because she was familiar with all the tribes in

Liberia. They had spent two years there after graduating from college, and they both went to volunteer for the peace corps, and that was how they met and got married. While in Liberia, they fell in love with the food and the culture, which consisted of sixteen different tribes; but before even going to Liberia, they had spent time in Rwanda, Congo, and a few other African nations but preferred the Liberian culture the most because Liberia was like America. It was where the free slaves who left America went back to and settled, and it was one of the freed slaves who became the first president, and they were called Americo-Liberians by the natives of the country.

Now the only problem with this was that the Americo-Liberians kept the natives, also known as the country people, out of the politics and refused them the ability to work unless in a domestic capacity, go to school, or anything that would help them prosper in life. So basically, they treated the natives just like they were treated by the whites in America. It was after years of abuse that the natives got tired of it, and in 1980, a coup took place. After the death of the former president Tubman, William R. Tolbert became president, and he saw the ill treatment and tried to make it better because he saw everyone as equals unlike Tubman, who was just a jackass—a real, bona fide jackass. Anyway, before any of his plans were put into gear, a coup in 1980 would cause his death and put in the presidency a sergeant named Samuel K. Doe, who was a complete imbecile and never graduated from the eighth grade. What a leader, right? And how does a moronic sergeant take over a whole country? So anyway, he went on to become the first native president of the country.

To show how much of an idiot he was, after the coup, there was an interview of him. By his side was his moron of a wife, but we'll get to that later. During the interview of the dummy—I mean, Pres. Samuel "Dummy" Doe—I'm sorry again, what I meant to say was Samuel K. Doe (not really), he was asked what his plans for establishing this new country would be and how he planned to reach out to other nations and to get his country back on track financially. Just to let you know, the question asked during the interview was a lot more complicated than that just so some Samuel K. Does out there may understand. To not want to look like an idiot, the new president said, "I don't know. That is a question for my cabinet head," but he made himself look like an idiot anyway.

After the interview, the bold new president slaughtered thirteen members of the former regime. What a guy. Not long after becoming the new president, the country started to flourish financially, which was not Doe's doing. I mean, the country of Liberia is a lot smaller than Rhode Island, so you really cannot have it as the fastest growing economy at the time, with foreign investors coming and depleting the natural resources. But Liberia was still the second largest producer of rubber in the world and also produced iron ore and bauxite, along with other minerals. Instead of letting these new investors only train and employ Liberians so there would be limitless amount of jobs for the inhabitants of the country, he decided to be greedy and take bribes and use foreign aid for himself.

Doe was from the Krahn tribe, and he only hired people from his tribe to be a part of his cabinet, leaving out the others. They ruled with impunity. Not too long after this, there was an attempted coup that was shortly stopped. The body of the leader of the coup was shown on television throughout the country and talked about on all radio shows. The people who started the coup were from the Gio and Mano tribes, so Doe sent his goons to kill all their family members or just anybody who was from those tribes, even if they were innocent. Tribalism in Liberia had never been an issue; if any, it dealt with friendly competition, with some tribes saying how they cooked the natives' food better than other tribes in the region. After the atrocities, it started to change little by little. Previously, it had not existed, unlike in other African nations that Ron and Susan had visited, and this tribalism led to wars or killings. These things would be a part of Liberia's history one day unfortunately, and Ron and Susan were not liking the new change, so after two years, they left to come back to the United States and were married shortly thereafter.

We had finally finished dinner, and Susan had baked an apple pie with ice cream and whipped cream for dessert. I normally had never liked apples, and I anticipated that I was not going to like this new dessert, but I decided even if I did not like the pie, I would eat it regardless because I really liked my new friends, especially Susan, and I did not want to offend her because dinner had been really good. Once I bit into the pie, I was surprised at how good it was. I did not even need the ice cream or whipped cream, but they just added it to the pie, and it tasted a whole lot different from the fruit. I had to tell Susan and Ron about my earlier fears about the pie, and to show my friends how much

I liked it, I had another slice and a third, and they thought that was so funny that they laughed until tears came out of their eyes.

Susan had packed me some pie to go home with, and since it was past eleven, Ron wanted to bring me home. I told him he did not have to out of fear that, because it was late, David would do something to me, and Ron may try to interfere, and David would hurt him. Even though Ron was more athletic and stronger, that still bothered me, and I also was a little embarrassed of my house, which led to fears that I would not be invited to their place again.

Susan gave me a kiss and a hug before we left. That made Ron say, "Look, you are you trying to take my woman," and they laughed, but I just gave them a half-hearted smile, which they both noticed but said nothing. My demeanor had changed from being happy and bubbly since I arrived in their house to seriously sad as it came time for me to go home.

When we started to walk, Ron asked if I was okay. I quickly nodded yes, but I don't think he believed me because he said, "Is everything okay at home?" I wanted to say no and tell him my fears, hoping he would let me live with them, but instead, I just nodded yes again. The pounding of my heart picked up and got louder with every step; it beat so hard that I swore Ron could hear it. I was now getting so scared. I felt like I had to urinate, defecate, and purs out at the same time. Tears started to appear in my eyes, and I could feel the cold liquid on my face and eyes. I hurriedly wiped them away before Ron saw them, and to be sure he did not know I was about to cry, I glanced up at him really quick, and he smiled back down at me.

We arrived at my door, and I felt trickles of urine inside my jeans. Ron knocked on the door, where I felt a few more drops. I heard the sound of the turning of the knob, as well as locks slowly unlocking, and I felt myself swaying forward at first and then backward and forward one more time. I knew I was definitely about to pass out, and then I felt heat coming from an open door, and my mother stood behind the door. Ron introduced himself and told her how we met and played ball before going to his house. He also told her what a great kid I was and how I was very respectful, which I had heard people tell my grandmother about me time and time again. Ron then told her I was welcomed back to his and Susan's house at any time. He also told her how he knew she was Liberian and that he and his wife Susan met there. My mom responded positively to that. So after about five minutes of dialogue, Ron said goodbye and rubbed my head, letting me know he would be expecting me the next day.

I walked in the house and saw David was not yet home and felt a little better. I knew I was in trouble with my mom because it was almost midnight, but she did not care and only said, "Is his wife Liberian?"

I said, "No, she is an American and a white lady," which was what she really wanted to know. Then she returned to her room. I sat my pie down and ran to the bathroom to urinate, and it felt so great. I could also feel that my underwear was a bit moist. I then I went to my room to change when I noticed I still had Ron's jacket. After changing, I went to the kitchen to find that my mom had cooked some beans *torborgee*. I ate again, being a glutton. I was still full, but I was not about to pass this up.

Returning home after school the next day, I could hardly wait to get to Ron and Susan's. I walked as fast as my legs would move, even running in between walks, before finally arriving at their door and knocking. Susan opened the door and welcomed me in with a smile and a hug; she then said she was making a little lunch for me, hoping I would stop by. I was happy to hear that. I put my book bag on the floor and sat down. Susan brought me grilled ham and cheese sandwich, juice, and more chocolate chip cookies. I immediately started to eat. Susan walked back into the kitchen and reappeared to take a seat next to me, and I noticed she had sandwich, juice, and cookies for her lunch as well. I asked her where Ron was, and she replied that he was still at work and would be returning later. She also asked me how my day at school had gone, which I thought was a silly question because she was not there with me, so she could never understand. I guess I thought that because no one had ever bothered to ask me anything about myself, so I told her about my day. She asked me if I had any homework. I told her I indeed did have a few assignments. She told me, after we were done, she would me assist with my schoolwork.

As soon as we finished our meal, Susan told me to go and get my homework from my book bag so she could help me complete my task. We began with an English assignment, such as sentence fragments, commas, vowels, subject-verb agreements, and some things that were not part of homework just so I could be a little more advanced than my class. We moved on to spelling after that, and when I did not understand something, she was patient with me and did not get angry and hit me or call me stupid and other names, like my mom and David would do. So because she was patient, kind, and able to explain things in a way I could understand, I was not nervous or afraid and do not make mistakes. Susan really made me a lot more advanced and increased my vocabulary by having me write down words I did not understand, find its meaning, write it down, use it in a sentence, and memorize it. Then we would have a spelling bee sometime in the week, and she would pick the day, so I had to be always ready, but she made it so much fun that I looked forward to it. The whole assignment became fun, so every day after school, I would look forward to doing my homework with Susan instead of being so scared that I did not let David or my mom know I had homework or that I did not understand anything in my schoolwork.

I only had one assignment left that we had to complete, but Susan had us stop at this point so she could start dinner. She saw how late it was, and Ron would soon be home for the day, so I asked her if she needed my help, to which she replied no. Then she asked me what my next assignment was. I took a seat at the bar that separated the kitchen from the dining room and the living room. I said it was just a writing assignment to just practice writing in cursive. She was confused that they had me doing that, which she figured was below my grade level. I explained that it was for an English for Speakers of Other Languages (ESOL) class, and she told me my penmanship was already very nice and neat, which was because my mom would have me write sentences over and over until my hands were numb, and—lord have mercy—if my writing was not up to her standards, I would get hit with something. Susan, however, was not like that at all.

As I sat there looking at her, I was wishing I were her child and thinking how wonderful it would be to live there instead of our house.

I could not help it. I blurted out that I wished she were my mom. She stopped what she was doing because I must have caught her by surprise or caught her off guard. She did not turn around at that moment but told me she wished I were hers too. I thought she was about to cry because her voice cracked, and her words came through trembling lips. Then she quickly wiped away what I thought were tears before she turned around, smiled at me, and repeated saying, "Thank you. I really wish you were my son, and the day I ever have children, I hope they are as smart, respectful, and handsome as you are." She then gave me a hug and a kiss before returning to her task.

We returned to her helping me with my ESOL homework, but I did not get a grade for it because the class was to help me communicate in my new country. Upon completion of that assignment, we moved on to the last one for the evening. As soon as we got started, Ron walked through the door with a cheerful hello, followed by him rubbing my head as I hugged his leg. Susan walked over from the kitchen to give Ron a kiss and a hug, which formed a sandwich with me in the middle. Oh, let me tell you, it felt so right. I could not explain it in this writing or even verbally. Ron asked us what we were up to, so Susan said homework, and then she told him what I said about wishing she were my mom. "That would then make you my son, and I could think of nothing better," he told me as he knelt down so he was eye level to me. "You are such a great kid." Ron rubbed my head and then excused himself to go shower before dinner.

With dinner started, Susan and I returned to the living room to play the game called Monopoly, which I had not heard of until now. So Susan explained the rules and how you would move and win the game, which took a while. We had finally begun to play when Ron came into the living room and wanted to play as well. He sat down so we could play, and we would have to stop now and again so Susan could check on dinner.

When dinner was ready, we put the game on hold so we could eat, and we sat around at the dining room table once again. It felt great that these people who had only known me for a short amount of time had welcomed me into their lives and made me a part of it. The situation was great, but it was still like being on the outside looking in because I knew sooner or later I would have to return to my life.

I mean, just imagine being a child or, better yet, a homeless child. It's around Christmastime, and it's snowing. You are walking by all these stores —some with clothes, some with toys, and some with television—and they have these big windows with different kinds of displays. Families are moving around you, shopping. You see kids pointing to things they want, and even though you can't hear them, you can imagine the conversation because you are outside, wishing that child were you. And the conversation, in your mind, goes something like this: "I want that one."

And your parents tell you, "Okay, son, no problem."

Then you walk to another store window, where you see a display of a family of mannequins sitting around a television set in their living room. The parents are sitting in a couch together with a Christmas tree lit up beautifully. Then you see the fireplace with a roaring fire going. Above that are four stockings hanging. The living room is decorated, and the two children, a boy and a girl, are on the floor, playing with their new gifts. And just for a few minutes, you manage to escape your reality because you imagine yourself as one of those kids or even hope some of the families moving about will see your situation and bring you home with them, but you know they won't, so you go back to the window.

Then all of a sudden, you are distracted by something; it brings you back to your reality, and now you are cold, hungry, and homeless again. That's what it felt like for me—being around Susan and Ron one minute and then having to return to my life afterward. Even though I was not homeless, my life living with a family that did not want me and abused me constantly was still a horrible life.

I had been visiting Ron and Susan for a month now until I came home one day to find we would be moving once again, so my last day to see Ron and Susan never came, and I was never able to say goodbye to them. I wish I knew their real name today so I could reach out to tell them how wonderful they were to this little African kid.

Before I knew it, my mom and David asked a friend of theirs, a young black couple, to watch me for a few days to allow them a chance to set up everything at the new place. It did not make sense to me, but I went along with it. I had no choice, but it did get me away from David and my mother. Honestly, I think this was their first attempt to get rid of me because a few days turned into a few weeks to the point where the couple, whose names I don't remember either, had to bring me to a family function or some holiday celebration. It was the first time I had eaten German chocolate cake, and it became my favorite cake of all time. So after a few days, it came time to leave, and one of their parents—I think it was the wife's mother—baked me some delicious cookies to take home with.

Upon returning to their house, they had been trying to reach my mom and David with no success and kept trying until they did. They had threatened them that they needed to come and get me because they really could not do much with me. That must have worked because, after a month and a few, I saw my mom and David, and they took me back. I learned I had a baby sister named Siya.

A few months after living with my new sibling, my mother informed me we were going on a trip; so the night before, she had me pack up all my belongings. I did just as instructed before going to bed. I was very eager to be going on this expedition because I was told I would be going to visit my grandmother, whom I had not seen or heard from in a couple of years.

I was awakened early the next morning to get ready, so I showered and brushed my teeth before getting dressed. Then my mother made me a sandwich on a bagel, wrapping it up, telling me to save it for the trip. I found that weird that she made me a sandwich because, usually, if I asked her to do something, she would tell me to leave her the hell alone or do it my fucking self. I took the sandwich she had made, putting it in a brown paper bag without saying a word. Before I had come to live with them, I was a sharp, happy child; but over the years, they had broken my spirit. Now I was quiet, withdrawn, scared of my own shadow, and afraid to make eye contact with anyone because during most of the abuse, I was told, "Don't look at me."

I took my bag to the car and loaded it in before getting in the side passenger seat, and we were off. The ride to the airport was very quiet; neither me nor my mother said a word the whole time. I looked at the time on the only gift I ever received from them, which was a digital watch, and it was only three o'clock. An hour later, we arrived at the airport. I quickly got out to get my bags because I did not want to make her mad and yell at me, telling me I was too fucking slow before slapping the back of my head.

We went to check inside the airport when I made a realization that I was the only one with a bag, and my mom did not. So I was afraid that I would get in trouble if I let her know of this error. It would come back to bite. I thought maybe she had told me to pack it in the car, and I forgot, and it was my fault. Even if she did not tell me to put it in the car, she would have said, "Of course, I didn't tell you. You were supposed to know that. You are fucking useless," and she would come at me with a barrage of hits. My heart was now beating hard in my chest as we went to sit down. At this time, I knew she came to a realization that her bag was missing; but instead, she informed me she would be right back, and she left after asking if I wanted a drink. I nodded yes as I watched her disappear around the corner.

After what seemed to be an eternity, I got worried and decided to go look for her but thought better of it just in case she came back and did not see me where she had told me to wait. I sat back down. Even more time elapsed when I persuaded myself to get up, fearing she may be in trouble, and I was going to save her; at least that was the story I was going to tell her if I ran into her and she asked me why I was not sitting down as she had instructed.

I had been walking around for a while now with no results. It was at that moment that I came to the realization that nothing around me was familiar. I had not remembered passing any of these places before, so I knew I was lost, and the airport was getting really crowded all of a sudden. I mean, I was able to see all the way down the hall one minute, and then I was not able to see much because the airport was full of adults; all I could see was above kneecaps. I decided to backtrack a little, hoping that maybe I would see something that would jog my memory, but instead, I got lost now more than I was before. I did see some police officers, and I wanted to ask for their assistance, but after my first encounter with them at school and the police headquarters when I had chicken pox, answering what I thought were innocent questions, which had been disastrous for me, I kept moving and never looked in the officers' direction. I was no fool.

About an hour later, I was still looking, and I was still lost, so now fear of being on my own set in. I know you are thinking I should be happy, but I was five, maybe six, at this point, and the only way to explain it to you would be based on a crime drama I had watched. These older kids between ages ten and thirteen take a three-year-old boy from his mother in a mall. They then bring this poor baby by the railroad and abuse him, and this poor baby is crying and scared, probably wondering where his poor mother is, so he goes to his abusers for comfort. Instead of feeling any sense of compassion for this poor child, they kill him. Just thinking of this is making me angry. So I think you now understand my situation a bit more. Of course, it was not what this child went through, but I was in an abusive home, and I was afraid all the time, but it was a home nonetheless.

My fear was now at its zenith, and I started to cry, knowing I was going to be lost forever. I tried to conceal the tears by quickly wiping them away and trying to muffle my cries. Still, with all my effort of trying to hide the distress, a woman walked over to me, bending over to ask if something was wrong with me. I quickly covered my face so as to not show any weakness, but she kindly removed my hand from my face. I smelled her perfume, which was very subtle, not overbearing. Her hands were soft with manicured nails that were painted red. She had a nice face with a little makeup. She had curly red hair that touched down to her neck. She had on a red dress suit that matched her fingernails and the color of her high-heeled shoes.

Now sobbing even louder that broke out into a full outcry with a stream of tears, along with a snot running from my nose, I told her in the best way I could between sobs that I was lost and could not find my mother. I was trying to catch my breath. She then wiped away my tears and nose, telling me, "It's okay. We will find her. You should not worry." She grabbed my hands as she stood up after cleaning off my face with a handkerchief she pulled out of her purse. As we walked, she asked me the last time I saw her, her name, and what she had on. I answered all her questions. She grabbed my hand, rubbing it, telling me everything would be fine. She squeezed my hand lightly to reassure me of what she had just said.

A moment later, we were standing in front of the two police officers I had tried avoiding. At this time, I was afraid because I thought I was in trouble for not staying where I was supposed to be sitting at. I had always feared law enforcement, especially in Liberia. Back there, the cops were corrupt and did not hide it. They also broke more laws than the whole population. For instance, if you were a child and your parents have beaten you and you were bleeding and if you reported it to the cops, they would tell you to get the hell out of their face, along with some other derogatory words, or they themselves would beat you and return you to the place of the abuse. So as you can see, it was not worth your while to go the police, and I thought all cops did the same thing, even in America, thus my silence when asked by one of the officers, "What's wrong?" I said nothing and retreated behind the lady who brought me to them. "It's okay, fella. We are here to help you." I still offered no explanation.

The lady told them I was lost and looking for my mother, and after giving that information, she told me it was okay to talk to these officers because she would leave my side. I did loosen up a bit but kept my guard up. That was when the same officer asked me what my mother had on. I tried my best to answer his question at this juncture, but I could not because I didn't want them beating me for looking at them, so I only gave a vague answer, like she had a white T-shirt with things on the front, as well as a pair of blue jeans; that was the best I could do. The officers then had me follow them to their office, where they took a report before announcing that I was a lost child and that they were looking for his mother. They also had security and police officers on foot and some in vehicles to search everywhere, including the parking garage.

The search had been going on for a while. I waited for news, but nothing came. All of a sudden, a cold chill came over my body that caused me to physically tremble. I recognized the cold chill to be fear. I knew that because it had come down my back before, going through the rest of my body. The only difference between this fear and the others was that I was scared for my mom rather than for me. I started to think, *What if she's been hurt and she's waiting for me to save her?* I also thought that since David would not have me to hit on, he may turn on her. With that, I wanted to find her as quickly as possible, but all I could do was sit all day until she was located.

Two hours later, officers and security people had looked through all the parking garages with little to no success. They had done their best to find her but had nothing. The day had gotten away from us with no fruit to reap from the efforts of all involved; most of the officers who had begun to help during the earliest of my case were now going to change shifts with the night-shift officers. The officers came to introduce themselves, asking if I wanted something to eat or drink, and I had informed them I was not hungry. I mean, put yourself in my position, feeling like you are alone in the world, as well as being lost. Food will be the last thing on your mind.

When the night-shift officers conducted the same search and followed the same procedure, nothing came out of their hard work as well. Now the lady who had come to my aid in the very beginning was still by me and was still trying to comfort and reassure me that everything was going to be okay, but there was a difference in her face, eyes, and the way she rubbed my hand, like she herself was not really believing what she was trying to help me believe. While trying to comfort me, the officers were still coming in and out of the little office we were in; and each time, they would smile and try avoiding direct and long eye contact before asking if I was hungry and saying I could have anything, and all I had to do was ask, but I think they really only came to get a look at me.

The head officer, I think he was the sergeant for the night shift, came. With him was a lady dressed in a gray pantsuit, holding a briefcase, some books, and what looked like the same folders I carried in school.

The sergeant offered the lady a seat and introduced her as being family and a child service officer who was here to take me with her because a whole day had almost gone by with no success of finding my mother. I would have to go with her until they could find her or a family member who would agree to take me. Upon hearing that, I immediately began to cry. So the lady from family services moved toward me, trying to calm me down, but I retreated as she tried to touch me.

The lady who had been with me all day told me, "It's okay. I will take care of it." Then she asked the social worker if she would talk to her outside for a minute, to which she agreed. She told me she would be right back and got up, but I refused to let go of her hand. I was starting to cry again, fearing she would leave too, never to return, but she assured me she would only be right outside and told me I would be able to see her right through the window. She pointed to it, causing me to look at the window. I had not seen it before, which was surprising because it was huge. So I agreed to finally let her hand go, and I walked straight over to the glass window, looking out, eagerly waiting for her return. I watched intently as they had a conversation, which I could not hear because the door was closed, and the window was thick. Although I could not hear their conversation, I knew they were talking about me because, every so often, they looked in my direction and pointed at me.

About fifteen to twenty minutes later, they walked back into the little office, and the social worker told the officer that she would be in touch on Monday because they were closed on weekends, and today was Friday. She shook the officer's hand and then the other lady's hand. I will call her Red because I don't remember her name, and she had a lot of red on.

When the social worker left, Red sat down to let me know I would be going home with her for the weekend while they looked for my mom. Hearing that had been the best news I had heard all day for some reason. I felt safe with her, and I thought I could trust her. With that, she and the sergeant helped me gather all my things, including all the treats and toys the officers had bought for me to make me feel better. After packing up everything and grabbing Red's things, the sergeant called a couple of his officers to help escort us to her car.

I did not know what was going to happen to me at this point, but I had given the officers the name of my father, whom I did not know was even in America at the time, along with my brother Samuel, whom I had only met in Liberia before coming to America. I also gave the names of a few others, but the craziest thing was the whole time, after moving from New York, my mother never let me know our address, so maybe she had been planning with David to achieve what they had done now, which was to abandon me.

The drive from the airport to Red's house was very long, and I had to use the restroom really bad. During the whole ride, she had held my hand, never letting go and keeping her promise of never leaving my side. She was able to get me to open up a little but only for a brief moment.

We pulled to a gate that looked as huge and important as the first building I saw in America. It was only the guardhouse. I knew that only because I saw two officers step out of it and say hello to Red, asking her who her friend was, referring to me. Of course, being introduced to them, I gave a half-hearted smile. Then she pressed some buttons, which sounded to me like pressing numbers on a phone, and the gate opened, which I thought was cool because I had never seen a thing like that before. *You can open something without a key!* So I thought she must be rich because she even had her own police officers guarding the gate. It's amazing the way your mind work and how far your imagination goes as a child, but of course, now I know better.

Anyway, we got to the house, and she pushed another button in her car. That opened up another door, and she parked the car in the house, which was even more amazing for me because I had never seen a garage before. I couldn't believe that this woman even had a house for her car. She must be the absolute richest person in the whole world. *This is fantastic*, I thought. Above all else, I thought that was just unbelievable that someone as important as this woman would take the time to help me of all people. I thought I must be the luckiest boy in the world, but now I'm a rational adult, and I realize that, because I had no one, God put the right people in place to help me along the way, so my belief and my faith are very strong.

When we got in the house, everything was nice, clean, and white. She had a big television in the sitting area with cream-colored furniture. From the sitting room, you were able to see the kitchen; even that was clean. There were no dirty dishes anywhere, and she even had pots and pans hanging high above a huge stove, but this stove was flat, and you could not touch into it; the whole thing was just flat. She told me to put down my bag and that she would show me the rest of the house, but I had to use the bathroom so bad that I started doing the dance we all do as kids when we need to go. So I swiftly interrupted her midsentence to ask where the bathroom was. She showed it to me with a giggle. I did not understand what was so funny at the time.

I quickly darted around the corner into the bathroom. It was even clean in there; her bathroom had the normal things in it that everyone has. The only thing that was out of place for me was that she had books and magazines in hers. At that time, I could not understand why anyone would want books that you touched with your hands, and sometimes you put your finger in your mouth to get it moist to turn the pages. I just could not grasp why you would put them in a place like this with the things that went on in there. After admiring the bathroom and how clean it was, I decided I would sit down so no urine would touch the seat or anything else and to prevent missing in my eagerness to relieve myself.

I finally came out of the bathroom, and Red asked me if I was okay. I nodded yes and decided to tell her to put her books somewhere because of the reasons I observed earlier. She giggled again and continued with the tour of her house. I loved every part of it and hoped I could live in a place like that one day because I knew that would be too good for me.

We then went to put my bag in the room she told me I would be sleeping in, and even that room was nice. It had a big bed that had steps on it because it was so high, and it had two desks on each side with lamps on. All were made of the same wood. The room also had a huge closet that I could walk into. There were desks and drawers, as well as light. My room even had its own bathroom with two whole sinks. I wondered why anyone would need two sinks and multiple rooms and bathrooms if just one person was living in the house. But I remembered she was rich, so she could spend a lot of money on unnecessary things. I thought I would advise her on being a lot more frugal because I liked her and did not want her wasting money. I also figured why she even needed to hire two officers when she already had a gate like that. You see, where I came from, because we had very little, we were sure to use everything and not waste any of it.

Immediately after stepping out of the bathroom door, Red asked me what I wanted to eat for dinner. I did not even know, but I knew I was very hungry, and the question kind of blindsided me because I was not from a home where children had a choice or asked how they felt about anything. Red asked me again what I wanted for dinner. I guess I must not have responded to her question adequately enough. I shrugged, saying I did not know. Red then said she did not know either, so she suggested looking at a few menus and ordering something we may find appetizing. We walked through the kitchen to get into the sitting area. After sitting, we started the search to figure out what we would order for dinner, and it was not long until we decided to order Chinese food, which I was fine with because it had rice.

As we waited for the food to arrive, Red put on a movie and popped some popcorn for our sleepover slash movie night. She also had a tent put up in the living room with a sleeping bag and then lit a fire in the fireplace so we could roast marshmallow to make s'mores, which I had never had before but kind of liked. We picked a movie that starred one of my favorite persons at that particular time in my life—Bruce Lee. The movie was *Chinese Connection*, and it became my favorite Bruce Lee movie.

Just as we settled down for the movie, the doorbell rang; it was our food that had been delivered. Red took the food from the young man who delivered it and handed it over to me. She then signed a piece of paper and gave it back to the boy, and he left. That was another thing that amazed me about Red. She was so rich and people respected her so much that she didn't even have to pay for anything. All she had to do was write a note to people, informing them that she wanted it or anything else she pleased. I had seen my mom pay for stuff everywhere. We would reach in a bag and pull out money. I also had observed my dad, along with a group of other men, pay for things by going into their back pocket and pulling out money from what my dad had told me was a wallet. However, he had failed to also let me know that you had to work to put money in there, so I thought that, since I had never seen any kid with a wallet, when you grew up and became a man, a wallet would automatically appear in your back pocket filled with money so you could pay for things with it, but I had never seen anyone pay for things by writing a letter.

Back in the sitting room or our campsite, we got in our tent, turning on our flashlights because we had cut off all the lights in the house, as well as the fire. We were cozy and very comfortable eating our food as we watched Bruce Lee beat a lot of people. The food was good, but it was nothing compared with the one in New York or as authentic as the one I had when a friend of mine had invited me to his house, but it served its purpose for the night. I had ordered the same thing I always did, which was shrimp fried rice with fried chicken wings. Red gave me some of her food, and it was even better. She said it was called sesame chicken, so I gave her some of my food as well. We then finished our meal but still had some of hers and mine left over, which she put in the fridge for us before returning to our campsite.

The Bruce Lee movie had finished, so we picked another one called *Commando*. I really liked that one, but even before it had begun, I started getting tired after the day I had. My young body was exhausted. I did not know exactly when it was I fell asleep. Red must have been tired as well because she fell asleep way before me, or at least that was what I thought.

Barely awake the next morning, feeling warm and cozy, I thought that the last days were nothing but a nightmare I had just dreamed of, so I snuggled even deeper into the warm, fluffy blankets and pillows to sleep for a few more hours. That was when it hit me like a ton of bricks. My bed was not nearly this big. Plus, I never had soft, puffy comforters and pillows, and my room was not this huge. I jolted out of bed, falling flat on my face, bringing me to the realization that the last hours were definitely not a dream, meaning my life was still the horrible one I had yesterday, today, and probably in the future.

Having been awakened and knowing that my life was still pathetic, the sudden realization of it brought back fear, sadness, and then depression, followed by abandonment and loneliness. I was now crying again, feeling the frustration and pain. I did not want to wake Red up or let her know I was crying, so I tried suppressing my tears and muffled any noise coming from my mouth, causing everything to just come streaming forward. I could no longer control any of it, and all of a sudden, I burst into full crying, mouth open, nose snotty.

Then I heard footsteps approaching my room, so I pulled the covers over my face because did not want her to see me at my weakest. She climbed up on the bed to sit next to me, and she said, "Knock, knock," but I kept crying, still trying to control it the best I could. Red told me how very sorry she was that all these were happening to me and how proud she was of me being as strong as I was because if it were her, she would not know what to do. She also told me my mom would be found soon and that she was probably out looking for me, worrying that she may never see me, but that I would be back home with her. Honestly, that did not cheer me up at all. It was only when she said she was always going to be by my side, even if they found my family, that I calmed down; she said she would always be my friend and keep tabs on me with an occasional visit. She then asked for a hug, wrapping her arms around me, pulling me up close to her, slowly pulling down my blanket off my face. She hugged me even harder, rocking me side to side, and then she made funny faces at me as she smiled, revealing perfect polished white teeth.

I was a little confused that Red had not taken off her clothes to make me do to her what my babysitter did. The only thing I did not want her to do was push my head between her legs. Red got up from the bed, telling me to get ready for breakfast so we could eat before we left the house because she had a surprise for me. "Call me if you need my help, okay?" she said, walking down the stairs.

I responded, "Okay," and got up to take a shower. The bathroom was even larger than what I had thought the previous night. I then remembered I needed soap, towels, toothbrush, and toothpaste, so I called after her to let her know what I needed. She told me that everything was already in the bathroom in the closet. I turned around to the room's doorway, where I found everything exactly where it was. I was really excited to see this surprise that Red had for me, so I quickly took my shower and did not do a very good job of it. Stepping out of the shower, I combed my hair, brushed my teeth, and got dressed.

I ran down the stairs, missing a few steps. That was when I noticed how really nice Red's place was as the sun shone down on me, emitting this light. I looked up to see straight out the clouds. At first glance, I thought there was a hole in the roof, but it was a glass roof. It was so nice. I studied the room. It had big windows, and I came to really fall in love with the house, wishing I lived there or hoping Red would keep me because I really started to like her. I told myself that one day I would own a house like this. At that very moment, I was brought out of my daydream by Red's asking if I was ready. "Yes," I replied, and she opened the door. We got into her car and drove out.

I looked out of the window to see other nice houses and beautiful grass, trees, and flowers; it was all truly breathtaking. Red asked me if I had ever been to a fair before. I had not. I did not even know what it was or heard of it until that very moment. We drove past another group of guys whom I had thought were Red's personal police officers, except this time I was paying more attention. The two officers were on my side of the vehicle now, allowing me to see from their head all the way down to their shoes, unlike last night when they had been on Red's side, and it was dark. One of the officers bent down to look in the car so he could talk to both Red and myself. He asked her where she and I were heading this early on a Saturday morning. "To the fair," Red replied. "Shawn has never been to one before." She rubbed my head, making me smile at her.

"Well, it's good to see you smile because yesterday you did not look too happy," the guard told me.

"Yeah, yesterday was rough for him," Red told him and then also gave him more information on my situation. If Red have told the guard or anyone else what happened to me the day before, I would have gotten sad all over again, and I more than likely would have burst out in tears, but today I was happy and really enjoyed being with Red. The guard felt sorry for me, and I kind of think he regretted bringing up a conversation that led him to find out about my situation. He didn't make eye contact and would only look down. He then quickly reached into his back pocket, pulling out and revealing his wallet, to get a twenty-dollar bill, handing it to me. I did not take it, and he offered it to me again, so I turned to look at Red for approval. She motioned for me to take it, so I did.

He rubbed my head, telling me, "Have some cotton candy," which was something I knew about, so I took it and thanked him. "No problem, buddy." He waved. "My shift is over. I'm going to go get some sleep." It was another thing I did not understand because he had come out of his home to greet us last night, and he had obviously spent the night at home, so why didn't he sleep? Then instead of waiting for the morning when his other police friends came to visit, now he was about to sleep, not even giving his friends some food. I mean, in Liberia, if anyone came to visit, we always gave them food, even before they asked for it. And hungry or not, they would eat so as not to insult the host.

Anyway, when the officer was walking away, I noticed he did not carry a gun, handcuffs, or any of the other things I've seen police officers wear on their belt. So now I was saying to myself, *What does he do after he catches a crook? How does he detain them to carry them to jail? I mean, because he does not have handcuffs, these criminals will escape, and the officer will get fired. That guy must be the laziest police officer of all time.*

Another officer came over to the car to talk to us, and he was not one of the officers from the night before. I knew that because, even though it was dark when we stopped, I knew they were both big men with higs and who were clean, and they both had big bellies and were much older than the new officer who was talking to us then. This officer was younger, tall, and slender. He had a full beard that made me not like him instantly because men only two categories for me at the time: good and bad. All men who were clean-shaven or just had a mustache belonged in the good category. However, any men who had a full beard with a mustache were all bad. I came to that reasoning because of my uncle and David, but through my life up to that, I had been correct. The officer tried his best to try to get a smile or some type of reaction from me with no success.

We waved at the officers, continuing on our journey down to this fair. Red told me how much I would love it. I turned to her and asked why the officer who gave me the twenty-dollar bill wanted me to eat cotton by telling me it was candy when everyone knew it was not a candy at all. Red chuckled before she told me it was not really cotton like the ones in the bathroom, but it looked a lot like it. I just said okay, and I think Red knew I did not understand, so she told me, "You are about to see."

We've been in the car for what seemed like forever. Red and I sang a lot of songs and played games like how license plates were from a different state than ours. We also played my game, which was us basically picking cars that we wanted to own, but the other person had to agree it was a great car. I really liked that game because I could daydream about how different my life would be when I grew up. Then I told myself I would buy Red a white car; it was what she wanted. I then quickly dismissed that way of thinking because Red was already rich and had the ability to purchase whatever it was that her heart desired. The last game we played was 'I spy with my little eye,' a guessing game where you give clues of the environment around you, and the other person has to guess what it is you see. It was Red's turn to describe something she saw, making it my turn to guess. Red's first clue to me was "What is it that my friend Shawn is excited to get to and see?" I did immediately start to guess as she spurted out a bunch of clues, until she pointed to huge wheels.

We got off the exit on top of a big hill, where I saw tents with people walking around with food in their hands and smelled delicious odors emitting from everywhere. There were children screaming as they rode on a bunch of rides. This place looked just like Coney Island, where my mom and David had taken me. During that time, we stood in line for food and drinks. I looked around me to notice my mother was gone, so I panicked and took off to find her. Shortly afterward, I was able to find her. I was crying, thinking I would never see her again. When I found her, she did not seem too concerned. Plus she did not react like a parent whose child went missing. Usually, upon finding him or her, they would scold their child because they were worried. Not my mom though. She acted like, "Oh, were you gone?" Yeah, that was her reaction.

I did not want to mess up Red's surprise or hurt her feelings by telling her, "Oh yeah, I've been to a place like this before," so I was still very excited. But I still did not know what cotton candy was. I never saw it at Coney Island, not that we bought food while we were there anyway. Red took my hand and pulled me close, telling me we had to make sure I did not get separated from her. I smiled at her and began our day with that. She asked me what I wanted to ride first. Without any hesitation, I picked the Mindbender, a ride that held two to three people in each sitting area; eight people were all connected to what looked like an octopus. Before we got on the ride, we needed tickets. We purchased a whole roll of them. I was happy to see that because I wanted to ride all of them, which I never got to do at Coney Island.

A full day had almost gone by, and after a day of rides, cotton candy, and a variety of different junk foods like funnel cakes, candy apple, and chili dogs, we had also played different games, such a dunking or shooting games, throwing games, and those that involved throwing a ring around bottles' necks. We played a game that gave you three tries to knock down some bottles or cans, and all had prizes for anyone who won. We had done pretty well, winning three prizes, which were all stuffed animals.

Time has really gone by fast today, I thought to myself, and I was very tired and continuously yawning, so Red said it was time to go. We left the fair to get to our car, which seemed a lot farther than I remembered. I think that was partly because I was very tired. As we drove away, I could see different lights bouncing around with the dark background of the night, making it look even better. And if I was not too tired, I would have wanted to be back to spend more time there.

I must have been asleep in the car on our way back because one minute I was talking to Red, thanking her for the day we had spent together and how much fun it was, and then I couldn't remember anything. She then asked if I was hungry, and I told her no. I mean, really, after a day of junk food, followed by sugary drinks, I did not want to even think about food because I was so stuffed that breathing was hard.

When we arrived home, I must have still been asleep because the next thing I remembered was waking up in bed, needing to use the bathroom. I got up and headed into the bathroom, and that was when I overheard Red talking on the phone. I knew they were talking about me based on what Red said like, "Yeah, he's asleep." I was the only *he* in the house. She continued on with her conversation, trying not to wake me up. She told whomever she was talking to about our day and the previous one, and then I heard her say something that made my blood run cold. She was told they found my family member who would pick me up in the morning. I really had to use the restroom. My heart was beating uncontrollably under my shirt. I did not want to be uprooted again so I could stay with someone else I did not know just as I was getting acclimated to a new place and person. I felt sick. My stomach was doing flips. I felt like I had to vomit.

I went ahead and used the bathroom and then returned to my bed. While lying, I was able to hear the last part of Red's conversation, which helped me figure out to whom she was talking. She asked the lady if we were supposed to meet her at the airport in the same office we first met. That was when I figured out that it was indeed the social worker because there were only two women in the office at that time.

I sat up in my bed still eavesdropping on Red's conversation, and then she hung up and headed into the hallway. I lay down, pretending to be asleep, but she was not fooled. "Get up, you faker," she told me, turning on the light. She climbed up onto the bed to sit next to me. "I know that you heard what is going to happen tomorrow." I nodded yes without looking at her. I was staring down at my hands, rubbing them together. She put her hand under my chin to tell me it was okay, turning my face up for me to look at her. "I will be right there tomorrow to put you on the plane." I also learned my father was coming to get me from the airport, along with my brother. I was immediately happy and could not wait to see them. It had already been two years since I had seen my dad and my brother, so I lay back down to sleep so I could go see them early the next morning.

Red woke me up at around four o'clock, which was too early for me because I had not really slept after Red left my room. I did try to get to sleep, but I was just too excited to close my eyes, so I sat up thinking about how good it would be to see my dad and my brother. Before I knew it, time had flown by, and the night was almost over, so I lay down to sleep, and that was when Red woke me up to get ready to leave for the airport for my flight.

At the airport, Red and I met the social worker before heading to the gate. Red sat me down to let me know she would stay by my side until my flight left, but before that, she said that she needed to speak to the flight attendants to give them some instructions on where I was going so that, when we got to the first stop for a layover because it was not a nonstop flight to New Jersey, they would make sure I made it to my next flight. Red returned to me so she could inform me of what was to take place when I started my trip. We sat in silence for a while, and Red would occasionally ask me if I was okay. Of course, I was, so that was what I told her.

But before I left her, I wanted to thank her for everything. In my mind, I tried thinking of how I was going to tell her that. I had butterflies in my stomach, so after ten to fifteen minutes, something told me to count to three and go on with it. I sat back looking at her hand as it held mine. I counted, *One, two* ... And before I got to three, I thanked her for the days I spent with her and for being with me the whole time. I also thanked her for the fair, the cotton candy, and everything else.

She smiled and thanked me. Of course, right then, I was unclear why she decided I needed to be thanked. She told me I was good and that she having known me was a great experience. Above all else, she told me she was already missing me as her home would never be the same. I saw tears coming down her face, and she tried holding them back. She told me, "When I have children one day, I hope they are like you." I thanked her again with a hug and tears of my own.

Then we heard over the intercom that my flight was about to start boarding. We stood up as an airline agent told me she would be the one who would put me on the plane. I hugged Red again as the agent asked me if I was ready. I said yes, and she brought me to the plane. I turned around one more time to look at Red, and she was still standing there waving goodbye. I waved back and then disappeared into the plane.

The stewardess took my hand and asked for my name. I told her, and she brought me to my seat. I sat down, and she buckled my seat belt, telling me to push the button above me if I needed anything. She also told me that, upon liftoff, she would come around to take food orders. I really was not hungry, so I really did not care.

The captain spoke over the intercom to let us know we were about to take off. He also told us how long the flight would be, which was about five hours. He even told us the weather. And when he had finished, the stewardesses told us about the safety guidelines, basically what we would do in case of an emergency. I did not really pay attention to any of that; my mind was somewhere else. When the safety instructions were over, they went to sit down, buckling themselves in, ready for takeoff.

The plane started moving slowly at first and then faster and faster; it was now rumbling loud and finally in the air. I was enjoying it all because I was once again by the window, staring out of it. I was already starting to miss Red because I knew that I would never have the capability to reach out to her and just thank her for everything.

Chapter 4

NEW BEGINNINGS

I arrived in Newark, New Jersey, at around three o'clock in the morning. I was instructed by the stewardess to not leave the plane until she could escort me so that she could make sure I was delivered to no one else except my dad. I agreed not to leave the plane until the proper time, but I was getting excited, ready to go see my dad and brother. Besides, I had been seated in the same spot for the whole six-hour flight. Imagine, I was only six years old, which meant my attention span was really short. I watched the other passengers getting off.

Before it was my turn, the lady came to me, asking if I was ready. I mean, did she have to even ask? She gave me her hand for me to take. Not wanting to make her feel bad, I took it, but I don't remember how long I held on to her because, upon getting off the plane and heading toward baggage claim, I saw my father, along with my brother. I ran, leaping on my father so fast that I could not believe it. My dad held me close, hugging me with love and compassion before setting me back down, never letting go of my hand as he picked up my luggage. As I pointed out my luggage, my brother came over, shaking my hand before hugging me as well. My father thanked the stewardess, and we went home.

Arriving in my new home, I was a little dumbfounded; it looked nothing like the places I had seen while with Red, but it was not too different from New York. Walking in the house, I met my uncle Francis, whom I thought at the time was the biggest guy I had seen. He came up looking down at me and said, "Did your father ever tell you about me?"

I replied, "No, he did not," and that was the only thing he said to me for that day, not that he was mean or unsociable, but he was just a man of a few words, which I liked because I was not talkative back then anyway. The next person I met was my aunt Melvina, who was very nice and spoke softly. The last person I met was my eight-month-old cousin Jacye, who was all over the place but would mostly go to my father but not too much my aunt and my uncle, and I would find out why later.

The next few days would be very demoralizing, and the next few years would be crippling. That morning, my dad knew my mom's number and address, so he called her to try figuring out what went wrong. She informed him that she wanted nothing to do with me. She told him how she had wished she had never even had me or even came to get me in the first place and that I was a useless, ungrateful child, along with some other expletives before hanging up. My dad was shocked as was everyone; he repeated the conversation and was also hit with disbelief. My dad and everyone who met me, interacted with me, or had known me did never see any of those things my mom had said about me.

The next day, a letter came addressed to my aunt and uncle from my mom basically reiterating the phone conversation from the previous day, along with some extra issues. The letter was eight to ten pages, and I heard every word of it. Even at that age, it hurt me, but I refused to show any weakness. After the letter was read, my father tried calling my mother, which proved to be a whole lot more difficult today than yesterday because the phone was disconnected, so he decided he would write her a letter to plead with her to take me back because he needed to travel and did not want to put more burden on my aunt and uncle as my elder brother was already living with them. Well, let me tell you, after writing that letter and overnighting it, the letter was returned to sender. It seemed my mother was ahead of the game and had already moved to parts unknown. So here I was, not exactly sure of my future or even that very moment, but there was one thing that was always clear to me: I was unwanted and a burden. These were two words I would hear throughout my whole childhood and thereafter.

The first month with my dad, brother, uncle, and auntie and the whole Spencer clan was terrific. We went out a lot. We were always fishing, going to the zoo, taking pictures. It was a family life I had only seen in white families. I myself never experienced them before. Also, the idea of having an elder brother was great. I looked up to Samuel, and he always protected me but, at the same time, instilled toughness in me. We fought a lot—I mean, physical fights with no holds barred. Even though we had issues, it was only momentary. I guess they happened because Dad had to divide his attention—an attention we both wanted. Then I learned I had an even older brother named Morris and a younger sister named Gartee, whom my dad had sent for so we could all meet.

The day they arrived, it was exciting. I mean, I was alone at one time, and then I had a lot of siblings. The first time I saw Morris, I liked him. He was that cool elder brother, but after a few hours with him, I hated his guts because he was a bully. I don't know if it was just teenage hormones or if he was just an ass. I just tried staying out his way, but Samuel had the attitude of "fuck you," and they clashed a lot more than he and I did, so we came together to battle a common enemy. My sister Gartee I always liked; she was really smart but laid back and a daddy's girl. Even at that age, I knew I could never contend with her when it came to getting Dad's attention, so I left that alone.

We had all been together for about a week, and the dynamics of the relationships that I had come to love started to change for the worst, especially for me and Samuel. It started with my brother Samuel; he was still peeing in the bed, and one morning my dad beat him with blows from his fist and kicks. I had never thought my father was like that, and I felt horrible for Samuel. The hurt and shame on his face was unexplainable.

After that horrible morning, we were supposed to visit a friend of my father, so we got ready to go. I was about to leave the house when my father stopped me at the door to tell me he did not want me going with him because he was embarrassed of me and was tired of people asking why my eyes were yellow at some points, but my uncle came to my rescue, basically scolding my father, who younger than him; our African tradition said your big brother was basically like a father. So that day, we went to visit my dad's friend, but I did not really felt I belonged among these people anymore. It was almost as if, overnight, they became strangers. My father fell into his old habits of hoe hopping and would be spending time more with different women than with us.

On the last day of Gartee and Morris's visit, we were supposed to go to the Bronx Zoo. Of course, we were excited to hang out with him; but once again, I was stopped at the door by my father, telling me I was not going with him because I was an embarrassment. And once again, my uncle came to the rescue. At that time, my father went on saying that if I was going, he was not. So my uncle did something I had never seen him do. He took time off from work to bring us to the zoo. My father did go with us. When that happened, he was bitter the whole time. That was the last time I would see my siblings Morris and Gartee, who by the way tried her best to make me feel better after the situation with my dad, but it really did not make too much of a difference to me, even though I appreciated her effort.

The month after Morris and Gartee left, a new school year started. And since I had nowhere to go, my uncle brought me to school to enroll me, but I was surprised to find out that I would be attending school alone. My brother Samuel had to attend a different school because he was two grades lower that I was, which made me feel a certain way because he was my elder brother. I knew his feelings were really hurt by that. I never considered how he must have felt back then; he was in the second grade, while I was in the fourth, and the nearby school called Hillcrest Elementary started from fourth grade to the sixth grade. Samuel was never a scholar academically, but when it came to street smarts, my brother was gifted. I also considered my brother only in a lower grade because of him peeing in the bed, which probably broke his self-esteem, but that was just my humble opinion. I was so excited at the thought of my brother and I being together in the same school and classes, but I was disappointed when I found out differently.

On the first day of school, I was surprised to see white children because, in my neighborhood, there were no white people. How was it that they would attend a school that was a fifteen- to twenty-minute walk from the projects we lived in? I placed the thought aside and proceeded to my classes. That was when I met Mrs. Pinder, who would become one of my, if not the most, favorite teachers. Then I met Mr. Kroger, who was my homeroom, English, and math teacher, as well as my second favorite teacher.

Mrs. Pinder was very slim and of average height and had brown complexion. She had cherry red streaks in her black hair, and it would change colors in the sun. Mrs. Pinder was a very pretty young black woman, and she even had a daughter who was a part of our class. Back in those days, the media was always advertising how beautiful and better-looking white women were than blacks, which we know is not true. I agree that there were and are beautiful white women, but I preferred my sisters, but it was not always like that. It was this time that I had my first crush on this white girl in my class. I was head over heels for her. It was not until I met Diana Hearts, a beautiful black girl, that I had bought that bullshit about my sisters because all the black girls in my neighborhood looked rough. This was the time of the crack epidemic, and a lot of parents were drug addicts, which led to neglected children. They basically paid no attention to their kids, leaving the children to groom themselves so they looked the part. Diana was a totally different case, and she did not live in our projects. She was also gifted with a beautiful voice. That actually made me like her even more; she reminded me of Anita Baker not just because she was a great singer but also because they actually looked alike. Diana could be Anita's daughter. She was a replicate of Anita and her hairstyle. I could never wait to get to school every day.

After my first day of school, I returned to find out that my dad would be traveling from New Jersey to London before heading to Liberia. The next day, one of his new girlfriends escorted us to get my dad to the airport. Gloria was crying from our house all the way to the airport and back home. I mean, really, bitch? Come on, is that even possible? Don't get me wrong, I cried as well, but it was not to that extent.

We arrived at the gate and went through security to his gate. I know you are reading this and saying, "No, you did not go see your father and his gate," but this was before 9/11. We all sat down to wait for my dad's plane to arrive, and we did not need to wait long. We said our goodbyes and exchanged hugs and kisses, and once again, just like that, he was gone, out of my and my brother's life. When I thought for the first time I finally had my father, he was leaving me again. We returned home from dropping off Gloria, who lived in the same projects, so we saw her every day. Even though my dad was not home, she would still come on over to hang out with my aunt mostly.

My dad used to come frequently, and it was a lot of visits at first. Whenever he was supposed to be with us, he would rather go all over the place with different women, and we saw him less and less. When he so-called came for a visit, he would be in New York, St. Louis, and California. He was all over, and then all the visits ended.

This was when the dynamics in the house had changed. My aunt and uncle fought a lot—I mean throwing knives and dishes or whatever my aunt got her hands on. The arguments were over another woman my aunt said my uncle was having an affair with, but he said he was only helping a friend of his wife; at least that was what we learned. The truth, however, was that my uncle was stepping outside his marriage. Now I'm not sure if that very thing was why she started to mistreat my brother and me.

One of the first rules that she put into effect was that we were not allowed to touch or open the refrigerator, even though my uncle was a chef, bringing home all sorts of food, such as Philly cheesesteaks, chicken tenders, and others from all types of cuisines. The next thing was when she put my brother and me on the couch in the dining room because she thought the bedroom was too good for us and because my brother was wetting himself still. Now dining room was horrible; the window was broken, and the floor tiles were old and mostly gone, so you can imagine how cold it got in the winter.

My aunt viewed us as less than human; we were her slave. She would make us hand-wash all her and her child's clothes, but before that, she would have hot, boiling water in the bathtub, along with a lot of Clorox, and then she locked us in the bathroom. Our eyes would burn. She also made us scrub until I had pieces of my skin come off, followed by my knuckles bleeding, and the Clorox made the wound burn; the pain was incredible. After hours in the bathroom, we thought that as the water cooled, the task would become easier, but we were wrong. Here she came with more hot water, along with Clorox. I was so happy to be done and get out, but before that, my aunt would have us stay in the bathroom as our eyes and wounds burned. She would also beat us for the craziest reasons. All I remember was my lungs felt as though it were on fire; every deep breath hurt. My aunt made us do this every day to the point I knew my skin would never heal. I mean, we got beaten because our blood messed up her clothes.

My aunt was definitely not human because she showed no empathy or sorrow for the children she was abusing. I tried to stay out of my aunt's way, walking on eggshells whenever she was around. Then she started hanging out all day; she would leave the house as soon as my uncle left, and he had two jobs and was never home. He did not deviate from his schedule, so my aunt came home a few minutes before he did, taking credit for the work she made us do. My aunt was the meanest, laziest bitch I had ever met. She used to beat me to the point of almost passing out, at which time my brother begged her for mercy, asking her to beat him instead. She would turn on him like, "Why did you interrupt me?"

Times just got harder for us. At school one day, a friend of mine named Jay asked me about some scars he saw. I told him about it, and he told me I should tell the teacher. I don't know what made me think this was a great decision, but after class, I waited until all the kids in my class were gone except for Jay, my cheerleader. I informed my teacher about the abuse and did not really get any kind of a response or concern. After opening my big mouth, I left for home, thinking, *Finally, this is going to be great. We would never go through these abuses again.* Boy, was I ever off base.

As I was coming up to the house, Samuel ran to me, telling me how I was in trouble and that my aunt was waiting on me, asking what had I done. Then he told me how a teacher called my house not to see if anything I said was true but to really just tell my aunt that I was talking about her. I immediately got sick to my stomach, I had diarrhea, and I felt as if I was going to throw up. I slowly came in the house. That was when I was hit from what seemed to be everywhere; the beating and punches were such a shock.

During that beating, I told myself I would not ever trust any secrets to anyone, but I blamed myself for not knowing better, and that would be my mentality for a long time. At this point, I started to hate women a little, not in the sense of "I hate you" but more like I had to proceed with caution and not put too much trust in the female because, at this age, there was only one woman who loved me unconditionally, so she would always be in my heart. That was my grandmother. The other abused me and threw me away. One took me in for a day and then was using her authority to abuse me, so it was not equaled out yet.

At school the following day, I ran into my friend Jay again and told him that I wished I had never listened to him. We were walking when another kid joined us. His name was Levar. We spoke for a minute, and that was it. Before heading to our classes, little did I know that this guy Levar and Jay would become my best friends, even though Levar and I were closer.

In another class was where I met Shawn; he was the kid I wanted to be. For one reason, he always had new sneakers every day and never wore the same thing twice. I, on the other hand, had only been going to school for a few months, and I've already worn everything I had over and over again because there was no way in hell my aunt would spend money for us. Her philosophy was that we were not her responsibility. So out of curiosity, I asked Shawn whether his parents bought his clothes. "No, I do my own thing," he said. He told me his mom was a crack and heroin addict, so he had to slang to take care of his younger sibling and buy supplies for his mom, her drugs, so she would stay home with them. After he explained all of this to me, I had no clue what crack or heroin was, let alone slanging. We did not have those in Liberia, at least not yet, so I asked him to explain it better. He said I should meet him after school.

So after school, I hooked up with Shawn to let him educate me since we lived in the same projects. He brought me to a part of the neighborhood I had not visited before, and there were a group of guys just standing outside. When a car stopped, someone would go to the car and hand them what I thought was sugar, and the person who got the sugar paid ten to fifteen dollars for a small piece instead of just going to the store, where you got a whole bag for two to three dollars. "What is so great about your sugar?" I asked.

And once again, he said it was crack, which people smoked to get high.

"It's a drug," he said.

So I said, "Like marijuana." That I knew about because it grew in my grandmother's backyard and all over, but nobody had to sell it. You just grab them from a bush. When I first saw my father and his friends smoke this plant in my grandma's backyard, I asked myself why anyone would smoke a plant; it made no sense to me, until sometime later my cousin explained it to me. From the perspective of weed, I understood crack and heroin; and as the years passed, I would not be able to duck it.

Shawn told me selling these drugs was how he bought all of these things, and he told me I could do it too. So when a few cars came through, I went to give them the drugs; and after I was given fifty dollars, I left because if I was not in the house thirty minutes after school, it was on. I put the money in my pocket and went home.

I pulled my brother to the side to tell him that we can make a lot of money by selling drugs, and then I showed him the money. That was when Samuel explained how wrong what I just did was, and he told me the police officers would come for me, but I did not believe him at that time. My brother was always in trouble, so who the hell was he to tell me no? I figured he just wanted to be the one to make the money.

That night, I really got a good look at what the drug game was all about when I saw two guys chasing one guy as they both opened fire on him. Then I saw him hit the ground, jump back, and continue running. My brother told me, "That's what happens when you sell drugs. People are always trying to bring about your demise or destruction."

This new way of life was going to be hard to adjust to. I mean, you had a neighborhood that pulled kids from broken homes, where a father abandoned the family, or the mother was a drug addict, so she was always gone, trying to get high at all cost, leaving a lot of very young children who were trying to seek their attention, sometimes from a negative standpoint. Nine times out of ten, that child would start acting out by fighting or just being plain disrespectful, and these drug dealers preyed on children like that. It was unbelievable how these people knew which kids they could mess with. They also knew which children they would not be able to attract into their nonsense, such as children from a two-parent home.

I was amazed to find out that a lot of my classmates were drug dealers. In our community, the only successful people were drug dealers; they had the best of everything, like cars, clothes, money, women, and so on. These guys had everything that a kid like me wanted, but outside of all of that, these superstars who were so madly admired lived in these places as us. It was an achievement that was possible for that very reason. Now these dealers knew about each and everything that went on in each of the apartment, and I don't know how they were capable of finding out this information, but they did.

So now put yourself in the position of that child whose dad is gone, and your mom is more into getting high than taking care of you and your two younger siblings. You know it's not going to be easy. After all, no one is going to hire you, so that's out of the equation. As you try to make things happen, you see your friends, along with some others, promoting their product, explaining how you can do the same. After that, you see the guy with all the things you want, an older guy who is like a father figure for these kids who are selling for him. Then every few weeks, he starts to reward the kid who made the most money for him by showering this kid with a lot of attention by picking the child up in his BMW, Mercedes, or whatever car that he owns that have rims and a loud stereo system.

Upon placing him in the passenger seat, the dealer brings him, his best salesman around, to all the drug corners he has workers on and tells the other sellers, "This is my lieutenant. He sold the most, and if you do better, you can be my next man." He then brings the kid to Foot Locker to purchase a few Jordans or some Adidas for him, as well as giving the new lieutenant an extra five hundred to one thousand dollars. He then goes to put his new and best dealer around a group of other sellers. Now that all the others see these things, they in turn want that attention and love because they don't get it at home. They believe this guy is the absolute best thing, which makes them want to please him. They believe this is what love is, and soon these kids see him as a father figure instead of a manipulator who does not give a damn about them whatsoever. The only thing he wants is money, loyalty, blind ambition. Nobody tells these kids the guy is wrong and not to follow him because only a few things will happen to them; those things are death, jail, or some more horrible things that wears your body.

So after starting at a very young age, you become immersed to the lifestyle; and by the time you are eighteen, your record precedes you, where you don't have many options. You suddenly have an epiphany, realizing that all of what you had been doing was wrong. And when you try to get a job, you are unsuccessful. After all, you have no skill, and no one will give you a chance because of your résumé. To survive now, you have to return to what you know.

This story is not one of a kind. Just look around. You've seen these children start young for a few reasons. Children make the best soldier. There is no better soldier than a kid who thinks the person who has brought him in this can do no wrong, and when that child is given an order, he will follow it to the letter to please this person, even if it costs him his life because children are unaware of their mortality. We were all young once and thought we were supermen and that we were going to live forever. The drug leader brought into the game a lot of kids simply because children were not prosecuted as adults back then, so they were used to do the killings for their father figures, as well as other tasks that were asked of them.

The days of living with my aunt and uncle was getting worse to the point where my uncle started to turn on us. It seemed that every night, when he got home, my aunt brought him to their room. And after being in there for about an hour, he came out mad. Now I don't know what she did to make him be like that, but I have my theories. My aunt practiced voodoo or whatever because, each and every year, she made food for some dead spirits. Of course, it was spread out, and no one would ever touch it. But after a day or so, the food was gone, never eaten by anyone I saw in the house. I know what you are thinking. I did not want to believe it at first, but every year, it happened. With that being said, I believe she would put my uncle under a spell to make him act like that. I used to look at his face when he came out of that room, and something else was controlling my uncle because it only happened when my aunt did things to him.

And when I thought that was as bad as it would get for Samuel and me, I had been sadly mistaken because my aunt was pregnant again. Each time she found out she was pregnant, my aunt would lie down from that moment until she gave birth. We were already doing everything in the house, including taking care of my cousin, as my aunt hung out. But now she was always home, and she was lazy. But that never stopped her cruelty. It had gotten so bad that one day, after my uncle had cooked so he could leave for work, exactly after he left, my aunt told us to fix her a plate and fix my cousin some so she could eat. But we were not going to be eating what she and her daughter ate; instead, she gave us rotten food that had been in the refrigerator for a while. We smelled the food, and upon taking a bite, we instantly knew it was spoiled, but we still had to eat it or nothing at all.

My brother devised a plan of jumping out one of the back windows, and then he would get us something, but it had to be something my aunt would not miss at all. So when my aunt fell asleep, we put the plan into effect. Samuel jumped out of the window and came back with two cups with rice. He explained we had to soak the rice in water, and when it softened a bit, we would add sugar to it and let it stand some more before we could finally eat it. I mean, where were we going to cook it? Besides, after a few more times of eating this rice with sugar, it became my favorite. It's amazing what you can get used to.

There was a particular night when it was raining really hard, and it became Samuel's turn again to jump out the back window and get us something to eat. As he stepped out on the ledge, he slipped all the way down. I panicked as I heard him moan and groan, so I quickly went to get my aunt, but she did not care and never came to check on him. By the grace of God, he got up with no injuries because if he had broken something, my aunt would just leave him with a broken bone.

It was just not an option. With his bruises and mine from all the abuse, I mean, my brother and I

looked like death. We were not taken care of the way I know now that children are to be treated. I just thought this was how life was for everyone, so when my friend Jay had instructed me to place that first abuse complaint and nothing came of it, I knew it was just because of that very reason.

My morale, my spirit was being broken little by little every day as was my brother's. We were in a situation that could not and did not allow us to relax in our so-called home, where we were supposed to be safe. Instead, my heart was always trying to jump out of my chest. There was no such thing as downtime, especially now that my aunt was pregnant. She did not leave us alone like she used to. Her being gone gave us a chance to relax.

I hated being at home. I could not wait until the next day so I could return to school. I began every day by waking up at five so I would start my walk to school. I was up early that no one had even gotten there except for a few teachers, along with the principal and the janitorial service, but I did not care. I was just happy to be there. When I heard the three o'clock bell at the end of the day, I became physically sick. My stomach knotted up. I felt as though I had to urinate and throw up as if I had diarrhea. With every step, I trembled. The closer I got to my home, the more I would violently begin to shake. Then I would get into the house and hear the closing of the door with the lock and chain, making sure I was not getting out. In that house, you could feel this thick dark fog that just lingered, and it was very heavy, almost to the point of madness.

The weekends were the absolute worst time for me and my brother. When the week was coming to an end, my classmates would get excited, talking about what they were going to do with their family. For me, however, Friday was just a reminder that I was going to be depressed and scared as hell, and I had this pain in my stomach that would not quit. It's hard to describe, but it felt like sharp, cutting pain or a deep stabbing feeling you could not quench. I don't know if my pain was more psychological or what, but I knew it was physical, and I always had this pain; however, it would get worse when I was at home, especially on the weekends or anytime we had breaks from school.

As my classmates discussed their up-and-coming adventure, I asked my teacher if I could be excused so I could use the restroom. "Sure, go ahead," he said. On my way out, I heard laughter and excitement all the way down the hall. I entered the bathroom just in time, where I vomited everything that was in me, and that was basically nothing because I did not have an appetite, so I did not eat my lunch or even the dessert, a big cookie with caramel that I would have devoured at any other time except on the weekend and any other day or time I knew I was going to be home.

After vomiting my insides out, I returned to a still excited classroom, with my teacher telling the class what he was doing for the weekend. And when he was done, one of my classmates named Fred asked, "What are you going to do this weekend, Shawn?" I was not really caught off guard because this happened every Friday, so as usual, I lied my ass off instead of just telling them how fucked up my family was; that was out of the question. So I proceeded to make up a cock-and-bull story about us going to a great adventure with all these rides with my best and perfect family, until I was reminded that it was too cold for great adventures. Now I had only said *great adventures* because I had seen a commercial a while ago and wished I would be able to go there.

I was also very aware that I would only go to a place in two ways. One way I could go was by using my imagination. The other was to be found by my real family who had lost me at birth because these people could have never been my real family. So one day there would be a knock on the door, and I would open it. I would see these two people who were unbelievably rich, and they had found me after all these years, and they would just take me away. But before we left, I would tell them I had a brother, and I would only go with them if my brother could go too. Of course, they would agree, and we would get in a limousine to drive down to his school to pick him up. We would not even have to pack our clothes, which we did not have much of anyway. I think between my brother and me, we each have two pairs of pants, along with a few shirts, which we had used over and over again. One time, a teacher asked me if the shirt I wore all the time was my favorite, not knowing I only had that one. I was embarrassed as everyone looked at me, so I replied, "Yes, it's my favorite shirt," while I felt beads of sweat starting to form on my forehead.

Now after lying to my friends and classmates about my made-up weekend adventure, I started backpedaling to tell them I was going to the one in California, where my brother and sister lived, and I only knew about that because they told us about it during their visit. After I saw that the class had bought my story, I had to reiterate to my classmates that I thought I was the luckiest kid alive. If only they knew, right?

Three o'clock was coming closer and closer, and any minute now, I would hear that bell causing my stomach pains. It's kind of unbelievable as I write it, but I never had to look at the clock to know it was time for my day to end because my stomach would just start aching, and then I would hear the bell. People used to call me slow, but I had to walk slowly because of the unbearable pain in my stomach. This pain would not quit; there was nothing that would ease it, and every movement hurt. The bell finally did ring as I sat there trying to hide how much pain I was going through. I sat at my desk pretending I was packing my book bag, waiting for my classmates to leave. Then my friend Jay and Levar came to get me, asking, "Why are you still sitting there? If I were going to California, I would run all the way home." I never told Jay and Levar everything that was going on, so if you're reading this and thinking I should have asked my friends for help, then you have not been paying attention.

I got up finally when I came to understand that I would be sitting for a long time if I just waited for the pain to stop, so I joined my friends in our ritual of walking home together and making jokes. However, I never really had much to say, knowing what awaited me at home.

My friends Jay and Levar did not live in my projects. From what I learned, they lived in a house, but I had never been to their home and would sure as hell never bring them to where I lived; my aunt would not allow it. As a kid, I did not understand why my aunt never allowed my friends to come over to my house, but now I know. It was for the same reason why we were never allowed to go to a hospital no matter how sick we got, especially me because people would see the abuse. Even if I were allowed to bring friends over to my house, I would not have invited them over anyway. Why would I? There were roaches and rats all over and shootings, drug dealers, and junkies all over the place. Would you invite your friends to a place like that? I don't think so. Oh, and let's not forget about the random violence and shoot-outs.

After a slow, deliberate walk, my friends and I reached a kind of fork in the road where we always parted; they went left, and I went right after our usual goodbye handshakes. Now I don't know if it was just nature or how things grew, but at the place that sent my friends and me in separate ways, there was a long, high hedge that ran all the way around their neighborhood, along with a metal fence, but you would miss the fence because of the hedge. I had never paid attention to the hedge until that day. I also saw that it grew all the way to the woods behind my school yard and formed an almost invisible gate, with just that opening where I parted from my friends. Also, it was very hard to see the neighborhood except for a part of one house, and people inside my friends' neighborhood could not see the projects. It was almost as if neither side knew the other was there, and the only thing that separated us all was a road.

When my friends and I separated, my walk was even more deliberate as my pain worsened the closer I got to my home, and I knew I was going to be beaten as soon as I got in the house because my thirty minutes were over. I was just not capable of moving any faster, but the beating did not even bother me anymore as I learned to immune myself from my aunt and all her cruelty. It's amazing what your mind can do when you are left with few options.

I could see the broken dining room window, which was also my bedroom. I started to cough and spit with what I thought was blood mixed in with my saliva, and then I noticed a little in my nose. I just paid no attention to it. I mean, it's not like I was going to tell someone, and they would say "Oh my goodness, we've got to bring you to a doctor." Yeah, right. Anyway, I pushed it aside. I stood straight, not slumped over anymore from the pain, just so I could not relay any weakness to my aunt of the hell I was in. The pain turned to pure rage filled with hate for all women. My pace quickened so I could get in the house and get it over with. Once again, I heard the chain and the locking of the door behind me; and even though it was only four o'clock and there were still sunlight outside, it was always very dark in my house.

I stood in the living room, which was the rule. We stood in the center of the room until my aunt came and was ready to beat me or my brother, depending on whose turn it was, and today was mine. I waited for about a minute when I heard something I never thought I would hear again. It was my aunt speaking softly and kindly to someone, and then I heard a man's voice reply to her before he said, "This must be Shawn." When I first laid eyes on the man, I thought he looked like Eddie Murphy in *Beverly Hills Cop*. He introduced himself as my uncle Richard, and apparently, my aunt and uncle knew him, and he had gotten permission from them to take us for the weekend. I thought, *This is it. This guy is here to bring me to my real parents, but the only way he can do it is by taking us for the weekend.* I really did not even care about anything after that. I just knew I was never coming back to this place again.

My brother and I were told by my aunt to go get our things, so we went to the dining room to look in the trash bag, where our few things were. My aunt let out a sickening, fake laugh and told my brother and me, "You know your stuff is in the room. Why are you over there? These children." She looked at my uncle Richard, so we knew now that she was trying to deceive him. We went to the back bedroom and found our few belongings in the closet. It did not take us long to gather them before we were ready to go, and we were eager to leave.

When we returned to the living room, I saw nothing but evil in my aunt's eyes, which told us, "When you get back, you are going to pay for this." Let me tell you, I'm almost forty years old at this point in my life, and that look gives me chills every time I think of it.

We were finally outside, but I could still not breathe. I felt, any minute, my aunt would come out to tell us we were not going and to get back in the house. As we sat in the car waiting for my uncle to start it, I was screaming in my mind, *Let's get the hell out of here! She's coming to get us!* And finally, I heard the car come alive before he put it in reverse.

When we started to leave, I could not help but keep looking behind me for my aunt. When we were far away from the projects, that was when I caught my first deep breath, and my heart started to beat regularly.

My uncle started to tell me that Kathy, his wife, was looking forward to meeting me because I was the only one who had no clue that they even existed and lived in Springfield, New Jersey, which was at least an hour or more away. My brother Samuel knew our uncle Richard and aunt Kathy; he had been the ring bearer at their wedding, and my uncle told me he would show me the pictures when we got to his house. As we sat in the back seat, I interrogated my brother about this new family when I remembered that my aunt had given us permission to go with him and wanted to make sure we were not jumping out of the frying pan into the fire. My brother, however, was able to ease my mind, telling me how nice our uncle and nicer our aunt Kathy were.

When we got to the house, I liked it and never wanted to leave. It was a very nice big house. My uncle gave us a tour of the house and showed us our room to put our things in, but we preferred to sleep in the living room next to the fire, so my uncle got us two sleeping bags, and he ordered us pizza, which was a rare treat for us, as we waited for Aunt Kathy. I asked my uncle how he and my aunt met, and I did not know she had already come in the house with the pizza. Apparently, she and the delivery guy reached home at the same time, so she paid for it and came in. "I will tell you how we met," Kathy said, making us all turn around.

When I first saw her, my jaw hit the ground. *She's white*, I said to myself. It was mind-blowing. I had never seen a mixed-race marriage before, and there was one in my family.

I think my auntie had a great sense of humor and a mind reader because she said, "I bet they never told you I was white." She put the pizza down to hug my brother and me. As we hugged, I felt at peace for the first time in forever. She took her coat off. She had long blond hair that reached her back, and she was slim with glasses and a few freckles. I thought she was pretty. She then kissed my uncle, and they greeted each other. They obviously were still newlyweds. She sat on the couch and snuggled between my brother and me. My aunt and uncle were really terrific to us.

"So tell us the story of how you met, Auntie Kathy," I implored her, and she began.

My aunt was visiting Liberia with either peace corps or a ministry, to the best of my recollection, and my uncle was in college. He was so smart, especially when it came to math. He was so brilliant that he was asked to take a teaching position, and that was how they met. My aunt sat in on one of his classes, and she was blown away by his charm and mostly by his mind as she was an intellectual herself, so they started dating. When my aunt was supposed to leave Liberia and return to the United States, she wanted him to go with her because they were in love and wanted to get married, but it was hard to get a visa to travel. So my uncle and aunt sought out my dad, and he was able to get the visa for him to travel.

When she was done with the story, we had almost polished off the pizza, and my uncle told us it was bedtime, but we protested that it was still early, only nine o'clock. Besides, there was no school tomorrow. If we had been with my aunt back home, we would have never even said anything; we would have just done it. So that goes to show how comfortable we were with Uncle Richard and Aunt Kathy. Now I understand why my uncle was in such a rush to put us to bed, and like I said earlier, they were newlyweds.

But to be fair, my uncle did tell us he would read us a story first, something that has only been done once before for me. I remember the name of the book; it was called *African Fables*, and the first story he read to us was "George and the Devil's Daughter." The story, if I remember correctly, was about a guy who made a bet about something, and if he lost, he would have to marry the guy's daughter. When he lost the bet, he found out he was the devil, so now he made another bet to get out of this situation. The devil agreed. Don't ask me what the bet was about because I don't remember. Anyway, George tricked the devil and wound up winning, which made the devil furious, causing him to go after George, but he couldn't because his daughter really liked George. She helped him escape her father's wrath by turning into an eagle or some kind of bird, and after the escape, he ended up falling in love with her, and they got married.

We were in our sleeping bags on the floor in front of a nice roaring fire, which just looked like it belonged on a postcard or a Christmas card. My aunt and uncle told us good night and that they were taking us ice-skating, something my aunt loved to do since she was a little girl. Growing up, they had a lake behind their house; so during the winter, it froze up, and they would go skating. I thought that they had to be rich simply because I never knew people could even own a pond, let alone a whole lake. I was really fascinated by that idea.

Before long, my brother and I fell asleep in front of the beautiful fire, which was pretty much dying out. It was not long after that when I was awakened by my aunt's kitten. It scratched me, causing me to jump up out of a sleep, followed by my brother, who was awakened by a scratch as well. I hated that damn cat, so my brother and I locked the cat in the other room until the morning.

It was not too long until the sun started rising, making me ready and excited of how great of a day we would be embarking on. Shortly upon awakening, I heard my aunt and uncle greeting us good morning. My aunt hugged us as did my uncle. It was just mind-blowing what was happening to me. If we were back home, there would be none of that. And I just knew that, even though neither my brother nor I said anything to my aunt and uncle about what we were going through at home, we had a feeling they knew. So for that reason, I just figured that we were never returning home again. I was enjoying myself.

We ate breakfast, which was another rare treat. It was a breakfast I would remember forever. If you ever read this book and you meet me twenty years after that and ask me what I had for breakfast that day, I will tell you it was French toast with bacon and orange juice. Honestly, up until that time, I had no clue what French toast was. I had never had it before, and my aunt and uncle let us help them prepare the breakfast, and we loved it.

After our breakfast, we went to shower; and in the bathroom, I noticed that it was cleaner than the one we lived in. I remember my aunt making us use our toothbrush to clean the dirt between the tiles, but years of dirt had been there even before I moved in the projects. On my first night, when I did take a shower, it was a quick one because I just hated how dirty it was, and I felt I was getting dirty in that shower, not clean, so I washed up in record time and got the hell out of there. But now after living there and going through what I did, I got used to it, along with a lot of other things. I know most people could never get used to that, but as I've said in this book over and over again, it's amazing what you get used to.

I took the longest shower of my life, so long that my uncle Richard told me that I was going to turn to a prune. I did not know what prune was, but I laughed because he did, and I immediately turned the shower off with soap on my body and shampoo in my hair because I thought he needed to use the bathroom. Usually, back home, when my aunt had to use the bathroom, it did not matter what you were doing. If you did not get out right then and there, you would pay dearly for it. So as I did at home, I exited the bathroom; but seeing me with shampoo and soap still on me, Uncle Richard told me it was okay and that I should go back in the shower and finish.

Honestly, Auntie Kathy, Uncle Richard, my grandmother, and others I would get to interact with once or a few times in my life helped me stay sane and human. When I started to go to those dark places, I looked at my abuser as someone who truly loved me, and the abuse and the hitting became a drug; it was euphoric, believe it or not. My thinking was that it was not my aunt's responsibility to take care of my brother and me, but unlike my mother, she had not thrown me away. So even though I was treated like I was not human, I was still treated in some way and being interacted with. So no matter how she treated us or how much she abused us, it got to a point that I transformed that into a sadistic kind of love—but love nevertheless.

Very confused and surprised, I did get back into the shower and finished washing and then brushed my teeth before finally getting dressed. When I was done, I went downstairs, where my aunt and uncle asked me who I was. I did not understand what they were getting at, and then my aunt said, "You're not my nephew Shawn. Just who are you?"

At the same time, Uncle Richard said, "I don't know. I saw Shawn go into the shower, but I think he washed away, and this is our new nephew. What is your name?" And they both started laughing, which was another rare thing. So I myself started to laugh, and it felt great.

My aunt and uncle put us in the car after fixing us lunch since we were going to be out all day, and that was when I got another one of those rare moments. My aunt and uncle asked my brother what we wanted to eat, something that caught us off guard. And together, we replied, "Anything." So my aunt told us to think and gave us some choices. To tell the truth, I was so happy that I was not even hungry. In all my happiness and joy, I could have gone without eating for days, and I would have not even noticed it.

To make it easier for us to pick what we wanted for lunch, my aunt and uncle gave us some choices, and we ended up picking some sandwiches, chips, and grape soda. To tell you the truth, anything would have been fine with us. That was just how happy we were. Anyway, we put coolers in the car, and we were on our way to the skating rink, which was a bit of a distance. We drove all the way to New York and somewhere I could not remember, but I did see it on television a few times because of one unique feature, and that was a statue of either a man or a woman. I'm not exactly sure, but they are kind of outstretched, lying on their side.

When we arrived at the rink, the first thing we had to do was get sign for our skates, which we immediately put on, eager to get on the ice, even though I had never been ice-skating in my life. My aunt and uncle were very supportive and patient, trying to teach me how to skate. And after about twenty to thirty minutes, I started to grasp the concept of skating. My brother, on the other hand, had been skating many times before at the home of Auntie Kathy's parents on their frozen lake, like she used to do as a child, so my brother was very proficient on the ice.

As the day moved on, I became better on the ice and started enjoying my time; but as with all good things, it had to come to an end. So we stopped to sit and eat our lunch before turning in our skates and heading back to New Jersey. It was around seven thirty when we got home and unloaded the car, taking all the coolers in the house. After we brought in everything from the car, we helped my aunt and uncle prepare dinner.

We were all still very excited, talking about how great the day went. And it was at this time I got the worst news I thought I would never hear. My uncle told us we had to hurry up to finish dinner because we had a school day coming in the morning and that we were going to be brought home. This new bit of information was demoralizing, and when I heard it, my stomach pain started again, and my heart started jumping. I felt sick instantly. I needed to sit down for a minute. All the happiness and joy I had enjoyed over the last few days were gone, replaced with depression and dread. I don't know if you guys have ever felt completely powerless knowing that the one thing you have hoped for was not going to happen, your nightmare was going to start again, and no one or nothing was going to help you out of it.

My brother and I instantly lost our appetite. When dinner was ready, we sat there at the table just playing with our spoons, but neither one of us touched our food. I knew that my aunt and uncle could see the change because it hung over our heads like a thick dark fog. I don't think we said anything else after that news. So after dinner, we put our food away. My uncle asked us if we wanted to wrap our dinner and take it with us, but we refused. It was the only thing we said that night. We went up to get our things for the ride back home, my house of horrors.

In the car, my brother and I sat silently in the back seat, depressed the whole way home, with my uncle trying to end the silence with an occasional question, like how school was or what our favorite classes, subjects, or teachers were. But all he got were one-word answers. To cheer us up, he told us that he would be right back to pick us up on Friday so we could come back and spend the weekend, which made us feel a little bit better, giving us something to look forward to during the week.

It seemed that the ride from Uncle Richard's house back to the projects was a lot faster than the ride over to his house the first time. When we reached the projects, my uncle parked and walked us into the house. For some reason, I just believed that my uncle was not really going to leave without us and that the only reason he had walked us in the house was to tell Auntie Melvina that he was taking us to live with him. We were all going to walk out of there with both of my middle fingers held up at my aunt as I walked out backward, just to see the helpless look on her face for a change. The thought of that almost brought a smile to my face, but that suddenly changed when Uncle Richard told Aunt Melvina how much fun we had over the weekend and that he would be back to pick us up on Friday. Then he hugged my brother and me before he walked out of the apartment and headed to his car.

My brother and I went into our bedroom, which was the dining room, and watched him get in the car and pull away. For some strange reason, I just knew this could never be and that, any moment, he would turn around and come back to get us. I kept to that dream until I heard that familiar voice, and the feeling of dread and despair came over me with the first words my aunt said, which sent chills through my body. "So you had fun right?" she asked as my brother and I looked at each other but said nothing. Then my aunt went on to tell us how Aunt Kathy and Uncle Richard could never really care about us, especially me. She pointed to me and got very close to my face that I could see the hate and disdain in her eyes for me. "Do you think it's possible for anyone to ever love you? Nope, no one will ever love you, especially if they really got to know you. You do know that, when you got here, your mother wrote me an eight-page letter telling me not to let you stay with me, and then she told me how much she hated you, and now I can see why. Hell, I hate you, but I'm the only person who would take you in. Your uncle who just left you didn't even want you with him because we asked them to keep you and Samuel, but he refused because of you. He was willing to take Samuel, but you are the only one he did not want. And now you think he and his white wife loved you? No, boy, no woman will ever love you. It's not possible. I mean, when a father does not want his child, I can understand that. But when a mother does not want a child, I could never understand that. So something has to be wrong with that child. Something is definitely wrong with you."

Then she started poking me very hard, and it hurt a bit, but what she was saying hurt more. I usually tried to never cry in front of my aunt, but when she was saying those words, tears rolled in my eyes because I believed every word of it, and I was not able to hold back my tears any longer. As the tears rolled, I really think she enjoyed it because she went on to tell me how she had wished that she had followed my mother's instructions to not let me stay with her, but she did not, and she regretted her decision. Now she knew that I was ungrateful, sneaky, useless, stupid, and some other expletives she used to describe me. So once again, she reminded me how it was impossible for anyone to love me because my mother hated me. No woman could ever truly love me no matter what. I would always be alone because I was stupid and useless, and she reminded me one more time that if a woman was to tell me she loved me, I should not believe her because it was just impossible. These would be the words I would hear until I left my aunt, but before I did, I heard those words every day without fail.

When she was done with her speech, she went on to tell us that we were not going to leave her with all the housework to go to Uncle Richard's house and think that was okay; she was not going to stand for it. I told y'all that my aunt was a lazy fat bitch, especially when she found out she was pregnant; she would lie down for nine months until she gave birth. So while we were having fun this weekend, my aunt took all her daughter's clothes and put them on her with no diapers so she could soil them all, and she would then make us wash them by hand. Now that we were home, she had the clothes in really hot water with a lot of Clorox, and she pushed us in the bathroom and closed the door. Our eyes burned so bad, but we could not open the door or the bathroom window. I mean, my lungs hurt trying to breathe in this air.

Once again, we started scrubbing the clothes, but the water was so hot because my aunt would boil it and then pour it on the clothes, along with almost a whole bottle of Clorox. When the water started to cool, she would then call us to get some more boiling water and pour them on the clothes. We were happy to come out of the bathroom even just for a minute. It was still great to be able to breathe in cool air even for a while. I remember scrubbing those clothes so hard that my skin once again came off. I saw blood run first, and then I felt the sting of the Clorox mixed with hot water. A new kind of pain hit me instantly.

We had been washing clothes for over six hours now before we were done. It was four in the morning, and in a few hours, we would have to be in school, but my aunt was not done with us yet. The next thing we did was scrub the kitchen floor, which was filthy. The linoleum was torn and moved as we scrubbed, so we had to place it back where it came from, but because it was a small space, we finished quickly. Then we had to wash all the dishes not just in the sink but also in the whole house. And when my brother and I were finally done, it was seven. We had to get to school and rushed to get ready. No, people, I did not have time for a shower. And no, I did not brush my teeth or combed my hair. I got dressed, grabbed my book bag, and ran to school not because my aunt said she would kill us if we were late but because I liked school. It was a place of safety for me. If you have not understood that by now, you are still not paying attention.

You can imagine how tired my brother and I must have been that day, and we were warned by my aunt that if a teacher called to say we were late to school or any class, she would remove certain body parts and put them somewhere else, and you know I made it to school in more than record time. *I should have tried out for the Olympic track team and made some money, and they should have had my aunt chase me around the track. I could have gotten the United States some more gold medals!* Yes, people, I was laughing. Laugh with me 'cause, trust me, if I did not, I would surely have gone mad.

While at school that day, my teacher reminded me of my sad life by pointing out that I was wearing the same shirt I had worn the last week; and once again, I was embarrassed. I really wanted to tell her to either buy me a new shirt if she was tired of seeing me in the same one or shut the fuck up, but you guys know I never did that. You know if I had, she was going to call my home, and my aunt would have used that as fuel to light my ass on fire. I want you people reading this book to know that my aunt could have afforded to take my brother and me shopping for school clothes, which she did, but it was at flea markets or yard sales where everything was between one and five dollars. But my aunt thought that was too good for us. So she went for the merchandise that cost fifty cent, and she would only get one or two things for my brother and me. Now that covered our back-to-school shopping. For her and her kids, however, they went to real stores at the mall, and they were all branded.

I remember one year when she bought us these shoes. I don't remember their name. Anyway, they were in a barrel for fifty cents, and they were pink, and we had to wear those shoes until the sole was coming undone. Once that happened, we would tape it or glue it. My brother and I used to joke that our shoes were talking. We made jokes about our lives all the time. It's like what I've said before. If we did not laugh, we would have gone insane, and then who knows what could have happened? We would have gone completely mad and become dark and evil. Thankfully, the ever-living God saw to it that this would not be my ending.

As usual, it was nearly three o'clock again. I knew that only for the same reason. My stomach started to hurt. Not only was I in pain again while walking home but I also was very tired. I wish it were possible to just go home and take a nap, but I knew very well that I did not live in that type of house with people who were concerned about us. I saw a few episodes of *The Cosby Show*. It was about this family that was close and loving toward one other. The parents even listened to their children and considered their feelings. Well, that was not my reality. So after that, I never watched it again, not that I could anyway.

As you know by now, we had no privileges in that house, and yes, watching television was one of those things we were banned from doing, so we only watched it when no one was home or in the middle of the night while everyone in the house slept. This was also around the time we would steal some food, and that took some doing because I really think my aunt was counting every item in her refrigerator. I know that only because, after four times, we got caught. My aunt told us what we had eaten and how much. I know, right? Let me tell you, we paid a lot for just a few grapes and two chicken fingers that my uncle brought home. It was free and plenty but not for us. We really paid for it. I still have the marks to prove it.

I stated earlier how I hated *The Cosby Show*. Well, I wanted to elaborate on that a bit. My reason for hating the show was it was giving me false hope. I had never seen a family like that anywhere before. Also, it had me daydreaming too much. That was when I got that stupid idea about some rich real parents of mine that lost me at birth, but they were globe-trotting, looking for me to come save me one day. It gave me false hope because I'm still waiting. You know, I was not really mad about the show itself, just about my life. But I did not watch that show again until much later.

I arrived home after a day that seemed endless. When I walked into the house, I was pulled in and then slammed up against the wall with such a force that it knocked some pictures straight down on my brother, who was already up against the wall. The next thing I knew was we were being hit and asked where the hell I have been and why I was I late coming home. My aunt then heard a key turning in the door, so she stopped all of a sudden, telling us to go sit and finish our homework. Then she moved as fast as she could and lay down on the couch. At the same time, my uncle opened the door, asking my aunt what happened. "Oh, nothing. You have to tell these kids everything," she told him and then yelled at us. "Hurry up with your homework so you can finish your chores and eat dinner! You know y'all have school in the morning." My aunt was fake and the best actress in the world. I mean, for a moment, I really thought she was coming from a place of caring, but those thoughts vanished very quickly.

My uncle was only going to be home for a few hours, and then he was off to the next job. He planned on sleeping for only three hours before leaving. I had to use the bathroom very bad. I was very scared, however, to get up and do so. The tense pain, as well as the throbbing of my bladder, soon overcame my fear. I got up, willing to take whatever. I also considered that my uncle was home, so my aunt was doing nothing to me because she had never done so in the past. It must have been our secret or something. I'm not too sure. Walking through the hall, I quickly darted in the bathroom to relieve the pressure on my bladder, hoping that it, in turn, would soothe my stomach. I don't know, I was desperate.

When I was finished in the bathroom, I cleaned my hand before eating. That was when something told me to walk toward the back of the house, where all the bedrooms were. Of course, we had no bedrooms, but something was urging me to go to the back anyway.

And for some reason, I did. I saw my uncle falling asleep, with my aunt standing over him. I watched as she quickly remove money from her wallet, as well as some from my uncle's. How much I was not able to tell. When she finished, she hid the money in my cousin's crib under the mattress. That was when she saw me standing there like a deer in the headlights with my jaw on the ground. I just knew I was finished. All I could think of was her flying from where she was all the way to where I was, like they did in those martial arts Saturday matinees. However, I was surprised to see her smile at me, but it was very sinister. She came out of the room, passed me by, and went right back to her seat.

I went back into the dining room, a.k.a. my bedroom. I hope you guys caught on to that. Anyway, I went back to my bedroom where my brother sat frustrated about his math homework because he just could not figure it out, and I was the one who tried to tutor him, but he was just not interested in bookwork. My brother was more street-smart, so we traded. He taught me what he knew, and I taught him what I knew, but most of the time, I just did his homework for him. I think that sometimes it bothered him that I, being younger, had to do his schoolwork for him. If that was the case, I never really saw it. Samuel was one of those people who envied no one really. His attitude was "If I have it, fine. If I don't, that's okay too." Mine, however, was "If I had it, great. If I did not, I will do my best to figure out a way to get it. Now if I keep trying and getting the same results, I may try to find another way. But if it becomes clear that it's just not happening, then okay."

One of those things I tried doing was finding a way to gain my aunt's approval, so I did my best in school, and I brought home academic awards and prizes, thinking she'd be happy and congratulate me. That, however, was not the case. So when that failed to work, I tried something else. I was able to go trick-or-treating one year. My brother and I amassed a lot of sweets between us, and when we got home, you know, we had to pay tribute to our oppressor and laid out all of our spoils to watch my aunt and my cousin pick through what they wanted. Had this been some centuries earlier and these spoils were gold, oil, spices, and those things explorers coveted back then, my aunt would have been the crown that invested into our voyages and would be now reaping those rewards of our findings. That was another short-term relief as, when the next day approached us, we went right back to where we were before. You know, in my mind at that time was *What the hell just happened? She still has candy, and she's still eating, so why are we not in a good place like we were yesterday? Bring yesterday back.* You know, yesterday was already far gone, just like the candy she ate. We also went trick-or-treating two more times the following years, yielding the same results.

I know I'm all over the place with my story, but I am only trying to keep your interest by giving you the best description I can. I hate stories where the author does not give a real description of what they are talking about, and it makes you feel as though you've missed something. Besides, I want you to buy my book, read it, and love it so much that you refer it to family and friends. But don't give them your copy; let them buy it so I can get rich. I've already suffered enough from a lot of things, and now I'm a father. I want to make sure my son does not even face any hardship, so please buy the book, people. I'm laughing right now. I told y'all earlier that if I did not laugh, I would have gone completely mad by now. I knew you guys are paying attention.

I came back to the dining room to complete our homework. That was when I heard my uncle come into the living room, where my aunt was. I got excited at this point because I knew my uncle would come ask us if we were hungry, like he usually did when he was home. But when he did that, my aunt would completely go loony tunes on our asses. When he left, it was bittersweet, like you are going to enjoy the food for however long it lasted, but then you would suffer a lot longer afterward because there was never a time limit on the pain. So basically, it reached a zenith where the cost outweighed the rewards.

My uncle did come into the dining room and indeed asked us if we were hungry, and we replied yes, so he started to make something. I had already told my brother about what I saw earlier, so he was aware that, at any moment, something would happen. My uncle, being a chef the night before, had prepared a sauce containing all types of seafood and warmed it up, seasoning it a bit, and then he filled five pieces of gyno and gave it to us. He told my brother and me we could eat on that through the day, and then he would come home later to cook dinner.

It was amazing how my uncle was always working even on his off days. He was incapable of just sitting down and relaxing.

It was exactly at three when we finished our very delicious meal. I wish I knew how to redo that meal he made. I got up from the table to put my dish away and was about to thank my uncle for the meal when I heard my aunt scream. It was so loud that I grew concern for my aunt. I knew she was pregnant, so the first thing that ran through my mind was *The baby is coming.*

"What?" my uncle hollered back.

"Mou," she said. Mou was my uncle's tribal name. My aunt went on to tell my uncle that the money she had in her wallet, totaling sixty dollars, was gone. Gone also was the money that my uncle had on him when he came home for his nap.

"What?" my uncle yelled, very upset. "Did you lose yours?" He was now heading toward their bedroom.

"No, it's gone, and I know they have it because they saw me hide it," my aunt informed her now very visibly angry husband. We had come into the hallway to see what it was my aunt had been yelling for when we became her scapegoats. At this time, I had already informed Samuel about what I saw my aunt doing earlier.

My uncle yelled at us, telling us if he did not get the money back, he would kill us. We were petrified, frozen in the spot. I even felt a trickle of urine in my pants. It was at the moment, in one swoop, he unbuckled his belt, landing a very harsh blow to Samuel's head, letting the buckle hit my brother. I saw blood streaming down his head onto the one good shirt I had, which was an all-white Run DMC shirt that I really liked and was the second of the only two shirts we shared. The white shirt was instantly red with my brother's blood. I immediately cried for him and wanted to hug him when the blow from my uncle landed on me as I looked at my brother, who stood motionless with a stone-cold look on his face. My uncle's fist hit me so hard that I was bounced off the wall, dazed and confused. Then more blows were landed on both of us.

I guess my aunt was satisfied with whatever it was she was seeking because she finally yelled out that she found the money. And just like that, the beating stopped, and whatever spirit my aunt had put in him for that time was gone, leaving him standing there looking at us as if he wanted to apologize, but he was ashamed and left the house. My brother and I gathered whatever dignity we had left, and we went back to the dining room to continue our homework as though nothing happened. That was the way it was for us. Our voices did not matter. Our feelings did not matter or ever asked about. There was no such thing as an opinion. Those crucial ways of communication and expression were denied to us, and we were delayed in those fields. So when someone asked us about our feelings, what we thought, or anything like that, we would be so surprised that we were not able to reply or react. We were stunted. Our growth was stunted.

Samuel and I sat at the table; neither of us wanted to cry, but seeing the blood still trickling down his face was my breaking point. The tears were coming more steadily now. I tried to muffle my cries with no success, so I ran over to Samuel, wrapping my arms around him. I'm sorry, everyone, but I have to put my pen down for a little while because I had suppressed these feelings for a while, and now as I write them down, it's still painful. This is not an easy book to write for me. So I wrapped my arms around Samuel, feeling so bad for him, but he just stared far away as though he had replaced himself with someone else. As I tried to console him, he was doing the same for me; it was unbelievable how much we used to fight, but when the chips were down, he was always the only one who stood up for me, the one who was always there for me outside of the Lord. Samuel and I held each other, never saying a word. I mean, really, what could we say? It was something we were too embarrassed about. "I'm going to get her fat ass," Samuel said staring very intensely at something I could not see.

I woke up early the next morning, looking forward to the end of that day because Uncle Richard had come to let us know that he would stop by to pick us up for the weekend, and for the first time, I could hardly wait for that three o'clock bell to ring. It seemed as though it would never ring, especially after I wore an outfit that I thought was cool, but I found out when I got to school that this was a baseball uniform. "Why are you in a baseball uniform?" My entire class asked, probing. I did not know what to say. I was getting hot and was feeling cold chills at the same time, and then the sweat beads started forming before another classmate asked if it was a softball uniform because this was the season for it. I nodded yes, and finally, all eyes were off me, and I was more than happy. It turned out that the uniform I had on came from a trash bag full of outdated things that was purchased for a quarter by my aunt. That was our back-to-school clothes for the year because we had not been shopping in a little over two years. After that day, I put that damn uniform away in the bottom of a trash bag that was supposed to be our closet because we did not have a real bedroom.

When the bell finally rang, I dashed outside to see if my uncle was there to pick me up for the weekend, and up I came through the second door, which was the last door before finally coming outside. I saw my uncle, and he had already picked up Samuel, who was smiling so wide now. I also noticed that there were no aches and pain in my belly, and I was very grateful for it. I got in the car, where I was greeted by both of them as I was handed a Whopper from Burger King. I remember, when I first got to America, my mother had brought me to Burger King for my first Whopper; and after one bite, I did not like it, and it took a few years for my taste buds to get acclimated to it as I would a lot of other things in my life, according to which happened first.

I took my Whopper and greeted my uncle as he gave me another bag containing fries. "Your drink is there," Samuel said, pointing at one of the cup holders. I asked my uncle how he had picked up Samuel so fast because his school was farther than mine. He answered me, saying that he saw Samuel about a mile from the school, and that was when he picked him up, asking how he got so far the school in such record time. Well, it turned out that I was not the only one who was eager to start the weekend, so Samuel decided to start running toward the same direction my uncle would travel, which was not too hard because it was the only way he could travel. So at one point or another, they would eventually meet. Once again, we were happy to be with Uncle Richard and Aunt Kathy. So now whenever my other classmates talked about what was going on with their family trips or where they were traveling and how much fun it was, I could actually have something to say without making things up.

The trip up to my uncle's house was a good distance, so as we drove, my uncle usually tried to entertain us with different games. I always played along with it, but more than anything, I paid attention to the road just so, on the day I planned on running away, I would be able to direct the cabdriver right to my aunt and uncle's doorstep. I knew they would be happy to see me and invite me to stay with them forever. The idea for that whole dream came to me after I heard Uncle Richard that he wished my dad made him and Auntie our legal guardian instead of Uncle Francis and his wife. He just did not know how much my brother and I had wished for the same thing. Uncle Richard then went on to say that if anything was to ever happen to my dad or to Uncle Francis and his wife, Melvina, he would love to bring us in. So you know, I prayed for that all the time, which was basically twenty-four seven.

We reached the house around six o'clock and raced off inside, where Auntie Kathy was busy icing some cupcakes; next to them was a huge chocolate cake that read "Happy birthday, Shawn and Samuel." I could not believe my eyes. "How did you know it was my birthday?" I had forgotten that my birthday was the very next day. There was never a time that anyone has cared about my or my brother's birthday, not that we did not care about it. I mean, how could children not look forward to their birthday, being the center of attention, getting a shitload of gifts? My brother and I never had that privilege of having anyone care about our birthdays. So year after year, we just forget about them.

It was not that Uncle Francis and Aunt Melvina did not celebrate birthdays. When it came to their children's birthdays, they would always order a cake from Carvel, a place that had great ice cream, as well as very good ice cream cake. They would then get gifts that they wrapped before having a party. As you know by now, my brother and I got the two smallest slices of ice cream cake and never dared to ask for another piece. After watching the festivities, my brother and I cleaned up and went back in our room, watching my aunt and uncle play with my cousin and the new gifts that had just been recently unwrapped.

Still in utter disbelief, I asked Aunt Kathy again how they knew our birthdays, and they said, "We are your aunt and uncle, right?" to which I nodded yes. "So then how could we not know your birthday is December 12 and Samuel's is July 26?" And of course, I asked them why they had not just celebrated Samuel's birthday when it came up. The reply I got was that they indeed had tried to, but Aunt Melvina kept dodging my uncle's calls when he was trying to come get us back then, but my aunt saw to it that it would never happen. After months and months of calls that led to nowhere, he was fed up, deciding instead to just come to the house. He was fortunate to have run into Uncle Francis, who had come home to catch a little bit of sleep, and on his way out, they bumped into each other. It was the time I walked in on them talking and laughing, starting the process of us spending weekends with Uncle Richard and Auntie Kathy. So now since I was younger, they decided to celebrate both birthdays on mine, and they had already told Samuel about their plans, which he was fine with. I told y'all my brother was really laid back about everything, but at the same time, he was still a child with feelings, and I think he held a little resentment and jealousy, which did not show.

We had finished putting the last bit of frosting on the last few cupcakes that totaled to four, and since we were so helpful, my aunt let everyone have one. Let me tell you, that cupcake was so good that I think I must have sucked the fingerprint off my fingers, and you guys do know I tried to get another one, right? But my aunt was over there, blocking the cupcakes, telling me dinner was going to be ready so we had to go upstairs to wash up.

We quickly washed up, ran downstairs, and prepared to eat dinner. My aunt and uncle had already set the table. I could see these little birds on each plate that I thought were baby chickens. I soon found out that they were called Cornish hens; whatever that was, I had no idea. What surprised me more than anything was that they were on each plate, so I asked if we each got our own Cornish hens, and the answer I received was yes. If this had been back at our house, there was no way in hell we would have possibly gotten our own bird. Things like these were rare treats. What my auntie would have told us was it was too good for us, and if she gave us any, my brother and I would have possibly gotten a wing piece, even if we had twenty of them.

Surprised we were all getting our own Cornish hens, my brother and I looked at each other, still not believing this. We sat down, and we started serving ourselves—another rare thing in our lives. And as you can imagine, we took advantage of these situations.

Before arriving at my aunt and uncle's home, we decided we should give them some gifts for being so nice to us. Since we did not have money, we went looking in this barrel at home that had nothing but books. They had come from this company my dad and aunt worked for, and they would bring home books, calendars, magazines, and other things sold there, even organizers. You remember those things we used to keep people's phone numbers and addresses in? You remember how you were capable of remembering over ten people's numbers? Then cell phones came, and organizers became obsolete, just like your brain. And you also became lazy —so lazy that the only number you remember is yours. And if you don't have your cell phone, you are completely lost. Yeah, isn't technology wonderful? It made all of us so pathetic. Technology is so wonderful because with your cell phone comes your GPS, which made maps obsolete. Before GPS, if someone gave you an address, you could find the place on your own. And after being there that one time, you were able to find the place again from your memory, which is another thing good old technology made obsolete. I mean, now all you have to do is type the address in that reliable gadget, and it brings you right to it. But the next day, if you have to find the place, without that GPS, you are completely dumbfounded. Okay, that's enough. You did not buy this book so I could insult you and your technology. I'm guilty of the same thing. Anyway, back to the story.

My brother and I had found some really good books and gift wrappers, along with those organizers. So we presented our gift to them that day. There was one more thing we found among those books in that barrel, and those were *Hustle* magazines. No, we did not gift wrap those, but they did come in pretty handy during this story. And no, it's not what you think, so get your mind out of the gutter. The magazine would help me out later.

After we presented our gifts to my aunt and uncle, they were really touched, asking us how we were able to afford these gifts. Of course, we lied, telling them how we had saved so much. They thanked us with hugs and kisses, and once again, there was calm and happiness. It seemed the only times those feelings arose in me were while being with these three people at that moment and time.

We moved from the dining room to the living room. We wanted to sleep next to the fireplace once again, imagining we were camping. My uncle went to go get the sleeping bags while my aunt finished the dishes. We unrolled the sleeping bags and positioned them parallel to each other, next to the fireplace. My uncle went to go get the book of African fables he had read us a story from the last time we were visiting. He opened the book to read us another story, telling us to get into our sleeping bags and lie down, which we did. As he started to read, my aunt entered the room and sat on the arm of the couch next to my uncle. I don't remember the name of the story he read to us that night because, shortly after, my brother and I were fast asleep.

The next morning when we woke up, my aunt and uncle had been hard at work decorating the house. I had even forgotten it was my birthday, and I was about to ask them what was going on when they started yelling, "Happy birthday!" I've got to be honest; it felt great, and now I understand why my friends would get so excited about their birthday. Until then, the only time anyone had even said anything about my or my brother's birthday was when my uncle gave Samuel five dollars as a gift; another time was when a classmate gave me a model car for my birthday that I had to be put together, and I cherished that car until my aunt destroyed it. I remember that car; it was a Ferrari Testarossa, and yes, it was red. I would always remember that day and my friend who gave it to me. He was this white kid with freckles. His hair was so red that I think his family was from Ireland. If I remember correctly, his name was Otis something, but he was only in my class for a short time, and I did not see him much after that.

When all the decorations were up, the house looked so good. I could not believe that my brother and I were worthy of someone going through all this trouble for us, but here we were. When we were done with everything, we went up and washed up and ran back downstairs. That was when I heard the doorbell ring, and I ran to answer it, only to find it was a friend of mine who was also a classmate, this white kid named Matthew. Matthew was the biggest kid in my class. He had shaved blond hair and the biggest smile, as well as freckles; it seemed all the white people I knew had freckles. When I heard the term *gentle giant*, he always came to mind. And like all white people, he and his parents brought a gift. Matt looked so much like both of his parents; it was crazy. They walked in, and I greeted him with a handshake. We thought we were all grown up when we did that. He asked where to put my gift, and my aunt showed him the way. Yeah, white people always bring gifts; black people just show up, asking where the food is. When you ask them where their gift is, they usually say, "I'm here. Am I not enough? I took a whole day off," as if that is something that they did for you when the truth is you are just the perfect excuse for them to do what they always do.

I was surprised that I had friends who had come to my birthday party, so I asked my aunt and uncle how they knew who to invite, and they explained that they had brought invitations to my class, which my teachers gave to the students I was friends with. So here they were, ready to party. Matt and his family had a prior engagement but pushed it back a bit so Matt could hang out with me for a few hours, and then they had to leave, so I walked them out and thanked them for coming. They thanked me for inviting them, and I told Matt I would see him at school before I returned to my party. It was an unbelievable feeling to be the center of attention, to have people who loved us so much that they put something like that together for us. I really believe it was these little things that kept me grounded and human no matter how much abuse and torture I had experienced.

Our party started to wind down a little bit. We had eaten so much sweets and so many sodas that I think we literally used all our energy, including those of the people around us and my poor aunt and uncle. I never really appreciated all they had done. What I mean is it made me very grateful, and I appreciated them, but it was not until I became an adult that I saw that, even though they worked all week and no matter how exhausted they were, they still took out the time to think of us. Instead of getting rest and spending quality time with each other, they put all of that aside to make us feel special when they did not have to. They did not even have children of their own. Recently, my uncle Richard had just come to Georgia for a wedding and stayed at my house, and he told me then how tired they were during those times, and it just made me love him and my aunt even more.

That evening, after opening all the gifts, I found out that I had over fifty dollars, and my uncle decided to open a bank account for each of us to save our money. We then went on to help clean up everything from the party. That was when a feeling of dread came over me. I think the same feeling must have overcome my brother because we both stopped at that very moment to look at each other. It was so spooky that I had to ask him if he was just thinking about the same thing. He slowly nodded and hung down his head afterward. It seems that whenever you go through traumatic experiences together, you form a bond that is so strong that you end up thinking and feeling the same things to the point that you can finish each other's sentences.

That feeling that came over me was always followed by a fiery, stabbing pain in the pit of my stomach that always put me down, stopping whatever I was in the middle of doing. If I had been home with Aunt Melvina, she would have started beating, slapping, and punching me for stopping whatever it was she was making me do. I sat down on a nearby chair because the pain was unbearable. Aunt Kathy asked me if something was wrong, but because I was not used to anyone asking or caring about my well-being, I just told her, "No, I am just tired." Even then, my aunt lovingly had me lie down for a while as she was aware of my medical issues. I really wished then I had told them all about this pain and how bad it has gotten, but I just did not want to be a burden, something I was always told that I was.

Our weekend visits at my aunt and uncle's house was always a bittersweet situation. Yeah, my life was an oxymoron. Once again, in the back of my uncle's car, my brother and I sat silently, knowing and anticipating what awaited us back home. We knew that my aunt hated to see us happy and despised seeing anyone wanting to do anything for us or with us. So on the days that Uncle Richard came to get us, she would give us a laundry list of tasks we needed to accomplish before we went anywhere. Then when Uncle Richard showed up to pick us up, she would transform in the blink of an eye to the nicest person ever, asking him how he was doing and if he wanted anything to drink. Thank goodness my uncle always said no because we were ready to get the hell away from her. But my aunt, staying true to that facade, hugged and kissed us before letting us go as if she gave a damn about us.

My uncle would always try to cheer us up on the way back to our hellhole by saying the weekend would be there before we knew it, but it never worked because, even though it was a quick week to him, it was forever for us. That would be like telling someone who was in prison for committing a crime he did not do after serving twenty years, "Well, we found the guy who really committed the crime, so as soon as we complete the paperwork, you will be out in forty-eight hours." To that guy, forty-eight hours would seem like an eternity—well, something like that anyway.

Back at the house again after a weekend of bliss and a birthday party, all the joy had been taken out of my brother and me once we saw those brown bricks, our hell. My uncle walked in with us as he had always done, except he did not make a lot of small talk with my aunt because he had to get back home, and the drive was pretty far. No sooner had he gone did we have to pay for the little bit of joy we had over the weekend. I never understood how come we had to iron my aunt's working uniform and shine her shoes when all she did was sleep, and she had not worked since the first time she gave birth and was pregnant again. My aunt took the toys we have received for our birthdays and threw them on the floor with one hand; with the other, she pointed to a bunch of clothes I had to iron, while my brother was given his own task. I could have become a professional dry cleaner by then with the amount of clothes I had to wash and clean by hand. I started on the clothes, knowing it would be another night without any sleep.

It was about four thirty when I was awakened with a kick and a slap that resounded in the whole room. "What the hell is this? Y'all don't know how to do shit, you fucking useless ass!" my aunt yelled. "Get your ass over here. I'm going to show you how to iron." She ordered me to plug in the iron and prop up the ironing board and to let her know when the iron got really hot, which was after only a few minutes. I was still groggy and sleepy, but I let her know they were ready. She took her uniform shirt, yelling at me, letting me know how useless I was and that she now understood why my mother want nothing to do with me, along with other things. I won't write it all here because I want to finish this book in one lifetime.

She proceeded to iron the shirt, spraying starch on it, telling me this was how she wanted it done, but I was so tired that I could hardly pay any attention. That was when she told me to give her my hand, and I did, thinking she was going to show me the form of ironing. Instead, I felt heat on the back of my hand, and I immediately tried pulling back, but she was stronger, and she held it there for a few seconds before letting go. She then yelled, "Are you paying attention now?" as she dropped the iron on ironing board.

I ran to the kitchen to run water over my hand as Samuel grabbed ice out of the freezer. Now I don't know what he was thinking when he did that except wanting to help me, but opening or touching my aunt's refrigerator was a no-no. When she heard the refrigerator door, she came right back to the kitchen, asking who the hell had opened it, and my brother told her he was just getting ice for my hand. The skin on the back of my hand was gone. She had taken of a pretty good amount of skin. I could only see the white part and some blood that the water had taken. As I looked at it, the meat looked disgusting. "Let me see. 'Ain't nothing wrong with him!" she yelled, so I held up my hand, still trembling with pain, so she could see. I think after my aunt saw how bad it was, she paused a little bit. I mean, I don't know what the hell she thought would happen if you held an iron that was burning on someone's hand, but she started trying to treat it, saying it was just a joke and did not mean for it to happen. Now as you read this book, my aunt is going to pull other painful jokes, so count this as one.

My aunt told my brother to get some rubbing alcohol. As if I was not already in a tremendous amount of pain, she poured the alcohol all over my hand, which looked as if something was inside because of the way it raised. It reminded me of this guy's foot I had seen when I was in Liberia. I don't know what happened to his foot or how he injured it, but one thing I do remember was that I saw maggots coming in and out of the infection. See? I told you it was disgusting. I had never seen anything like that before or since.

My aunt had my brother get some gauze so she could wrap up the burn, but before doing so, she rubbed an ointment on there that looked like Vaseline or something like that. My arm hurt so much that I could not keep from trembling every time she touched it. It felt as though the iron was still on my hand. I could literally still feel the heat; the burn was at least a third-degree burn simply because my skin was completely gone. I saw that part of my skin was still on the iron, which was now lying on the floor next to the ironing board, which was also knocked over as I had tried getting away from my aunt while she held my hand and burning me at the same time.

When she was done dressing my hand, I cradled it very close to my body and limped back to the couch, where I lay with my brother, who comforted me with a hug. I could see the anger on his face, which told me, if he could have his way, he would have definitely done something terrible to my aunt for what had just happened, as well as the other mistreatment she committed against us over the years. My brother had always been my protector. He would take beatings for me when I could no longer stand. He would ask my aunt to beat him instead, and she always did without any hesitation. My brother and I lay on the couch, talking about how much we hated our lives and could not wait until that day when we would grow up and leave or until we had enough so we could just ran away from home, whichever came first.

The next day while at school, I felt sick all day, and my hand was throbbing. It was in one of my classes that a classmate pointed out that my hand was leaking. There was blood, along with some other creamy green ooze, which turned the white gauze dressing all green and red. My teachers, as well as some classmates, were asking me what happened to my hand. And of course, you know I lied and made up a story about how I burned my hand trying to cook something. I was never going to tell anyone what was really going on with my brother and me at home. I was no fool. My teacher reminded me to be more careful the next time I decided to cook, as well as to make sure that an adult was present to assist me on my next cooking adventure. Then she excused me, telling me to go see the school nurse.

I got up and headed straight to the nurse's office to see about my hand. There, I was asked to repeat what exactly happened to my hand, so I reiterated to her the story I had just explained to my teachers and classmates. The nurse, just like the others before her, told me to be careful. She then proceeded to remove the old dressing of my hand, but it was dry and had gotten stuck to my hand. I could the see under the gauze, and it looked disgusting. She tried wetting it with some kind of cleaning solution, but even then, only a small portion came up, with skin and an oozing mess. The dressing was actually embedded inside my hand. The nurse added more of the solution. This time, she poured it all over my hand using the whole bottle. That must have done it because now she was able to pull up more of it, but the process was still painful, pulling more of my skin with it.

It took a little over thirty minutes for her to finally remove all the dressing. She then washed it again using some swabs, and then she put a generous amount of some ointment to keep the dressing she put on from sticking on to my wound. When she was done dressing it, she wrapped my entire hand so, when it started leaking, there would be a good amount of dressing to absorb it. "There," she told me as she handed me a handful of ointment, dressings, and cleaning solutions that she put in a bag.

I was about to get up and leave, though I was still not feeling well, when she told me she was not done yet. She wanted to take my temperature because I felt warm to her. She moved over to one of the white cabinets that had a glass covering, removing a thermometer that she placed in my mouth and then took out to read. "Oh my goodness, you are burning up." She told me that my temperature was 103.7. I was told to lie down until she could get in contact with my parents.

Lying there, I started wishing that I had never walked into that damn nurse's office, especially now that they were about to involve my aunt. I could hear the nurse on the phone talking to someone about me, explaining how bad my hand was and that my temperature was really high. She also explained to the person that I was really sick and would need to go see my pediatrician. Now I have no clue what a pediatrician was, but one thing I could have told the nurse just so she did not waste her time was that I was not going to the hospital because there was no way my aunt would let that happen, not in a million years.

When she was done, she came back to the room where I was lying down. I could see the frustration on her face as soon as she walked through the curtains that separated us. She explained to me how my uncle was out working in New York but would come to get me. She also told me she spoke to my aunt, who could not come because of her pregnancy. Just hearing my aunt's name made my belly start hurting and my heart racing. The nurse told me how bad I looked and that I looked worse now versus when I first came in, so she repeated taking my temperature, which had elevated a bit more. If that nurse only knew that her mentioning my aunt's name was the reason for the pain in my stomach and the spike in my temperature, she could have saved me a lot of grief by never talking to my aunt at all or saying her name in my presence.

School was almost out, and my uncle had finally walked into the nurse's office. I woke up to hear the nurse talking to him. Apparently, my lack of sleep the previous night had caught up with me. When they were done, my uncle and the nurse walked back to the room. I could see the anger and frustration on his face. I got up, picked up my book bag, and walked over to him. We exited the room, heading to his car, which was now parked where all the buses were now picking up students, as well as parents coming to get their students after the school day was out.

On the drive back to the house, I got an earful about how much of a burden I had become. He also told me that he could not be leaving work to come and get me. When he was saying all of this, I just sat there looking down. Tears were brewing in my eyes upon hearing once again that I was unwanted. It was right then I heard something I had never heard before. My uncle told me that my father had stolen over seventy-five thousand dollars, which he had given to my father for both of them to start a business. Instead, my dad took the money and fled, and that was the reason we had not seen or heard from him. I was shocked and angry after hearing that, realizing now that my father was the cause of all this bullshit we've been going through. At least now when I looked at the situation, it made sense. All this abuse was not the fault of my abusers. It was just much easier to understand. It was also a way to take the sting out of my being unwanted, even if it was just a little bit and for a short time.

When we got home, I think my uncle felt bad about the way he had talked to me because he fixed a place in the living room for me to lie down. He also cooked me something to eat, and then he went out to get me some juices and some pills for fever. I took the medication, but I was not really hungry, so I let my brother eat the food since my aunt was gone. I don't know where, and I did not care. I was just happy she was gone. I was getting pretty sleepy, so I gave the remote control to Samuel since my uncle had given us permission to watch television and told Samuel to take care of me until he and my aunt returned later.

It was at around eight o'clock when my aunt returned home from wherever the hell she was. She was not alone. My uncle Richard was with her, so once again, she was fake as hell, laughing and pretending to be the most caring human being on the planet. She came over to me and proceeded to feel my forehead, causing me to flinch because I thought she was about to hurt me. "What's wrong?" she said, now feeling my head, gently telling me she came home from my uncle's house as soon as she found out I was not feeling well and that she wanted to make sure I was okay. So now if you've been reading the book and paying attention, you must know this is bullshit and that my aunt did not give a fuck about my or my brother's welfare. Besides, as you can remember, the school nurse had first talked to her before they reached my uncle. When the nurse had talked to her, she said she could not move because of her pregnancy.

Feeling my head again, my aunt asked me what happened to my hand as if she did not know. I wanted to tell her, "Bitch, you know what the fuck happened to my hand." I was no fool, however, so I just told her I burned myself while ironing, and I was not paying attention when it fell on my hand, burning me. She reminded me to be more careful.

When she was done with her act, my uncle gave my brother and I a checkbook, along with some other documents in reference to our bank accounts he and Aunt Kathy set up for us. I took the documents with the other paperwork. I was looking out of the corner of my eyes, concentrating on my aunt's anger that was coming out, and I just knew we were going to get it as soon as Uncle Richard left us to deal with this situation. "Oh wow, look at you, grown men with your own bank account. I remember that day when I had opened my first account. I was in my twenties. You guys are going to be rich. Just remember me and your poor uncle, making sure we are given very good treatment like we do for you," she said.

I almost fell out after hearing this, so to make sure I did hear it right, I asked my brother way later instead of right then and there. We were proud to have our own bank accounts, and my uncle had placed in there the money received during our birthday party. All the money equaled to a little over a hundred dollars. When he was gone, my aunt took our bankbook, saying we were not worthy of it. She also asked my brother if we were better than her and her children because they had no accounts of their own. After that, I was told to get off the couch so she could use it. That made no sense to me because, when my uncle told me to lie down, I picked the smaller chair, which was just a love seat, leaving the bigger couch empty for her.

Lying down on the floor once again, I fell asleep, so my aunt decided to fix me when she approached the couch I was sleeping by. She decided she wanted to sleep on the bed inside the couch, so she removed the cushions and pulled out the bed, bringing it down very hard right between my eyes, causing me to jump out of my sleep. I was startled, confused, and in pain as my blood trickled down into my eyes.

I screamed in pain while I ran toward the bathroom to see the damage that was done. I could see the imprint of the bottom of the leg, and I even saw the "made in China" writing that made a mark on my face. I quickly washed my face with my brother's help, and my aunt asked if I was all right, acting as though she did not know what had taken place. The blood was coming down profusely. I could smell it as it burned when it got in my eye, trickling down to my lips and into my mouth. I licked it; the salty taste of my blood was something I had tasted before. I cried out in agony, and snot ran down my nose, mixing with my blood as they both were washed down in to the sink, spinning and disappearing down the plumbing together to whereabouts unknown. I was, with my brother's help, able to clean up my face with my blood coagulating.

We went out of the bathroom into the living room, and I saw our bank documents in my aunt's hand; she was still asking us if we think we were special and better than other people, including herself. She then reminded us of how pathetic, useless, and unwanted we were. "Especially you," my aunt said, pointing at me, repeating what she had told me over a million times and what I would hear from her at least twice or more times a day in the future. My aunt continued telling me how I could and would never be loved by anyone. She walked over to me, putting her face close to mine. "Look at you with your yellow eyes. Damn, you're ugly. If I were your mother, I would have left you too. No one wants you. I'm the only one who does, so you should be grateful to me for that."

When she finished her insult, I thanked her for keeping me. I mean, after all, I had no one except my brother, who was in a different situation. I convinced myself that my aunt really did love me because I was still with her and her family in her house. I also came to the conclusion that all these things were indeed my fault and that if only I was a better person or tried harder to be better, then none of these things would have taken place.

With that, I apologized to my aunt, promising her I would do my best to do better so that I would not be such a burden. I felt better after that, especially when she told me to sit down on the couch, allowing my brother and me into her presence. All her actions had really confirmed to me again that what I had just convinced myself of was true, and basically, that was it was all because of me. After all, look what has happened when I apologized like that. Sitting there watching television, talking to my aunt, and even sharing with her things that happened at school gave me the motivation and the fuel to say that I would start a new day trying to satisfy my aunt and become a better person so I would not frustrate her and make her life difficult. I just did not understand that my opportunity was heading my way.

Chapter 5

THE BANDWAGON

The next morning, I woke up with excitement and joy to start my personal mission to do better and be better so I would not be a headache to my aunt. My brother and I had sat up most of the night talking about our plans. We were both very excited the next day. I actually remember smiling for the first time in a very long period.

School let out that day, and I headed home without any sickness or stomach issues. When I entered the house, my aunt was lying down on her couch. I started my chores like I always did every day, asking my aunt if she needed anything as usual. I looked for new ways to appease her, but I really did not know what else to do because we were already doing all that was possible for us.

That was when my uncle walked in the house, huffing and puffing. He was definitely angry about something. It seemed that the only time my uncle would get seriously angry was when he got home, and my aunt would bring him in their bedroom for about an hour or so, after which he came out of the room fuming mad.

My aunt was a big follower of voodoo; she would cook food for the dead every year, and when I say cook, I'm talking about a four-course meal. It was for the dead that no one was to touch. The food sat in the room for a week, and it would be consumed by someone. That was why

I really believed she had some kind of spell on my uncle. My reason for thinking that way was very simple. My uncle was a nice guy; he was known for that by anyone who had a relationship or some kind of interaction with him. All of that would change when he got home; he was still the same person until my aunt brought him in that damn room. When he emerged from there, he was angry, not the same person who had just walked in the house.

His anger this day had nothing to do with my aunt. My uncle was upset because his eldest brother, whom everyone called Mr. Spencer, said his second eldest child, called Ricky—who was his father's namesake— was somewhere in New York, homeless now. I don't know if it was his brother or his brother's wife who contacted him to go retrieve Ricky to bring him back to the house. The reason for his anger was that he was treated worse than a slave while he lived with his brother and his wife. He complained about how he would never lift a hand to help any of his family members with all of that money. The only family my uncle came to help was the family members of his wife because she did not allow anyone to do anything else.

While living there, the cost of tuition was something my uncle's big brother could afford with no problem, but he refused to help him or any of the Spencers, not even his eldest son from a previous relationship. I heard this story time and time again from so many people. Their mother had fourteen children altogether and was my grandfather's thirteenth wife. My grandfather had over fifty children, and they all did not know one another, leading to a funny story that happened to Uncle Francis.

One day my uncle decided to take a trip to Sierra Leone, a small West African country they were from. So while on vacation, he ran into a pretty young lady whom he liked very much, and she was as enamored with him as he was with her, and they started dating during the two weeks he was there. When those two weeks ended, he was to return to America, so they exchanged names and addresses. He was surprised to find that this young lady had the same last name as him. The name Spencer was not very common, and he had never met anyone out of the family with the same name, let alone spelled identical to his. Reading and paying attention to the last name, shocked, Uncle Francis instantly asked her who her father was. "William Herbert Spencer," she replied. My uncle was devastated when he heard her just say his father's name.

"Oh boy, I can't believe this," he said, sitting down on the bed, distressed and confused. When he was finally able to relay to her that the name she uttered was his father's, it caused her to break down as she sat next to him. They embraced and cried to each other for hours. It was hard for my uncle to comprehend he had been sleeping with his sister for a whole week.

I do not know a whole lot about my grandfather, but what I do know is that William Herbert Spencer and his younger brother, whose name I am unaware of, set sail from Jamaica all the way down to the country of Sierra Leone in West Africa, where they settled down. It was there where he built his wealth. He was able to own hundreds of acres of land where he built his plantation. He was able to own acres of tobacco, banana, cotton, and many others. My grandfather had never planned to marry thirteen wives, but because he was very wealthy, other citizens wanted to be associated with his name. Whenever he visited any city, the town chief—mayor in America —would offer his most attractive daughter, obliging my grandfather to marry her. For my grandfather to marry any other wives, his first wife had to agree; and if she did, the new wife would be groomed for marriage into the family.

Uncle Francis left the house to go get his nephew Ricky in New York, and they both returned later that night. My first impression of my cousin was a good one. I liked him instantly. He was dressed sharply with shades on. He greeted us all before my uncle brought him in the back to show him the room he would stay in. I thought that now that my cousin, who was twenty at time, was staying with us, it might put an end to our abuse. But it only took one look at my aunt to see the hate, anger, and disdain in her eyes for my cousin. I knew that look since I had seen it time and time again; the only difference this time was that it was directed toward someone else when usually it was for me or my brother, sometimes individually, other times for the both of us.

My aunt had always talked about Ricky's mother, whose name was Princess. Aunt Melvina would say how mean Princess was to her, and when my aunt left Sierra Leone, the only thing Princess gave her was a stick of gum. Telling us about how mean and evil Princess was, I thought, *Look at the pot calling the kettle black.* One thing I did not understand of my aunt Melvina's story was that she was mad at Ricky for something he had not done. My aunt explained that a bit more by saying that Ricky was treated like a prince; my uncle was making a lot of money as the vice president for Citibank, and his children went to the same school as the president of the nation's children, as well as that of other dignitaries. I was still confused about Ricky being at fault for whatever it was his mother did, and soon my brother and I would become pawns in a war she was about to wage against Ricky.

In the beginning, my aunt struck the first blow by telling Ricky he was going to be responsible for paying rent when he was not working. The guy was on the street, homeless, so exactly how the hell could he be charged rent? I mean, really? If he had a job, I'm pretty sure he would not have been on the street. Am I right, people? Don't y'all agree?

Tasting how awful life was going to be for him, Ricky immediately got a job, deciding he was going to get the hell out of Dodge City. We profited from Ricky's new job at McDonald's. He would bring home all kinds of treats, like apple pies, Big Macs, and fish filets, along with everything that was on the McDonald's menu. Ricky would always take meal orders from my brother and myself, and like clockwork, we received it every night he came home. Even if we were asleep, Ricky would wake us up to make sure we had eaten.

My cousin was more like a big brother. The refrigerator was always packed with foods from his job, which was why I came to hate the things my aunt made us do to him for her enjoyment. Melvina was visibly angered of my cousin's bringing home food for us. My brother and I would become enthralled by my aunt's war against Ricky. To tell you the truth, we became close to my aunt at certain points in my life, which were very few. For the first time in a long period, we could breathe a bit.

I recall the amount of times my aunt was able to say something bad about Ricky, looking at us to cosign her agreement. We were instructed to tell her anything that he did that she could use to accomplish her goal of getting rid of him, but it was never beneficial, causing her anger that was armed toward us. One other thing she had us do was stealing from him. So after a very long day, Ricky returned home absolutely exhausted, letting us know that it was time to sleep. We never wanted to do any of these things to my cousin, but I was only seven and scared. So when the person who was the bone of my existence wanted to befriend me and all I had to do was inform her on another person to alleviate the pressure and pain, my brother and I quickly followed suit, falling right in line. Every morning, we would each take twenty dollars from him. We never let my aunt know we had found more.

I started wishing I did not have to continue stealing and selling anyone, especially someone who was a family member and someone I liked. Above all else, he was a cousin who looked out for me on certain situations. After we discussed it, my brother and I made a promise to each other that we were never again to steal from Ricky or tell on him, even though we knew very well the consequences. We did not have to wait long for what we knew was her wrath. The first thing she did after she beat the crap out of us was tear up our bank account documents, and that was the last time we had laid eyes on it.

The bell rang for the school day to begin. Instead of going to our class to begin the day, everyone was told to report to the gymnasium for some special rally. Entering the gym, we saw a huge banner that read "DARE (Drug Abuse Resistance Education)," which was the program in effect during the eighties when the Pres. Ronald Reagan initiated the war on drugs.

In my neighborhood during this time, people were being killed over different territories and over a new drug called crack. The so-called government believed that if children were educated early enough, the drug problem would be done with, but they missed a few things. First, all these white people who came to save the poor black niggers had never lived in the same places where the drug dealers and drug users lived. Second, they never interviewed the kids who were on the corner selling for someone and killing for the same person. If these people did ask these kids why they were involved in this life, the answer would be those kids had no choice. When their mom was on crack and their dad was gone, these children had to eat, so the person who put them on the corner to make sales was an answer. These people were father figures and all other things these children needed. Who else was going to employ these children and feed them?

In my neighborhood alone were four different drug gangs that fought one another, and they divided this place, even though it was only one complex. You could be killed by going into the wrong place, even if you were not involved with any of the gangs. The name of one gang was called SGP or South Grove Posse. They were in the section I lived in, and they were the bigger, better, and well-armed gang among all four. The leader of that one was an eighteen-year-old kid called Antonio, who I thought was the coolest. He never wore the same shoes twice. He had a Benz and a Jeep and had lots of money and girls. Antonio lived next to my apartment; he would occasionally buy me candy or ice cream from the ice cream truck. Everyone in our hood liked him.

The police officers started the program, telling us that most people using drugs were about our age and also that if they were not careful, they could be killed by overdosing. I, of course, did not believe it because I had not seen any kid do drugs or even die from it. In my neighborhood, crime was really high, and there was shooting at least once a week. There were sometimes bodies in the garbage cans or in the stairwell. That was true. I experienced those with my own eyes.

As the officers talked, one of the other officers walked around, holding an open briefcase, showing us all the confiscated drugs, such as crack, heroin, and marijuana. The officers did also inform us that two officers would always patrol our neighborhood, so if we had questions or simply wanted to talk them, they would always be available and ready.

Another item the police officers showed us was pictures of people before they started using drugs and after; those pictures scared me so bad. One of those pictures looked like Freddy Krueger; it was good enough for me to never use drugs. I was also told if we did mess with drugs, we would go to jail with bad people who would do bad things, and they were very graphic to us. I was scared straight after that. I had always tried to be good; now I would be super-duper good, especially since those officers really did patrolled our neighborhood, asking if all was well. It was a constant reminder to be good.

The program lasted a whole week, and once we completed it, we earned a certificate of completion. We then took a class picture, and each student got one with a black DARE T-shirt, which I really cherished since I did not have clothes. Every day of the week during the DARE program was almost like a free week since we had no schoolwork. When I got the certificate, I brought it straight to my aunt, thinking she was going to be pleased. However, it was not the case. She did not even look at it, but she did ask me if Ricky was doing something bad, so I told her yes without her asking what exactly, and I returned to stealing money from him.

Ricky had been living with us for a little over two months and saved enough money to buy a very expensive mountain bike so he could get around since he did not have a car or able to afford one. After another whole month, he saved enough to afford an apartment. He did not have money to furnish it, but he decided to live there; he could buy furniture a few at a time until it was fully furnished. Who could blame him, especially with the way Melvina treated us? She could not do anything to Ricky, and he was able to work and save to move out. I felt kind of lost when he left, and I always wished that I could work, but who was going to hire me?

Ricky's departure put my aunt's attention to us. She basically blamed us for not getting something on him that she could use to destroy him and even for not stealing so much, making it hard for him to save. That was another thing I was puzzled about. She always complained about him not paying his rent, making her get angry at him, but now she was mad about him leaving, so she punished us for failing.

With all that going on with Ricky, I had to ask my aunt about my money and the account Uncle Richard had established for us. My aunt went crazy, yelling at me, cursing, telling me never to ask her about any damn money. She asked who I thought I was to even ask her about the money or the account. It was the last time I had heard of it. I wish I really did have it. I'm pretty sure the interest from there to now would have made me a nice little amount, but I don't remember the bank's name or the street it was on. That was never to be since my aunt did something with it.

While I was contemplating about the location of bank, another idea hit me, and I instantly realized that Uncle Richard had not been around recently. After that realization, I tried to think what could have happened to him and Aunt Kathy in a little over two and the half months. Uncle Richard had always gotten in contact with us if he was not going to make it, and he would not let almost three months pass without so much as a single word.

Life was getting a little out of control, with violence increasing in the neighborhood. I heard a few terms that upset me. One of them was *statistic*, which was a way of saying if you were a black person, all hope was lost for you. Another term was *natural brain killers* as if we came out of the womb sagging, smoking a blunt, taking a gun, ready to deal drugs. Still another was *thug*. You guys know its meaning, and I know you people are educated, so I won't be explaining this one for you.

With my cousin now moved into his own place, my aunt started to brutalize us, especially after giving birth to her second child, named Joey, after my aunt's father. Shortly after the birth of her son, she started to hang out once again, leaving my brother and me to take care of an infant. As soon as my uncle left for work, she too left the house, returning a few hours before he was due to be back. It was only by the grace of the Almighty God that nothing happened that we were unable to handle. I was happy that she was out of the house for those long period, but those days were cut short one day.

When my aunt left the house, she took her kids out with her. My brother and I were not invited, which was not really a surprise. What did surprise us was when she told us we could not stay in her house while she was gone. Nope, we would have to wait outside in the cold until she returned home. I could not believe that we really had to wait outside during a snowstorm in New Jersey. That was the longest day of my life, but what could we do? My aunt told us not move, and if she came home to find we were not where she had instructed us to stay, we would get it.

By the time my aunt and children had gotten home, I was pretty close to hyperthermia. My toes, fingers, and face were frozen solid, especially since we did not have coats, scarves, gloves, or anything you needed for the cold. Shit, we hardly had any clothing. It took almost the entire night for me to stop being cold. The window in the dining room was broken, allowing more cold air in the house. Even with the heater on, I was still cold as was Samuel.

I needed to get used to being outside every time my aunt left the house, and she was gone no less than eight hours each time. As a matter of fact, there was one particular time when I was so cold that I got brain freeze, like you do after drinking a cold beverage too fast. With my health being as bad as it was, it did not take very long for me to get sick. While I was at school, having to return to the nurse's office to get my temperature taken, the nurse told me what I already knew. I had a fever of 104°F. The nurse asked me if I had gone to my doctor since the last time she saw me. I lied, telling her yes. She told me I needed to go back to get checked up. She then wanted to call my legal guardian to tell them to come and get me from school because of my fever. I lay down in the office again, falling fast asleep like the time before, waiting on my uncle. I knew my aunt was not going to interrupt her day for my sake.

A few months had passed by with everything getting worse instead of better. I was just in a slump, depressed all the time, as well as in constant fear. It was something I still did not or could not get used to. We had still not been lucky to hear from Uncle Richard, and since we had not been to his house over the weekends, giving us something to do, now I hated weekends, vacation days, or just anytime we were out of school. The beginning of the weekend was coming, and when that bell rang, all I was able to think of was spending my weekend with her, and then my stomach started hurting again.

The year had gone by very slowly for me, having to spend all my weekends, vacation days, sick days, and bad weather situations, mostly snow, with my aunt. And now approaching was the end of the school year. That only meant spending every waking day and night in the house with my aunt except for those days she went out as soon as my uncle left for work. I had noticed that, because I was in the house more, my stomach issues returned with a vicious ferocity that was unlike anything I had felt before. With my stomach like this, I started noticing blood in my urine, as well as in my feces. I knew something was definitely wrong, but what could I do about it? Who could I tell who would care outside of my brother, who had no kind of power, resource, or capacity to help himself, let alone me? It was one thing for him to take a beating or something, but that was a whole different territory, so I simply kept quiet, choosing to suffer in silence.

Chapter 6

ON MY OWN AGAIN

School let out for the summer, so a few minutes before that three o'clock bell rang to end the day, each of the teachers had the children explain to the class what they and their families had planned to do for the summer, which was something the school asked every year. I sat there listening to each classmate, like I did each year, and I hated it. No one was going to think of me as important enough to even walk me across the street or to the track, let alone bring me to any place I was going to enjoy or have fun in. So I watched all my classmates finish explaining about the wonderful things that they were about to embark on with their loved ones.

When everyone finished, it became my turn to get up in front of the entire class to talk about something I knew nothing about, and I would have to take bits and pieces from the stories I had just heard, allowing myself to paint a picture of the perfect family or just an okay family I wished I had. I went ahead to give people a portrait of my family going on a tour and visiting Disney World as I always wanted to do, and then I told my friends about going back to visit Africa, along with some other places.

It had been a real dream of mine to join the gymnastics team not because I thought I had any skills but because my gym teacher believed in me to the point he wrote a letter to my guardian begging them to let me join and even called and stopped by my house to beg. I was not able to do it. The price for joining the team was less than fifty bucks because the coach was willing to pay for most of it. My aunt did not think I was worth it; that was what I was told.

Whenever I received any letters from school for any activity that cost ten dollars or less, such as field trips or parties, I would not bring home the paper. I would throw them away because I was taught that I was useless, unwanted, and unlovable. If there was a letter that might have made me see myself in a positive light, I threw those away as well. I never believed in myself. Those points had been driven home so much. Those words were part of my proverbs or psalms. Hell, it was my bible. And I know you guys reading these words are asking yourself, *Why does this guy always repeat these things damn near through the whole book?* I don't know what else I can say to drive home this idea to you. I mean, this was what had been preached to me since I was five, and now at forty, it still resonates, kind of like the church back in the day lying to you that Jesus was white, but now people know better. The elders who came up back then still believe that even though they see, it's not true.

Here is a better analogy. I don't know how many of you guys saw the movie *Unleashed* with Jet Li. In the movie, Jet is taken at a young age after his mother's pimp kills her, and then he puts a shock collar on Jet to make him fight to win. And if he loses, he's punished; but even if he wins, the treatment gets no better. Even though Jet becomes a great fighter in the movie, he never attacks his boss, who's mean to him, even with the leash off. Then he meets a kind family man, Morgan Freeman, who shows Jet a better life, but the whole time, Jet thought that was how everyone lived.

The three o'clock bell rang, excusing us from school for the summer. Even though we had a party with cakes, drinks, and games and everyone was happy for the break, including the teachers, I was not happy, but I was not going to show my depression. Once again, as students celebrated, signing one another's yearbooks, I was left out because I could not afford one. It seemed I was always the odd guy out or standing on the outside looking in, the unwanted one. My friends walked out of classes, running outside to parents, awaiting their loving hold. Some of my classmates started their trips immediately after leaving school. I walked home slowly, with some of my classmates asking if I was okay because of my pace and gait. It was my abdominal pain as usual, but I told them that I was okay and that I just had a lot on my mind, thinking of my upcoming trip. That point was driven home one day after a few classmates who lived in my projects saw me enter a Porsche 411 that my uncle was driving for his company, so automatically, they came to the conclusion I had money, and I did nothing to dispel these false truths. Instead, I informed my classmates it was ours, which would become mine when I turned of age, and I even had a key to it because my uncle was so cool that he let me drive it around a little bit.

My brother and I arrived home from school at the same time, both of us having cakes, candies, and other sweet treats from the last day of partying at our school. We took all the treats and laid them out in front of my aunt for her to pick through what she wanted for herself and her children. After making her choices, we took the rest of them for ourselves. My brother and I would routinely do something like that whether it was a party like we had for the last day of school, some student's birthday party that their parents organized to celebrate their child's day with us, or trick-or-treating for Halloween. We did it to try to gain favor, hoping to get on her good side to ease the beatings and other abuses that she only did to us but not her children. I can't even begin to tell you how many times we tried befriending her. Our attempts to befriend our aunt lasted for a few minutes or however long it took her to polish off our treats.

During our few minutes of peace, I could hear an ice cream truck coming up our street. As soon as my little cousins heard the song from the truck, they started chanting, "We want ice cream. We want ice cream," over and over again. My aunt told them to hush because she did not have any change for the ice cream truck, only making them to chant louder. That was when I remembered I had some money left from the theft of my cousin's money. I'm telling you I will have to pay this guy back one day. So I told my aunt I had a dollar or two in change from the money Uncle Richard had given me a while ago, which was a complete lie. I don't even think she cared, telling me to bring her fat ass a giant ice cream sandwich. That alone was two dollars. Thank goodness I had a twenty-dollar bill.

My brother and I walked out to the ice cream truck. There was already a long line that had started to form because the trucks did not come in our neighborhood often for two reasons. The first was the violence that had escalated in our hood from the crack epidemic, and the second reason was the fear of getting robbed. The robbery of a few pizza delivery guys by children happened so much that, in the beginning, drivers would turn their cars off during a delivery. What used to happen was someone would make a large order of pizza costing over fifty to a hundred bucks, and then they gave the guy an address of an abandoned apartment. So as the guy made the delivery, knocking on the door, a bunch of kids ran out and grabbed all the orders; and by the time the deliveryman returned to his car, all his products had disappeared. We did not get any more deliveries after it happened a dozen times.

While standing in line, we heard some guys arguing, which was nothing out of the ordinary; it was just the norm around our hood. Then the argument got louder, with pushing and shoving, and before we knew it, we heard popping noises. They sounded so soft at the time that we all thought it was some guy who had bought these little poppers we all used to get from the ice cream van, and they were like very small firecrackers that had to be slammed on the concrete to make them pop. That theory was soon proved false when one guy in the altercation yelled, "They shot me!" So soon after he said that, we started to hear louder pops that I had heard often as did everyone in the hood. We knew them to be gunshots, and it was a free fall after that, with bodies running in every direction. I was so frozen with fear that it seemed as though everything was happening in slow motion, and I could not move my feet at all as if the cones grew hands and held me in place. My heart was pounding as though I just ran a relay race or a marathon or something. I tried catching my breath with no success.

It was at that very moment it occurred to me that I did not come out here alone and that I had to find my brother. Not really thinking anything was wrong, I started to finally move now, and time had moved back to its regular speed. That was when I looked down to see my brother lying at my feet. It did not register that anything was wrong. I extended my hand to help him up, but he never moved. So again, I stuck out my hand, this time laughing, telling him to stop playing around. "Come on, or I am going to report you to our aunt." If nothing else was capable of making him move outside of the Almighty, it was the threat of telling my aunt. With that, I took a few steps, thinking he was going to be right behind.

Then I remembered I had not gotten my aunt's ice cream. Now I was trying to come up with a reason she would be satisfied with, and then I told my brother the same thing, still thinking he was behind me. So I turned around to see why this guy had not answered me. Was he worried about not getting the ice cream too?

And when I looked down, he was still lying there, except now blood started forming under him and I mean a lot of blood. Still not thinking he was dead or I just did not want to accept it, I started yelling at him to stop playing around, and I was starting to really get angry at him because he's played so many jokes on me before. I kept yelling at him to get up or I was telling out aunt. Tears had started forming in my eyes, and I was crying and yelling, not believing that the one person I had in the whole world was gone. I sat next to him and was completely lost. I'm sorry I have to put this pen down. It's hard to write this. I got tears in my eyes and can't see what I'm writing.

I sat next to my brother, staring in space. Sewer people came up to say something to me, but I did not hear anything. It was not until the cops showed up to take him away that when I lost it, telling them to leave him alone and I had to bring him home with me, but the officers kept telling me he could never go home with me again. I did not care about what they said or how it was said. My brother was not leaving me, and I would not leave him. He was always playing around. I told the officer he was going to be okay.

Now I knew my brother—my protection, my only family and friend in the whole world—was gone, but the pain, sadness, and loneliness was not making it easy for me to just let him go. If I did, I was unwanted, and I really felt it even more now. I was alone and scared, and I knew I was next.

The thought of death scared me. It was something I had brushed off when they told my grandmother I was going to die. It was something that I was not going to be associated with. Now it was staring me in the face to let me know it was real. For the first time at such a young age, I knew my mortality, while other children had no clue what that was. These were the children who did not live in my neighborhood, and they were mostly white because the only whites in my hood were the cops and the people who collected rent or bought drugs who thought every black child was a dealer. I had several of them asking me to let them buy something off me, and I hated it, but I told myself when the next white asshole would ask me to do that, I would just take their money and run.

About an hour after my brother's death, I saw him covered up and loaded in a bag that looked like some trash bag. His small frail body was picked up as if a sack of laundry and put into a lonely cold van's floor that read "Coroner." I did not know what it meant right at the moment, but I would come to learn and see it more times than I cared to. Their next order of business was to interview people, asking if they saw anything or anyone right before or during the shooting as if, while these assholes were trying to annihilate one another, someone decided to take a look around just in case the cops asked some information on what the fuck had taken place, and then he would go even further as to risk his family's lives, including his own, to tell on a group of guys who would kill in front of the police for the simple reason of being the man and being cheered on as a legend in his group—a group the cops themselves couldn't contain or didn't want to because they served the public by annihilating each other, along with rest of us.

Covered in his blood, I walked in my house with officers right behind me. They introduced themselves to my aunt, asking if she was my guardian or the parent of Samuel. She replied yes. They asked if they could sit, to which she said yes. After taking their seats, an officer said, "We are sorry for your lost, but your nephew—" Even before finishing his words, my aunt broke down or at least acted like she was just fucking devastated, crying on the floor now. The only thing that ran through my head was *Is this bitch serious? She's sitting there crying like they had told her one of her kids was dead when she knows that she couldn't care less if my brother was dead or not. She did not give a fuck when he was alive.* They asked all their questions when she had calmed down. I don't remember what. I was not even in that house, even though my body was standing right there in the living room.

When they finished, the officers said their goodbyes and that they would be in touch. I didn't hear anything from those fuckers again. Anyway, when her guests leave, my aunt came back in the room, starting to talk to me about some bullshit. I did not even hear what she was saying because I was gone, and the only thing I remember her saying was "Go wash yourself off." I then remember my feet moving toward the bathroom, and the next thing I do recall was just breaking down, crying. I was in that shower for about an hour, trying to get it together to wash off this blood. I thought of him even more. I would not ever hear his voice, see his face, or even have him around when and if I had children.

After my shower, my uncle came home to find out that Samuel was gone. Now my uncle is not very emotional and does not know how to express himself. Shit, I wonder where I get it from anyway. I was in the dining room when my uncle walked in. He did not know exactly what to say to me, so he fell back on what he knew, which was him asking me if I was hungry, but I did not respond. I just sat in the chair, staring blankly into space. He asked me again if I was hungry. Without looking at him, I slowly shook my head no. He then said, "You need to eat, Shawn. I know you love Samuel, but he's gone." All that did was to make me cry again. Now I don't know the idiot who said that time heals all wounds, but that person is full of shit.

My uncle left the dining room. I don't know where he went to, but it must have been very late, at least around midnight. I went to lie down, but all I saw was the empty part of the couch my brother once slept in. I started getting an eerie feeling telling me I was going to die, and then through the thin see-through white curtains hanging on the window in the dining room, I saw human forms, a lot of them. Then they started to reach through the curtain with their white skeletal hands, so I ran to the light switch to turn it on, but that did no good. These things were there, so I went to the couch and cried all through the night until the sun was coming up.

Even though the night was over, I knew those figures would be back that night and those after that and that there was no running from them. Sooner or later, they would accomplish their task. I knew for sure, as there is day and night, that these things were going to get me because it was crazy that my brother died that way. It was only after his passing that we learned he had a hole in his heart and that his heart had gotten so big that if he had not died from a bullet, he would be gone in a few days. So now I don't know if he would have suffered more that way. I had no clue; all I knew was that my brother was gone and that I would never see him again, causing me to break down. I started to cry again.

For the next few months, all I did was cry. There was not a day that something did not remind me of my brother, causing me to break down and cry. I was not really worried about them seeing my weakness. Before, I did not want my aunt or anyone to see me as being weak; therefore I never allowed myself to be seen in that light. But after my brother's horrible death, I started to cry and not really give a damn.

Nighttime was the worst time for me not only because I was all alone or that I was deadly afraid of the things that come to me at night to let me know I was going to die exactly as my brother had. No, it was not that. I mean, those things were horrible, and I would cry myself to sleep. But the one thing that bothered was the fact that my brother had just been murdered, but the world kept on moving, not giving a damn about my pain, making me believe I was the only one mourning my brother, my best friend. No one cared of his passing, not even those in the house with me. It seemed the only time my aunt showed sorrow was to put on a show before an audience of detectives. I really felt alone. Hell, I was alone in my personal hell.

I had cried for almost three months, and all my crying and mourning had resulted in a headache that seemed to have no end. I also had to deal with my stomach pain, which continued to worsen from day to day. I spent my night alone and scared of those things that I was seeing each and every night, so I got no sleep. And when I would cry myself to sleep, I had horrible dreams of those creatures taunting me, telling me I was going to die the same way as my brother. I would then wake up in a cold sweat, but it did not make me feel any better to know it was just a nightmare and that I was safe. Even awake, I was still in that nightmare, waiting for that first light. By then, I would breathe a sigh of relief, but that too was short-lived because, even though the day chased away those ghosts and creatures or whatever they were, I still heard the voices and sounds they made.

Can you imagine going through life afraid every day without anyone to talk to, with no one to protect you or to let you know everything is going to be okay or those things that every child should hear from the people who are supposed to take care of and protect them? I had none of those things, and now the one person who had tried to be those things for me was gone forever, leaving me to face all of these things by myself.

I faced each new day as just an ongoing nightmare; today had been no different from the day before. Even though there were people around me, it made no difference. I might as well still be alone because those people served no purpose, nor did they try helping me in any way. With Samuel's death, I was left to deal with my aunt's abuse alone, and she did not let up despite this. I think she got worse with me when she said that my uncle had shown me a bit of sympathy, which must have made her angry. It had gotten so bad that I thought that I might be better off dead so I could see my brother and be with him, not having to deal with this nightmare.

So I read up on the most dangerous elements known to men or ways to commit suicide, and I found out that mercury poisoning had been a reason people had expired. I knew there was mercury in the thermometer, so I put it in my mouth and broke it, hoping it would pour into my mouth, killing me. I also wanted to punish my aunt. I wanted her to feel bad of how she had treated my brother and me. I hoped she would spend her life feeling bad about all of it, and I wanted her to feel life without me, and she had to be the one to do all the things I had to do, like scrubbing clothes to the point it made her knuckles bleed because she had scrubbed the skin away. I wanted her to feel the burning of that Clorox with hot, boiling water. I wanted her eyes to burn as she sat in the bathroom with the window closed. When my plan of breaking the thermometer did not work, I realized how God had always been my protector. I did not realize it then because I was not wise enough to know. But now looking back on my life as I tell you this story, the picture becomes clearer to me.

Another night had ended again with no sleep and with constant crying. I had cried so much that I thought all my tears must have been used up and that I could cry no more. After almost three nights, that was when I came out of my world to see my aunt happy while she sat on some old lady's lap. I had no clue who she was until my aunt called her mommy. Apparently, my aunt had convinced my uncle that she needed help around the house and with the kids, which I really did not understand. She had never taken care of the house or the children; all of those things were my brother's and my responsibilities. Usually, when my uncle left the house, she was right behind almost an hour later; then she returned home at eleven, an hour before my uncle was due to come home. And she was the one who needed help? Really, lady? You cannot be serious right now.

Anyway, all of these things had taken place as I was in my slump. All the tasks my brother and I had to do now rested square on my shoulders. So as I was expected, I went to say hello to my new tormentor, at least in my mind. I figured that my aunt must have learned her cruelty from somewhere, and this must be it. After introducing myself, she asked me why I was so sad, and my uncle told her what had transpired with my brother. She said in very broken English, along with Creole—which was a tribe and language in Sierra Leone, where she had just come from—how sorry she was for me, and then gave me a hug.

I returned to my fortress of solitude, the dining room, and sat by myself, leading my aunt's mother to ask me why I was sitting alone while everyone was in the living room. My aunt, being as fake as ever, never missing the beat, explained how she had always asked me to join them in the living room, but I would just sit in there by myself. Now if you've been paying attention to what you have been reading, then you know she just lied and that she was full of it. That lady had never thought of my brother and me as human and had never invited me anywhere, except some time when she visited Gloria, who had been one of my dad's former whores and who became my aunt's best friend. She thought that my aunt was the best thing since sliced bread and could do no wrong.

So one day while visiting her and her mom, I just sat there with my hands on my cheeks, thinking. Gloria's mother asked me why I was sitting like that, looking as if I was in complete disarray and depressed when my aunt was so good to me. So I took my hand off my cheeks and put a little smile, the only bit I could muster up, thinking, *If this old lady could only read minds, she would see the person she was talking about was evil.* When a few more minutes had gone by, I forgot about everything, and I went back sitting in the same position with my hands on my cheek and elbows on my knee. Once again, Gloria's mother chastised me, asking me if my aunt was good to me. I nodded yes. I mean, what else could I say?

That night, I was awake once again, crying and afraid, when the lights in the dining room was turned on. It was my aunt's mom, asking why I was crying. I told her about the nightmare, the ghost I saw at night, and the voices telling me I was going to die as my brother did. I was surprised that, after telling her all these things, she allowed me to come in her room to sleep on the floor. I did not hesitate and followed right behind her, and that was the only time I was able to sleep through the whole night in almost three months, but I made sure to get up before sunlight and return to the dining room before my aunt found me sleeping in her mother's room and put a stop to it.

Even though it made the nightmares go away that night, I still had to deal with them by day. I still heard the voices, and I would cry in the daytime, but I made sure no one saw or heard my cries, and I did not fully trust my aunt's mom because I figured she had only been nice to me when my uncle was home, which was the same thing my aunt would do. I know you guys know the saying "The apple does not fall too far from the tree," so I had to see what her motives were since I did not trust people, especially women.

Chapter 7

NEW BEGINNINGS

The summer seemed to have sped by since the death of Samuel, and because I had spent my days and nights in my personal hell, I did not pay attention to too many things. This new year of school came with different things; now I was in junior high. I had to ride the bus since the school was farther away, which meant I would meet new people, but I still kept the same friends I had gone to elementary school with, including Jay and Levar.

On the first day, they came up to me because they thought something was wrong with me. I was not my usual bubbly self and joking, which was because I was away from my aunt, making school a sanctuary. I explained to them about losing my brother Samuel, whom they both knew because they met him one day as we walked home when my aunt had sent him to get me because our cleaning of their clothes was not up to her standards. They both told me how sorry they were that this had happened because they knew how much my brother and I loved each other, causing me to start crying again. They tried cheering me up, and then Levar asked if I would like to come over to his house after school to play some new game he had received for his birthday. I agreed, and the bell rang, ushering the beginning of a new school year and the start of classes.

Now that I was in middle school, we did not have classes as we did in elementary school. In junior high, we had seven classes, including homework. The bell rang to signal the beginning and ending of each class, which was an hour long. And we had several teachers, whereas in elementary school we had one teacher for all of our class.

Once again, the school day ended with the ringing of a bell, but I do not need to hear a bell to know the school day was done because my stomach let me know that without fail. The pain was unbelievable; it felt a little worse than it used to when I had gallstones living with my mom and David, and I had to have my gallbladder removed. I had my locker, which was another thing about junior high that was different. We even had gym lockers, but they were fifty cents, which I could not afford. And besides, gym lockers were supposed to be a place you kept gym clothes in as we were supposed to change into our gym clothes every day, but I barely had regular clothes, let alone gym clothes. So every day, when my PE teacher asked why I had not changed, I told him I forgot my gym clothes at home. After a few months of that excuse, I had to find a different one to use, and that was that my doctor said I should not do strenuous exercises. Since he had been the coach of my elementary school, knowing me to be constantly sick, he allowed me to sit out of gym classes.

While standing at my locker, thinking about Samuel, causing me to cry yet again, someone tapped me on the shoulder, making me wipe away my tears so I could turn around to see who this was. It was my friend Levar, and he saw the great depression on my face. "Yo, man, I'm really sorry about Samuel. I liked him a lot, and you guys were so close I wish I had an elder brother like him," Levar told me. He was trying to empathize with me in the best way he could. After all, he was just a kid too.

Levar then asked me if I was still coming over to his house. At any other time, if I was asked this very question, I would have turned him down in a flat second because my aunt required that we be in the house thirty minutes after the school bell rang. At this point in my life, however, a lot of things made no difference to me, for example, the beatings. My aunt was still abusing me. The only thing that changed in that routine was the fact that I did not cry or show any kind of reaction or emotion; neither did I cry and yell out loud, lying and rolling around in the ground. I used to roll all over the floor from the pain of her beating me with kicks and blows, and I thought she enjoyed seeing the pain she was inflicting on me.

Levar was still trying to cheer me up, asking if I was still coming over his house, but he let me know that I could come over on another day when I felt better. I told him I was going to come on over to his house. After all, I did not really care of what my aunt was going to do to me.

Levar put his arm on my shoulders to let me know that all would be all right as we headed out of the school's double doors that led us to where our bus waited. We got on and sat next to each other as we did each morning. I knew that going over to my friend's house would definitely get me in real trouble with my aunt and her thirty-minute rule. At this time in my life, with Samuel's passing away, leaving me on my own like I had been done by a lot of people, I just did not care anymore. I lived my life with constant crying and grieving. I was always in a fog, where days and nights went by without me noticing. It was the zenith of all I could and would take. I cared about nothing anymore, especially with the voices telling me I was going to go as my brother had.

The worst part of my grieving was that I was the only one who did. I mean, nobody else even acknowledged it or me. The world just kept going, while I was in turmoil, crying and hurting from real physical pain, as well as emotional and almost spiritual pain, if that made any sense. My emotions are coming out really fast, and I'm trying to describe it to you so you can understand my every pain. Also, it still hurts to put down on paper some of these things, so I have to take a pause in telling you my story. Just imagine I'm with you wherever you are at home, on a plane, or whatever, telling you, my friend, a story.

I suffered from all this pain. The physical pain was horrific, but that other pain I could not touch or reach, but the worst part of it was I did not know what or where it came from. It was more than just losing a loved one who was everything to me. Making it even worse was the fact that I could not express it in words. With all my aunt did to us, the first thing she taught us was that we better never show any weakness and that any expression of such things was indeed weakness. The second thing she taught me was that I was unlovable. So now imagine hearing that your whole life in an environment where your thoughts, feelings, and opinions did not matter. "You're not human. You are just a kid whom nobody wants, but I took you in because I'm your best friend, and all I do for you is not appreciated, making you an ungrateful child." Hearing this for years and years would stunt your emotional growth, along with other things. I'm not a psychiatrist, so I don't know if my mental growth was not developed because of this environment and circumstances.

We had been on the bus for almost thirty or more minutes because Levar's bus stop was the second to the last. As we rode along, I started to pay attention to the things and places we passed. I saw beautiful houses with big yards that were manicured neatly. There were beautiful bushes, with some of the best-looking flowers I had ever seen. Even the grass on each house was all in pristine condition. The place was unbelievable. This was not like my neighborhood at all. There were no crackheads or other junkies hanging around, and trash was not thrown all over the place. There were no drug dealers leaning on their cars, drinking, and slanging dope. For those of you who do not understand street vernacular, *slanging dope* means to sell drugs.

My friend Levar's house was the one right across from where the bus had dropped us off. Getting off the bus, I almost fell while trying to take in all the beautiful scenery that was in front of me. I had been to other places, but they were not even this nice. My uncle Richard's neighborhood was not this gorgeous. Another thing that threw me for a loop was that Levar and Jay both lived in this neighborhood, and they were black. I had come to be taught and believed that only whites could live in areas like this, and places like where I lived were only for black people. I mean, after all, I had never seen white people in my neighborhood. The only whites I ever saw were police officers, mail carriers, or the manager of the projects, but none of these people lived there. They always came and left every day, so at such a young age, what else was I to believe?

My environment told me black was ugly and bad, every negative stereotype. And the worst thing I was taught was being African and black was the lowest of low. And at home, I saw that. On top of all these things was how worthless, useless, and unwanted I was—a lesson from my aunt. So if I couldn't get any nurturing outside and none inside, where was I to go? White was the total opposite of black, so white was wonderful and truthful. You can tell a little white lie, but lord have mercy on you if you told a black lie, no matter how small. They even told me and showed me the Son of God was white, contrary to what it was said in their Bible. Oops, I forgot. As long as the Son of God was white, everything is fine and dandy. But if he is black and you try to prove it by showing it to them in their Bible, all of a sudden, race does not matter, and it always does. Old black people who hold steadfast to this belief would argue with you all day about who the white guy is that they put on their wall as if he is some relative.

Looking around Levar's neighborhood was just unbelievable, and then we entered his house, and I could not believe what was ahead of me. Levar's doors were French doors with a painted bird on the glass portion of it. Then there were stairs leading straight up and another that ran down to a lower level. We climbed up the stairs, and when we reached the top floor, there was a nicely decorated living room with antique furniture, which blended well with beautiful curtains that ran down to a carpet. On our left was a hallway leading to a room. I only saw the open door and the edge of a bed. In front of us was a little pathway with two wooden glass cabinets with some beautiful designs.

Levar led me into the kitchen, where he asked if I was hungry, and I told him yes, so he opened the refrigerator. When I saw him open it, it was like getting hit with a bat. I was stunned. It was at that moment when his mom walked in, and I almost peed my pants and sock myself. I knew for a fact we were dead. She asked in a real soft voice, "What are you guys up to?"

"Shawn and I are hungry, so I was going to fix us a sandwich with some chips and drinks," he replied.

"Okay," she said and was leaving when Levar introduced me to his mother. "How are you, Shawn?"

Still very afraid, my voice cracked as I said, "Yes, ma'am. It's a pleasure to meet you."

"Well, a real gentleman and polite. I like that. Now how long have you known my son?" she said, leaning down to shake my hand.

"Remember when I told you about him, Mom? He's the kid from Africa," Levar reminded his mother.

"Oh yeah, okay, now I do remember with you telling me that. Well, either way, make yourself at home," she said, leaving the kitchen for a second time. Levar's mom was very tall. Well, I guess everyone is tall when you're a kid. Anyway, she was tall and dressed in a robe that ran all the way down to her feet, her hair was a little past her shoulders and very well maintained, and she had a nice face with glasses. I came to find out later that she was legally blind. I did not understand what that was at that time.

After his mom left, I could not get my feet to move. I was so scared. In my house, it was known that we were not supposed to touch that refrigerator or even look at it unless you did not value your life or your hands. It was also very surprising that, when I saw Levar talking to his mom, he did not have to look down. Instead, he was staring directly at her. If that had been my aunt and I looked up at her while she was talking, she would have taken my eyes out of my head to throw them of the floor. Also, there was no way I was to reply to anything she said. All I was supposed to do was look down and listen because I was less than human; my feelings, opinions, and emotions did not matter because I did not matter, and I was useless.

We finished our ham and cheese sandwiches with chips and drinks, and we headed to his bedroom, where I saw a television on a wooden drawer with books on shelves below. It was also decorated nicely, and on the left of his bed was a bunch of toys. Above all his toys was this spooky-looking clown, which just hung there with some strings. On the right side of the room was a door leading to his closet. I was really amazed that my friend was able to do things that, in my house, I would have gotten my teeth kicked in for doing.

After everything, he asked me if I wanted to play a game. I replied yes, thinking it was a board game, so it kind of surprised me when he turned on his television because I was thinking, *How are we supposed to play a game and watch television at the same time?* But he handed me this rectangular thing with buttons labeled A and B; another group of buttons had arrows pointing in all directions. Levar called it a controller, and then he put in this box that was below the television a cartridge that I thought was a cassette tape, but it was a lot bigger.

All of a sudden, I heard a voice say, "Double Dragon." You guys must know that I lost my damn mind because I loved the game. At the only time I ever was at the grocery store, when we went to help my uncle with the grocery, he gave both me and Samuel fifty cents apiece to play the game, and we became instant fans. I could not believe how this kid had an arcade in his room. Plus, he had twenty other cartridges that I learned were all different games.

He asked if I had a Nintendo, which was the name on the controller, so you know I lied my ass off, saying, "Yeah, I got one."

"So you know how to play then?" Levar asked again.

"Yes, I only played this game on the big machines at the store," I informed him, hoping that this would get him to teach me to play the game because I was clueless, and it worked because he told me this one was a little different from the arcade, and he proceeded to show me to do combos, as well as other moves.

"What games do you have?" he asked.

Now I had to think quick because, not too long ago, I had no clue that there was an arcade for the home called Nintendo, so I blurted out some games I had seen at the grocery stores but had never played, such as Mario, Zelda, and a few others. "But I don't have this game that's why I don't know how to play it," I told Levar. He went to explain that most of the games were played basically in the same way as any other ones; it was only the combination of the buttons that mattered.

We spent the whole day playing games at Levar's house, and since it was a Friday, meaning we were not going to school the next day, we kept on playing. His mom checked on us occasionally, which was something else that surprised me. Then one more thing caught my attention, and that was how clean Levar's house was compared with mine. There were no roaches running around with or without lights. Not only were there no roaches everywhere but there also were no rats outside or in the garbage just running around. Most rodents run from any noise but not these project rats; they did not fear anything. They would sit there looking at you like, "What the hell do you want?" Not only were these rats not afraid of shit but they also were huge, so big that I had seen cats and dogs run away from those ferocious rats. Shit, I don't blame the dog and cats. Hell, some of those rats were bigger than the cats and dogs. Man, I used to hate taking out the trash because our Dumpster was the headquarters of all big ass rats from New Jersey and New York.

I had been having so much fun at Levar's house that I did not cry the whole time I was there. I had no headache or stomach pain. It was at that time when Levar's mom, whom I had come to call Mrs. Pompey, came in the room to ask if we were having fun and what we wanted for dinner. I almost fell out of my damn chair. I started asking myself, *Where the hell was I? If this was a dream, please, Lord, don't wake me up. If this was heaven the Lord had taken me, please, Lord, let me see Samuel to prove to me this was real.*

When his mom left the room again to answer the ringing phone, I leaned over to my new best friend, and I asked him, "Does your mom always ask you what you want for dinner?"

"Yeah. Doesn't your mom ask you that?" he asked me.

"Well, yes, but I live with my aunt and uncle," I told him, lying again. Visiting Levar's house was something I never thought I would do for fear of my aunt killing me, but now I was happy to have done it, and that was only because I lost my brother, and I really did not care for anything. I just did not give a fuck anymore, and I was going to be treated like shit anyway because I did not matter. Shit, I was barely human, according to my aunt. I was happy to have learned that not all children were treated like my brother and me because, all this time, I thought that all children went through the same things I endured, so there was nothing wrong with the way I lived. However, this was a double-edged sword because learning all of these new things would give you that feeling of worthlessness. I did not even feel human, and my aunt had been correct in describing everything I was and everything I was not. My thinking was that she was correct in all she said that I was, had been, or would be. It was a glass-shattering moment. I cannot even begin to tell you how low my self-esteem was. It was already in the toilet and flushed away low. But now after learning all these new things, it fell so much lower that it had no signs that could detect its frequencies.

Mrs. Pompey returned to the room after she was done with her phone call and asked us if we decided on what we wanted for dinner, so Levar started out saying a bunch of foods, and then his mom interrupted him, telling Levar that he should let me pick because I was the guest, which made me almost fall out of my chair for a second time that night. But it was the next thing Mrs. Pompey said that made my heart jump into my throat and wet my pants. "Do you want me to call your parents to let them know where you are and that you'll be staying for dinner?"

"Yeah, and you can sleep over since tomorrow is not a school day. Can he stay, Mom, please?" Levar asked his mom, now begging instead of asking.

"Well, he can if his folks say it's okay," she told him.

Now I had to think fast. On the one hand, I wanted to stay right where I was with Levar and his mom; but on the other, if I stayed, Mrs. Pompey would have to call my aunt to ask her if I could stay in a place in which I was not supposed to be in the first place. However, I could fake-call my house and pretend in front of Levar and Mrs. Pompey that I was getting permission to spend the night; but then what if Mrs. Pompey wanted to talk to my aunt? I would look like a liar and would never be welcomed back into their house, which to me was a bit of heaven that I could visit whenever I wanted to. So I told Levar and his mom I could not stay because my aunt was taking me and her children on a trip tomorrow, but I did not know where we were going because it was a surprise.

"Aww man. I really wanted you to stay so we could stay up playing video games. You sure you can't stay?" Levar told me, looking seriously disappointed.

"Yeah, I know. I wish I could stay, but my aunt has been planning something for us to do after my brother passed away to try to cheer me up," I told them, lying again.

"Yeah, I'm so sorry. Levar told me about the death of your brother. I know Levar said you guys were very close and that he was a nice young man," Levar's mom told me as she took my hands and rubbed them gently. Hearing Mrs. Pompey speaking of my brother like that brought back all those feelings I had forgotten about for the hours I was over their house, and I did all I could to hold back the tears until I left the house.

While I was packing up my things, I kept my head down, looking under the bed as if I lost something, but I was only trying to wipe away the tears now flowing down my face. My friend, Levar, was still trying to get me to stay. It was this moment that I accidently lifted my face, and his mother saw my tears. That was when she told Levar to leave me alone and that he needed to understand that this was an important trip to me. Besides, we could have a sleepover any other time.

Levar finally relented, saying, "Okay, man, maybe next time." I could now see the disappointment in his face after I had finished wiping away my tears and standing up. Levar reached out his hand, and we did this little handshaking formula we made up after seeing Will Smith on the show *The Fresh Prince of Bel-Air* do his handshake with his best friend.

After our handshake, he walked me down to the door, with his mom right behind us. That was when she noticed how dark it was outside, and she asked me if I was okay with walking home in this darkness and thought that maybe I should call my aunt to pick me up. I reassured her I would be fine going home. I told her I did not live too far away from there. With that, she was okay with it and finally let me go.

When I was out in that darkness, fear had consumed my thoughts. At that very second, I asked myself, *What the hell were you thinking coming over to Levar's house and staying so late, having to now walk home in the dark?* My fear became a physical one. I could feel the eyes in the darkness looking at me, trying to grab me and pull me into it. I now felt fingers moving from the small of my back and up and starting to clutch the back of my neck. When I felt that, I took off running through the darkness. I was so scared that I could see those same things that I saw behind my curtains in the dining room. Now they were right behind me, chasing after me.

When I looked back, trying to see my pursuer, they had all disappeared. And when I turned around again, it had gotten brighter. The light was now chasing the creatures away. That was when I saw that the streetlights were now coming on, and that made no sense because it was after eight, and the other lights in the opposite direction from the way I was going had all come on. So the ones I was now under should have been on a long time ago. This was how I knew my heavenly Father had always been with me every day of my life because he knew I needed him, though I did not know that much about him except the little bit of what my grandmother taught, which was not much because I was only with her for a short time. However, he knew everything about me and had been with me thus far, always saving, protecting, and carrying me at different intervals of my life. And as you continue to read through this book, you will absolutely see the wonderful hands of the Almighty God working in my life, guiding the ship that is my life through the rough seas, which are the obstacles that the enemy used to try to block my way, but God sailed me through it all.

I ran so hard and so fast that I could see the lights of my project building and those unforgettable brown piles of bricks that made up my personal hell. Even though I was terrified out there, I ran two miles in about a few minutes. Normally, when you are in a situation like the one I have been an unwilling participant of, you are happy to see your home because it is a place of comfort and happy memories; and most importantly, you feel safe and secured there, and no one is able to deprive you of that. In my case, things were vastly different; those brown bricks meant being unwanted, fear, terror, feelings of worthlessness. I could spend the rest of this book listing all the things my house was not.

The reason why I take time to talk to my reader is so you can get an intermission—you know, like the way they do at the movies—and I also do that when something I am about to write or have written is hard for me. You see, for a long time, I just pushed these memories as far away from myself as possible; but now as I write or tell you this story, it is like what I have said before—I pretend I'm talking to friends of mine. So please don't get confused when you get to portions of this story, and you think, *Is he talking to me?* The answer is yes. I am talking to you, but I know you have been paying attention, and I don't have to tell you over and over again.

The brown bricks of my building were now even closer, and the little light I had seen from far away was now so close that it felt as though I could reach to it and grab it. The moon was now out as well. A few minutes ago, there was none, so the Lord must have been watching over me.

My stomach pain was at full throttle to a degree that it caused me to stop, vomiting all I had eaten that day. Usually, when my stomach was about to start aching, I felt a small gradual pain starting from the center of my chest into my sides, going farther down my stomach. Now it was different because it blindsided me. I wanted so badly to lie down, hoping that was going to help me, but it never did no matter what I did. My pain had a mind all of its own.

My door was now in arm's reach. I stood up prepared to take in all the blows and kicks that I knew were coming to me as soon as I entered into my house. The pain was now so bad that it almost buckled my knees. I was able to get myself stable as I entered the door.

The hit I received was very unexpected, even though I had spent time preparing to take it, but when my aunt hit me, she did it from behind because she had hidden herself behind the door. That first hit landed with such ferocity that it picked me off my feet, thrusting me forward, and caused more of the food from earlier to come out of my stomach to my mouth and on the floor in the living room. "Where the hell have you been? Haven't I told your stupid ass that you should be in the house thirty minutes after the school bell rings?" she said, bringing her other fist around, landing it on my mouth.

The only thing I saw after that was light. I then put up my hand to try to protect my face from another hit while still on my knees, trying to explain my tardiness, but I made that mistake of looking her in the eyes. A number of hits were directed to me, landing every blow. "Who do you think you are? Haven't I told you to never look at me, huh?" She was still continuing to hit me. I was so weak and out of breath at this time that I collapsed on the floor.

That was when I heard my aunt's mom walk into the living room, inquiring what was going on. I was so happy about the interference because I could stand no more from this beating. When Samuel was alive, this was usually the time he would chime in, begging my aunt to beat him instead, and she would turn loose on him so fast and hard that I would cry seeing how bad she hit him. My aunt did that to tell him, "How dare you interfere me?" Now thinking about it, my heart breaks for him because, even though we never knew before he died that Samuel had a hole in his heart that was killing him and making him sick, he was going through all of this abuse while he was so sick. I can't help but feel guilt and responsibility for all he had to endure. If only I were a stronger younger brother, I can't help but think maybe he would still be here. I would have my best friend, and a mother would have her baby.

That is another problem because Samuel's mother lived in Sierra Leone, which was plunged into a brutal civil war lasting ten years. The war was so savage that I fail to believe humans can do what these people did to innocent civilians. They would chop off the hands of men, women, and children because they voted in an election where the motto was "The future is in your hands." So these bastards chopped off everyone's arms and legs off. The sons of bitches were and are less than human; they are lower than waste. My brother's mother lived in this country during a war that started in Liberia and made its way to Sierra Leone because both countries are very close. I don't even know if she is alive; and if she is, she does not know her baby is dead, and I've made a promise to my brother that one day I will go and seek her out so I can let her know. I don't even know how to begin because so many people were killed in countries that are smaller than Rhode Island. The population, if I'm not mistaken, was about three to five million, and over two and a half million people were simply slaughtered and thrown away like trash, or bodies were left in the streets. Just to give you an understanding, the human waste of rotten corpse brought out vultures that feasted so much on people that they could not fly because they were so stuffed, and this was just in one country.

When she saw me, my aunt's mom helped me up to my feet, but I was still not able to stand on my own, so she put my around her neck to help up and sat me in a floral love seat I was not allowed to sit in. I knew for a fact this old lady, whom I was finally able to see, looked a bit like my grandmother, but she was very short with all-white hair that looked like cotton candy. Her complexion was light brown. I had never looked at her before because, when she first arrived, I was in a fog of depression, and I was crying so much that I could see nothing.

Sick or not, I jumped out of that chair because I was not allowed to sit in it, and I knew for a fact this old lady was not going to be here to defend me all the time. I also thought she was just like her daughter and that one day she would see I was worthless and that I could not do anything right. She would also see I was ungrateful and unwanted and that no one could ever even love me. I knew that her helping me was a short-term situation, and before long, she was to start abusing me too. The only thing was, back then, I did not see it as abuse. I simply thought it was my fault because I was never able to do anything right, making my aunt angry, so she would beat me. Thus I needed to do better, and if my mom only loved me, I would not be such a screwup.

After getting up from the love seat, I went over to my aunt and knelt down in front of her. I grabbed her hand, and I apologized to her, telling her I was going to do better and that I was going be a better human being. Believe it or not, I was afraid that she would get rid of me like what she talked about. She said she was going to take my brother and me to a government agency to tell them our parents had abandoned us, she did not know who our parents were, and she could no longer care for us. Abandonment was the one thing I was deathly afraid of since it was the one thing that made me unwanted and worthless, and my aunt was all I had, so I could not stand the idea of losing her.

After my apology, my aunt told me to get up and go sit down, but I had to clean my vomit off the floor. I ran off to the bathroom when I felt like throwing up again; it was while I was in there that I heard my aunt and her mom arguing about me. My aunt's mother basically was asking my aunt why she would beat like that when I was just a child. She said, "You beat him like he's your enemy, worse even." My aunt then retorted that children get stolen off the street all the time and that she was worried that something might happen to me. Her mother told her that she did not need to do that; all she had to do was to sit me down and explain her worries and the dangers of being on the street. Honestly, my aunt did not give a damn about what happened to me; the only thing she was worried about was me telling someone about what she was doing to me and them seeing all my bruises I made excuses for. Then the abuse would be revealed to proper agencies.

Even after that took place, I still did not see anything wrong with my life. If only my aunt knew that I was so afraid of losing her and that everything I did was for her to love me. After the death of my brother, I did not care about anything; but when I was out of my fog, seeing how mad I have made my aunt, I went into super overdrive to do better because my aunt was right; something was wrong with me, and this beating happened because of my fuckup.

As they argued, I ran back to clean up my mess. As I cleaned, I tried to explain to my aunt's mom it was okay, saying that this was my fault. "So please don't argue over me, please," I begged her. And after a while, they did stop, something I was glad to see because I was so sick that I needed to lie down. And since it was so late, everyone was ready for bed and went into their individual rooms.

That night, as I sat in the dining room, I could not help but think of what I had experienced in Levar's house. He and his family must be rich with how big his house was, and he even had his own arcade, and they had a television in every room when all we had at my house was one. Levar was even allowed to eat anything in his house, including opening the refrigerator. At my house, the only food we could eat was what you were given, and anything else was off-limits. Special treats like ice cream and other desserts were seen as adult food. My uncle would bring home food by the bagful like Philly cheesesteaks, shrimp in all kinds of sauces, and an array of many other foods, which were also off-limits to just my brother and me. But my aunt and her kids could eat all they wanted. I guess that was why she was so fat.

It was a little after midnight when my stomach pain was just so atrocious that I could not sleep. It was an absolute horrible night. No matter what I did or whatever position I lay in, the pain would not let up, so I sat up. That was when I heard rain. The rain was calming to me, and I loved it. When I lived with my grandmother, whenever it rained, my cousins and I would take off our clothes to go play in the rain. We would run around the whole neighborhood for hours before returning home to take a warm bath. Lying in my bed, listening to the rain on a tin roof would always put me to sleep. I don't know if you guys have ever heard the sound of rain on a tin roof while in bed. Oh my goodness, it is awesomely cozy. You guys should try it once; you will fall in love with it, trust me.

I walked over to the window, opening it, letting into the house the beautiful and pleasing sound of the rain, which was now getting louder and heavier. It was as if God himself was taking a handful of water and dumping it all over us. I stood there staring blankly into that dark night, watching puddles being formed by the rapid drops of rain that fell with such ferocity and with such power now that the wind had increased in strength. I saw young saplings and bushes dance to the beat of the rain.

I looked on, deciding to do what Samuel and I had done numerous times whenever it rained. We would sit on the window with our legs dangling above the ground. The window in our projects had a brick extension on them that allowed you to sit or stand on it. I climbed up on my windowsill and sat on the ledge, with my feet getting wet from the rain as I swung them back and forth. The window was also getting very wet as the wind picked up, now splashing rain on my chest also. While I sat there trying to forget about my stomach, which did not do much for me, I decided to live with it.

Sitting on the window's ledge, I noticed a black jeep pulling up into the parking lot next to our Dumpsters. The first person to exit the vehicle was someone I instantly identified because I liked him and thought he was just too cool. He lived next door by himself. He was always dressed up well and never wore the same shoes twice.

During this time, Run DMC had exploded on the scene where they were known for the shell-toed Adidas and just plain ones. Not too long after that, another shoes had become very popular in hoods all over the place, and that was a model of Nike called Cortez; but in the hood, they called them Dopemans because most of the people who wore them were indeed dope dealers or, for a better translation, drug dealers. Don't worry, white people, I got you, and I will make sure to always translate the hood language for you, if I have not done so already. Anyway, they had an assortment of colors, but the shoe itself was white but the check mark of the Nike symbol came in different colors.

Antonio, the kid who lived next door, always had different colors of Nike shoes, as well as other brands. He had an athletic build; his hair was wavy and was always covered with hat or a do-rag, which is a hair wrap; and he always wore these big gold chains on and rings on each finger. Antonio reminded me of LL Cool J, especially when he wore those sweat suits with Kangol hats. I admired him from afar, even though he lived next to me. But

I was afraid that if he got to know me, he would start to hate me because of all my flaws, so I was just quiet. Every time he said hello, I would wave my hands, not wanting to look him in his eyes, and I did not want him to see my yellow eyes and see how ugly and weird I was—another thing my aunt would tease me about, telling me that I was really those things.

Another thing liked about Antonio was that no one told him what to do. He lived alone and was always driving different cars with stacks of cash. Some of the money were held together with rubber bands; others were held together with what I came to understand later were money clips. They were all fourteen-karat gold with an *A* for Antonio, and little bits of diamond outlined the *A*. This guy was so fresh he even had gold watches with diamonds in them. I did not even know there were such things as gold watches.

I would see all these things when the ice cream truck came around our neighborhood, and if I was outside and he was around, he would always ask me if wanted ice cream. I would nod yes. He would then walk me down to the ice cream truck and give me a twenty to purchase my ice cream, and if there were other kids around, he would give me give me one to two hundred dollars to buy ice cream and candies for all the kids. Once that was done, he let me keep whatever change was left over, and Antonio would only get these ice cream popsicles that had two of them stuck together; they cost only twenty-five cents. He always wanted the grape flavor.

Antonio was well-known and respected by a lot of people because he paid people's rent and drove old ladies to the store to help with their groceries; that was my reason for liking him and wanted to be like him. I wanted to do good things for people and help others if I could. Besides, what's the point of having all that money if you don't help anyone? I also had a not-so-honorable reason to be like him; that was so I can have class and money to buy everything people needed so they could love me and never leave me. I would have all they needed right there, so they would never have to go get it at any other place.

As I watched Antonio go behind his jeep, opening up the back of it, I saw two young ladies exit the vehicle at the same time. Antonio turned on some music, now exploding from the speakers in his truck. The sound coming from the truck was muffled by the storm. Antonio walked back to the front of his vehicle, which still had the headlights on. With a girl under each one of his arms, they started dancing and enjoying the rain. Each one of the girls were competing for position and for his attention, and then they both were bending over, shaking their butts into his groin as he slapped both of the girls' behinds. They shook even harder, and it did not take a rocket scientist to tell you he was enjoying himself.

While the dance competition went on, I sat enjoying the rain and the cool feeling it had on my face. As I tilted my face up toward the stars in the heavens, Antonio and his girls never noticed me sitting there on the ledge. I was as invisible to him as I was to everyone else.

A few minutes had passed by, and the rain was still as strong as when it began. I told myself I needed to get to bed so I could get up on time, but the rain felt so good that I wanted to wait for five to ten minutes more, and then I would go inside—at least that was what I told myself.

As I sat there doing a monologue on why I should get to sleep and how many minutes I was going to wait before doing so, I saw a car that had been on top of the hill, which was the entrance to the parking lot. It sat there for a few minutes with the headlights on, and then it started to slowly move down the hill and had now turned its lights off. I had never seen this car here before because I would have remembered it. Samuel and I used sit on the ledge looking at each car and deciding if we would buy them or not once we became adults, so I knew all the cars. So I just thought they were coming to visit someone; that happened all the time. However, they turned off their headlights and still proceeded down the hill. In my neighborhood and hoods in all projects, that means only one thing, and that was someone is about to have a very bad day because he is about to get shot.

I stood up on the ledge, now watching this vehicle still proceeding down the hill, and I started to jump up and down, flapping my arms to get Antonio's attention. But because I had the girls, his music, and the rain fighting against me, he did not hear or see me. I held on to the building and jumped even more instead of yelling because, even though they could not hear me yelling outside, my aunt and everyone inside my house could, and the absolute last thing I wanted was to wake her. So I jumped high and flailed my arms all about.

Finally getting his attention, I immediately pointed up the hill to the car now closer. I did not know the model. However, after a flash of lighting, I saw it was a four-door cream-colored car. It had three passengers sitting on the door of the car, with their legs inside and their bodies out. There were guns in their hands, which were resting on top of the car.

When Antonio saw me pointing at the car, he must have thought I was waving at him because he waved and went right back to watching the show these ladies were putting. I was so angry at him at this point. I mean, here I was jeopardizing my life to warn this moron, and all he did was wave at me. Can you believe this bullshit? Besides, who stands outside in the rain doing such things instead of going inside? That's what I would have done. I know I was only a kid, but if I had two fine girls in front of me, we would be inside in the bed. So yes, people, I was horny as hell back then. I was a young kid, but don't act like I'm the only one, y'all. Go ahead, put your hands up if you were like that. Don't worry, I won't tell anyone. This stays between friends and readers.

I tried once again to get this idiot's attention, but instead of him looking up at me, one of the girls did, so I frantically pointed at the car again. This time, she patted his hand and pointed at me; and once I had his attention, I was not going to let it go, so I pointed at him once and then up the hill twice. I did this repeatedly. My last attempt had worked because he looked up the hill to see the car with the guys sitting on its window and guns pointing at his direction.

Antonio did a quick series of moves, pushed down the girls, and drew his weapons. At this time, the guys in the car started shooting at him. I don't know why he did what he did next, but he moved from the cover of his vehicle to the next vehicle. I guess he did this to draw fire from the girls, or he did not want his vehicle. I don't know, but what I do think is he did that to save the girls because Antonio was always in new cars. He changed cars like he did his tennis shoes, and the reason why he did that so often was so his enemies could not link him to one car, like a lot of the other dealers in my neighborhood who had a one-of-a-kind car that stood out very loudly from the others. It was easier to kill those guys without a shadow of a doubt. Sometimes they would let their girl or friend drive this unique vehicle, and the target's enemies would sometimes kill the person driving that car, thinking they killed the target. I think Antonio had seen enough dudes getting killed all because a vehicle was tied to them, and he decided this would not be his fate, so he changed vehicles often. That allowed him some more privileges than the other guys. He could go anywhere to expand

his empire because he would make new contacts and better deals and even have a chance to spy on his enemies. While the other dealers swam in their pond, he was swimming in the ocean.

Another thing about Antonio was that he did not have a lot of enemies, especially since he was in a business that warranted this type of lifestyle. I saw guys who came out to fight him, and he would beat their ass, and then he invited them to work for him, making more money than with whoever they previously worked for. The next day, you would see the guy working for Antonio. The thing about Antonio was he wanted everyone to eat. He was not greedy at all, and he knew these guys were just jealous of him. So instead of them coming to him, saying, "Yo, Antonio, hook me up," which they were too proud to do, they came for a fight. And after they get their ass beaten, he would hook them up. And if the guy he just hired did not own a vehicle, they would be driving around in his car afterward. Then you would see Antonio with a new car.

After these guys started to work for him, they became his most loyal, honorable workers and friends, and these would also breed a lot of jealousy from the leaders of the other drug gangs because their workers, whom they were abusing and paying minimum wage, started jumping ship, hoping Antonio would hook them up, which he always did. Now the new people who jumped ship were making money; they had cars, jewelry, and wealth they did not have before. So now they were loyal in many ways. They would feed Antonio about the movements and dealings of the crews they just left. They would even make deals with suppliers at great prices. So he had so many connections that when the other guys had no work or drugs for my white readers, Antonio's gang was still working. These guys who were trying to kill him that night must have been part of those other groups.

Being kind of young at the time, I did not understand it so well; but from what I knew, Antonio did not only have the lowly soldiers jumping ship but he also had taken away from the other gang the man who had the connection for the drugs and had helped the gang make a lot of money. But when the money came in, only one guy ate well, leaving his crew with scraps. It was not Antonio's intention to take these guys away; he was just a better businessman and employer. It was jealousy that prompted these boys to come through, trying to assassinate him this night, and I also think there was a reason why God had me sitting there.

The guys had now put their car in reverse when they realized he was no longer by his jeep. Antonio started to shoot at his attackers and must have hit the driver because now the car was in drive to supposedly turn around but instead hit the Dumpster, causing one of the guys sitting on the window to fall out, but he quickly jumped back into the car. Once again, they moved forward, making a U-turn, and the driver slammed on the gas to get the hell out of the parking lot, causing the tires to spin like crazy because of the rain, but it finally caught some of the pavement. The car then fishtailed, hitting a few parked cars and, with great speed, pushing them forward before stabilizing.

At the same time, Antonio came out shooting, causing one of the passenger windows to explode, hitting one of the guys sitting on the window. He then changed position to start shooting from behind the car. A bullet ripped through the back window, hitting the driver because he slammed into a few parked cars but very quickly got the vehicle under his control. Antonio was not done with them. He ran up the hill, shooting, and then he stopped, bent over, and came back up with two guns and emptied both clips at the car.

With all this noise, nobody woke up or called the cops. It was raining, and there surely was thunder and lightning, but not even one person witnessed this except me. The whole time, I was hiding; and other times, I peeked out of my window as if I were a news reporter or something. If cell phones were as popular then as they are now, I could have recorded this gun battle and sold it for big money. I must be dreaming, right? Even if cell phones were popular and free back then, my aunt would have just taken it from me.

Still standing in the middle of the parking lot, Antonio stopped again and picked up another gun from the ground that had apparently been dropped by his enemies, who were there to end his life but failed miserably. Most the people in other gangs liked him not only because he was tough but also because of his ability to think ahead and move around certain obstacles without the use of force, thus making everyone involved a lot of money. Anybody who knew him was aware of what was to come after a stunt like that. People were about to get it, and they knew it better than anyone else. Antonio was no punk. The only other times I saw a gunfight like that were in movies. The only difference was that there was no explosion.

The other thing that was crazy about the attack was if these guys just sat down to talk with him instead of trying to murder him, Antonio would have made a way to see that all the parties involved got what they wanted. Now they had to deal with a retaliation that was 150 percent coming to a hood near you. But the crazy thing about that vengeance was that it was not going to be dealt out by Antonio. No, I told you a lot of people were loyal, dedicated, and willing to give their lives for this kid. Those were the people who would enact the revenge, putting

Antonio in the middle of it as he tried to broker a peace even after what had happened. Of course, anybody would be upset, and Antonio was angry, but he would always wait for everything to calm down. He believed that any type of gunplay was bad for what he was trying to do now. That did not mean he did not resort to that; it was just that he always investigated to make sure the right people paid for their crime instead of innocent people, and that was the reason he and the people who were sent out to take care of business were not allowed to drink or smoke before any mission. Now what they did after finishing a job was their business. The reason for putting that stipulation was because there had been times were different crews going for a job got high on drugs and alcohol and ended up killing innocent people, so after seeing things like that, he enacted these rules.

If he had decided he would get a legit job, Antonio, who has been a great detective, would have excelled in this field because he had eyes all over the place and was able to get information from people that no one else could. All these people respected him so much that they did not even charge him for the information, like they did with other people in our hood.

Antonio stood in the middle of the parking lot while I hid myself, still peeking over my windowsill. Then I started to think, *What if those people saw me and are mad at me because I pointed them out to Antonio?* I knew that one day they would definitely come looking for me, and when they did, it would be bad for yours truly. My heart was beating like crazy after I saw this intense gunfight. It started beating even harder at the thought of retaliation that would surely take place if they had seen my face, and I was certain that they did, making what the voices were telling me after my brother's death more feasible. After the death of my brother, the nights were longer as I sat in the darkness, scared for my life. The monsters in my dreams were also there in the dark, telling me I would die in the same manner as my brother did, so it became more truthful at this time with the gunfight I just witnessed, and I was sure those men had seen me.

After all of what had taken place in my life, causing me to have those horrible nightmares night and day as I walked around in a fog of tears and mourning, I was shown some light at the end of this tunnel. Then without any provocation, I had been pulled down farther in the tunnel, making that light more distant and finally disappear to never be seen again. With all of these thoughts running marathons in my mind, I was a lot more afraid now than I had been.

Once again, I took a peek out of the window, and I saw the ladies Antonio was dancing in the rain with running up to him, and he received both girls with kisses. I could not hear what was being said, but one of the girls pointed in my direction. So as he turned to my location, I quickly ducked back down so he would not see me, but I knew he had noticed me already. I did not know my reason for not wanting Antonio to see me. I guess there were a lot of different thoughts going through my mind at the same time.

In my neighborhood, I had often witnessed or heard of someone getting beaten or killed for seeing or talking about a situation that they witnessed. Now I feared that might be my reality soon enough regardless of the fact I had saved Antonio's life. Even doing good things would get you killed, and it did not matter to these savages. If you were a man, woman, or child, all of these things meant absolutely zero to people without souls or had evil souls in them or possessed, for want of a better word, because I just refused to believe that a human being—a creation of the Lord Almighty—was capable of doing to another all the things I had heard of or witnessed. I just could not accept it.

The next day, I was extremely tired. I looked over my shoulders, expecting to see that four-door light-colored vehicle with guys hanging out of the windows, but the only difference was that, this time, I expected the guns to be pointed at no one but me. You cannot even start to imagine all that went through my mind. Not only was I dealing with the fear of living in my house with my aunt and in my neighborhood but now the only place that was safe to me—my school—was not safe anymore as well because a lot of the drug dealers in my hood studied there with me. News traveled fast on the streets because the shootings the previous night were being whispered around my school. So I was going to school with people who may have known the guys in the car, and of course, they wanted retaliation as was the rule of that concrete jungle and in that life they lived. I wanted no part of either one of those things after all of the craziness that had happened in my life recently, especially that Samuel was no longer around for me to tell him my fears or for him to protect me.

I loved my brother, and I know he loved me, even though we fought a lot. I just saw it as him trying to toughen me up and basically telling me, "Little brother, we are all alone in this life. And for that reason, we can never show any weakness no matter how much something might hurt." That was not how I saw it at the time, but I saw it when he passed. There were times I hated him and told him I wished he were not my brother and that, if he was gone one day, I would not care. But man, was I so wrong. Then when he was gone, I had those creatures in my nightmare that bothered me day and night, with the echoes telling me I was going to die in the same manner as Samuel had gone.

For a long time and even now, I've blamed myself for his death because, a few weeks before his passing, I had a nightmare where Samuel and I were outside getting ice cream as we had been doing that day. All of a sudden, someone tried to shoot me, but Samuel saved me by getting in front me, winding up getting shot and killed. The night before that, we had fought; so in the morning of his passing, I was mad at him, so I did not speak or even acknowledge him. We went our separate ways to school. When we got home that evening, we went out to get ice cream, and I still was not talking to him. I even refused to buy him any ice cream or candy because I had the money, which we were arguing over, until I turned to a different direction, pretending not to hear him. Then right before he was killed, he showed me something he had gotten me. It was something he was going to give when we got home but never got the chance to do so.

Looking back on that situation, I have blamed myself for his death because I should have done something. After all, the whole thing seemed to be in slow motion; and in my mind, I could have jumped in front of the bullet. Even after getting hit, I would still live, and I would get up to chase those people down, tying them up before the cops came and arrested all of them. Yeah, I know what you're thinking. I had seen too many action movies. Well, at least the few I watched when I was woken up by Samuel after my aunt was asleep, which we would do as often as possible.

Yeah, I really took Samuel's death hard. I even still do today. I don't know if you guys have been in a situation where you could not depend on or trust anybody except one person, and that person was everything to you until you did not miss any of the things that were missing in the first place. He was somebody you could talk to about things no one else would ever understand because it was just too unbelievable, but you knew your secret was safe regardless of what may have happened or would happen. Well, my brother Samuel was all of those things and more. Then just like that, in a twinkle and in the blink of an eye, someone stole him from me forever. How do you go on when you are only ten years old and there is no one to hold you, to comfort you, and to tell you everything is going to be okay because the person who tries to comfort you and tell you it is okay was gone? And even if he were alive, he was just a kid himself. I'm sorry, y'all. I have to put my pen down because writing this is still hard for me. And as I said before, I don't know who the hell said that time heals all wounds. I don't know what the hell they are talking about because it still hurts.

Through school that day, I listened a lot closer to any conversation I thought might be over the shootings that night and if they saw an eyewitness, but most people could not believe how they slept through the whole thing. It was crazy that a thunderstorm was what covered a war. It made no sense. What I came to believe was that people in our predicament have become used to gunfights to the point of sleeping right through them or not even caring about them anymore. Every kid in my hood were giving these outlandish stories of what they saw and that they were right there and there, even stories about them being involved in the shooting and saving the lives of some other eyewitnesses. But I knew they were all full of shit, but I did not say a word. What went through my mind after hearing those stories was that these guys were purposely putting these stories out to get somebody, mainly that eyewitness, to come out to say what really happened. Then they would kill them.

I, however, was no idiot, and anyone who was from my hood knew it did not pay to run your mouth. After all, the people who were doing most of the killings were children because, back then, children were not tried as adults. These drug gang leaders knew that, so they put that to the test by having nothing but kids on the street selling dope but always had an older gang member along on the ride to make sure it all went the way it was supposed to go.

That was what I was dealing with on top my nightmares, and my stomach became worse, along with my headaches, which were now causing my nose to bleed. I think it bled at least three times that day. I know what you're thinking, but I was not digging in my nose.

After the three o'clock bell rang, I would not regularly want to go home, but today going home was the lesser of the two evils, at least that was what in my mind. Even though my aunt abused me, I did not think she would kill me, or at least I hoped so. I rushed to my bus and got in, making sure to sit in the back; that way, I was able to see any and every one coming in. I had even planned a great escape, at least I thought so. Again, I figured I could use the emergency exit door situated at the back of the bus. If that escape plan was fruitless, I decided to use the windows. So to prepare, I went ahead, putting the window down on my side, as well as a few more on both sides. I kept my head down during the ride home, which was something I had always done. The only difference was that I was doing it for my safety. Usually, I kept my head down because I was picked on for my clothes and a laundry list of things. My lifestyle made me so worthless. I figured I deserved it and that all of these things were indeed my fault.

Getting home that evening, I was looking over my shoulders, with my heart jumping at every noise or movement, making my mind start playing tricks on me. I was in such a horrible situation that I did not notice the two-door red car riding next to me with some guy trying to get my attention until another kid tapped me on the shoulder. I looked up, and the kid I knew pointed to the car running next to me. I looked over and saw that it was Uncle Richard, whom I had not seen in quite a while. Then all of a sudden, there he was again calling my name, telling me to get in his car, which I was more than glad to do. I wished that he was there to tell me he was back to take me to go live with him and my aunt.

We drove until we got to a Pizza Hut, where we parked the car and went inside, sitting down at one of the available tables. My uncle started to explain why he had not been by. He said that, one Friday, he was on his way to pick us up, which was the week after the birthday party. He had called my aunt, asking her if she was okay with him coming over earlier so he could wait for us to get home and leave with us right away because the house that would be visiting was far away, and my aunt said okay. So my uncle said he jumped in his car with his and Aunt Kathy's things because we would be heading out to pick her up next. Upon his arrival to our house, before he got a chance to get out of the car, he saw my uncle approaching him, with my aunt shortly behind. So Uncle Richard walked up to shake his hand, but Uncle Francis knocked his hand away, which puzzling him. Before he could ask what the problem was, Uncle Francis told him he was no longer welcome to the house, he could never pick us up for anything, and the next time he talked to Aunt Melvina and disrespected her, he better be ready for a fight. My uncle could hardly believe what he was hearing and did not know what Uncle Francis meant about disrespecting his wife. He had always respected her every time he spoke to her. He tried to get Uncle Francis to listen to him so he could tell him he had never or would never disrespect his wife. He just valued them too much to do that. My uncle did not want to hear anything Uncle Richard told him, especially with Aunt Melvina behind her husband yelling out that Uncle Richard was lying.

After several more attempts of him trying to convince Uncle Francis that he would never think of doing any of the things he was being accused of, Uncle Francis was just getting angrier and had removed his shirt like he was about to fight. Uncle Francis was a very imposing figure. He had played football most of his school years and continued to work out throughout his life. So yeah, he was pretty big. With that, Uncle Richard left, not wanting a confrontation. Plus, he wanted for everybody involved to calm down so he could call later to explain his side of the story. That, however, was another flop because Uncle Francis got angry again or was still angry, which was not really like him. It was for this reason I believed my aunt was controlling him with voodoo or something. It just made no sense the way he would flip. After my aunt brought him in their room for an hour, he would come out mad as hell. I thought any amount of time back in that room would make any man happy, but apparently, my aunt and uncle were using the room wrong.

Later that evening, Uncle Richard tried calling the house, hoping everyone was calmer and he could explain his side of the story. But once again, all that he got for his effort of trying to keep the peace was nothing but yelling and vulgarity, with Uncle Francis telling him never to come to the house or get us for the weekend. If he did, Uncle Francis said he would hurt him. So with nothing else that he could do, Uncle Richard stayed away, hoping time would resolve the issue. But after a long time with nothing and after hearing of Samuel's death, he had to find a way to reach me.

Uncle Richard came to my school to try to see me, but it seemed Aunt Melvina was a step ahead, telling the school to not release me to anyone except her and her husband. So once again, he was fooled. After telling me his story, a lot of things began to make sense because I remember meeting Uncle Francis at home in the middle of the day, and he was very angry for what I thought was something I did. Then Uncle Francis came up to me, saying, "You'll never see your uncle again, and if he knows what's good for him, he will not come around." He then turned his attention back to my aunt, and they both laughed as if there was some kind of inside joke. I put it out of my mind. After all, my brother had recently been killed. I did not give a damn about too much else. As a matter fact, I just didn't give a fuck.

After telling me all he went through just to see me that day, I wanted to tell him about it but quickly decided otherwise because I did not want anything to interfere with him taking me as I just knew he was here to do. A waitress walked up in the middle of our conversation, asking what kind of pizza we wanted. Uncle Richard pointed at me to tell the waitress to ask what I wanted. I casually turned to the waitress because I was so happy to be connected with my uncle again. I ordered sausage pizza with black olives and extra cheese.

I remember that very day because, up until then, I had only been happy a few other times in my life. Those were days I never saw too often, so I can only count two or three other times that I was ever really happy. It seemed my aunt was the one person who would decide that I should be always miserable, and if there was anything or anyone who made me happy, she would be sure to remove it. This was the reason she made up the story of Uncle Richard disrespecting her, which was full of shit, and it was practically our own fault.

Every Friday, Uncle Richard would come to pick us up without fail, and my brother and I would rush home to wait for him; but while waiting, we talked about what we would be doing that weekend and how happy we were. It was something my aunt saw and wanted to put an end to. That was the reason for the story she concocted about my uncle disrespecting her; it was just impossible to believe. She was that angry over the little bit of joy we did enjoy, which was not a lot. She had always found a way to foil any attempts of us being happy. I don't know why she was like that or who made her that way, but in the end, it was my burden to bear.

I was starting to see a cycle happening with me, so I came to a conclusion on why nobody wanted me, and it was because I brought misery to any and all around me. It was true from my mother and David. I made their situation worse. I was constantly sick or messing up at school, and then I used up all my mom's time at work by having her come and get me from the police station. Oh, let's not forget the social worker who was coming by the house. I was useless and ungrateful. These were all the things my mother wrote in the letters to my aunt, telling her not to let me live with them because I would be nothing but a headache and to make sure she never be found, so no one would ever be able to bring me back to her. She packed up in less than a day to move, even changing her phone number.

Now I was here with Aunt Melvina and Uncle Francis, and even here, I was still useless and couldn't do anything right. My aunt was right; no one would ever love me because there was something wrong with me. I had managed to make my own mother not love me. Besides, who would want to love me anyway? Look at me. I was dumb and ugly with freaky yellow eyes. Even my father was right. I was an embarrassment. My brothers and sisters were not an embarrassment and a disgrace, just me. That was why he was not around, and it had nothing to do with the money he stole. He wanted Samuel. He had sent one of his girlfriends, named Emily, to come and get him. But because Samuel got in so much trouble, she brought him back. That was what my aunt told me, and I knew that was the truth because Samuel and I were surprised to see her at the house out of the blue, and she did take him and brought him back a few months later. He was killed not long after that.

My aunt had informed me about a lot of things, and I had witnessed a lot of it, so she was all I had; there was no one else. I wanted her to want to love me, but I was never good enough, but I kept trying. I know you guys reading this may be a little confused on why I would want this love from my aunt so bad. Remember, I was just a kid and had mostly been rejected instead of being wanted, and what my uncle did and said would prove that to me in so many ways.

After getting the pizza, I ate a slice, happy that Uncle Richard was back in my life, and I knew he was here to take me with him to get me out of this hellhole and to go live with him and Aunt Kathy forever. "Let's go," my uncle said. "Are you ready?" I eagerly nodded yes, and we started out.

I grabbed another slice of pizza out of the box, and I was happy thinking I would not be seeing those brown bricks of my former hell again. I was so excited that I almost jumped the gun and asked my uncle if we could stop by the house so I could say goodbye to my aunt and grab a few meager items of mine. But no sooner had I thought it, we pulled up in my neighborhood, and I was thinking, *Wow this guy is already thinking a step ahead of me.*

So I was caught off guard when he said, "Okay, my boy, I will try to come back to see you. Oh, by the way, I'm sorry about your brother's passing. I was really shocked, and I know how much you loved each other. I know it's hard, but you've got to be strong." With that, my uncle left; and with him, he took my appetite, my hopes, my dreams. Everything was gone. I even threw away the pizza I had just eaten a slice of.

My uncle leaving me proved my aunt's point; no one wanted the burden of caring for me. If they did, why have none of these so-called people who said they loved my brother and me come to take us to go live with them? And as time went on, my aunt's point was made over and over again. I was not wanted by all these people who said they would take me if it was needed, but even if I did need it, they still did not want me. I was even convinced that my grandmother was happy to get rid of me and was no longer held down with having to care for me.

I stood outside in the parking lot watching my uncle leave. Yeah, I would leave me too. I didn't even want myself. I did not even want to see my own reflection. I can't even describe the way I felt. *Unwanted* was not even close. *Worthless, useless*, or any other words with *less* at the end did not even describe me.

With the pizza now wherever I had flung it, I began walking in the house, determined to do better so the one person who did want me was going to keep me. As I thought of it, my aunt did what she had been telling Uncle Francis; she was disrespected by Uncle Richard because I think she was afraid we were getting too comfortable with him and Aunt Kathy and that her abuse would be revealed to them, causing the law to come down hard on her. But if only she knew we had never talked about it to anyone, including Aunt Kathy and Uncle Richard. That was not to say we did not trust them, no. It was because we were so relaxed and comfortable whenever we were at their house that we did not even think of it because we had so much fun. Also, we did not want to do anything that may have gotten in the way of our weekend visits.

Besides, not wanting to disturb our visits was another reason we never said a word to anyone because all you had to do was look at my brother and me to see something was obviously wrong. Most people who saw us would inquire if we were sick or a myriad of other things. We wore the same two jeans and shirts for so long that holes began to appear on them. The one good thing about that situation was that holes on jeans were a fashion trend in the eighties and nineties, especially when George Michael popularized it. So other kids thought we had fallen into the fashion trend because of the rips and tears on our jeans, not knowing they were there because of overuse and the inability to get some new ones. We wore our clothes so much that we were afraid to wash them for fear of them falling apart, so we washed them only if it was necessary.

I watched Uncle Richard drive away, hoping he was coming back to take me with him and that it was all a prank, but I knew otherwise. Believe it or not, I was not mad at him as I was mad at myself. After all, I opened myself up to love and get used to someone. Tears rolled down my cheeks as I vowed I would not let anyone be close to me. The thing that hurt me even more was that people were leaving me, but I kept going back to get my feelings hurt. Hell, if my own mother did not love me, why would anyone love me? I did not care about anything that I did not even like myself, let alone love myself. *Man, you're an asshole. Do you ever learn, moron?* I scolded myself, going so far as to punch and hit myself to the point I started to feel pain. I was crying really hard now, mad for letting my guards down, having let someone in too close. My cries were bitter, and I was crying so hard. I could not contain it anymore. I finally burst out a loud cry. *No one wants you around or needs your worthless ass. You are taking up space that someone else could be using now, you fucking idiot!*

More time had elapsed with me just standing there looking blankly into space, still crying and weeping, totally confused about my life. Then a foreboding feeling came over me as I realized how the rest of my life was going to be wasted at my aunt's house, being abused and mistreated, and that I would always be trapped in that cycle of bullshit.

The next morning, after cleaning the entire house, I was given the chance to sit on the first few steps in front of our building. I took that opportunity. My aunt was not being nice; she just did not want me to follow her because she has taken her kids out that day and did not want me to come along. They were all in the house, excited, preparing for their day out. I would not lie; it hurt me to be excluded from what would become or had already become a normal situation, a norm, around me. When they were ready, they came down the stairs, passing by me, telling me they would be back as if I gave a flying fuck. The only thing I was so grateful for was they left the door open so I could go in, and even that was not an act of kindness. No, it was not. The reason for that was my aunt was expecting a very important call. But I had taken some precautions by leaving one of the windows unlocked, so if I got too cold, I could get in through the window, where I could exit as well to run and sit back in the place my aunt had ordered me to.

I watched as my aunt and her children pile up in my aunt's silver cutturs and leave. I did not move from my seat only because I was in deep thought. I was trying to figure out why I was unwanted by everyone. What was I doing so wrong that caused anyone to not want to be around me? Why didn't anybody love me? Even those who said they did wanted nothing to do with me. Everyone could not be wrong. After all, even those who were obligated to care for me would leave my life sooner than later. *Pathetic, pathetic*, I told myself. *You are just plain pathetic and useless.* As I said that to myself, tears began brewing in my eyes, and I asked myself why no one loved me.

I had been outside for about an hour and a half. I was beginning to get very cold, so I got up with tears in my eyes, making everything I looked at blurry. At my door, I started turning the doorknob, about to enter my dwelling, when I heard a voice call out. "Yo, little man." I turned around to see who was being summoned. I saw a group of guys, totaling almost ten, but no one said anything, and whoever it was who had been calling after me I did not know or could see because all of those guys were far away from me. I turned around again to open the door, and once again, I heard the call. "Yo, you little man." This time, the voice was a lot closer behind me, so I turned around to see who it was, and I saw Antonio standing there with the crowd of people behind him. I stood there scared as he walked up to me.

"Yo, what's up, little man? I've been trying to catch up with you to thank you for that night," Antonio said, holding out his hand, and I shook it. He proceeded to tell me about the guys in the car that night. They used to be his friends, but they wanted more money than what they deserved. Antonio said he did not mind people saying what they were worth, but he was not about to give out money because someone thought they should get that dough for just knowing him or because they grew up together or were related to him. "It does not work like that. Right, little man?" I nodded yes, agreeing with him.

"See? Even this young brother knows that," Antonio told his entourage. "That's what I'm talking about, man. What's your name, little man?"

"Shawn," I whispered.

"What?" he said. So I spoke up, telling him my name. It took him a few times of me pronouncing my name over and over again before he got it.

Antonio then instructed me to follow him. With nothing else to do or fear, I followed him as did his crowd of associates, friends, workers, and bodyguards. We walked up the stairs, leading me into his house. When I reached the top of the stairs, I could hardly believe how nice his place was. He had a television that you could not pass by without noticing. The television was seventy inches and sat on the floor, and it was still taller and bigger than I was. The televisions back then were not light as the ones today, nor could you hang that up. That was why they were called floor television or floor models.

The next thing I noticed was the giant fish tank with a bunch of tropical fish, even octopus. The tank was also filled with a small wrecked ship, like the real ones you see in the ocean. I saw so many kinds of fish I had not seen on National Geographic. The living room was decorated with black and white leather sofa. He even had an all-white rug in the center of the living room with a round glass center table. In the dining room, I saw a huge table with at least ten chairs and plates, napkins, and silverware as if someone was about to serve dinner. The next room I could see was a huge kitchen with a bar separating it from the dining room. I did also notice that his apartment was bigger than ours or any other apartment in the project. Antonio's place was better, bar none, and I noticed there were no cockroaches running around. It was as if even the roaches knew not to fuck around with Antonio or in his house.

When I was finished looking around, Antonio offered me a seat. His guys turned on the television, and I was asked what I wanted to watch. Since it was a Saturday morning and they used to have a Saturday morning cartoon lineup that included *Looney Tunes*, *GI Joe*, *He-Man*, and a list of others, I told them I wanted to see cartoons. It was crazy that everyone in the house wanted to see cartoons. I forgot that all of these guys were kids as well, but because I was younger, I only saw them as adults.

While we watched television, a conversation began among Antonio and his friends over who they thought would win in a fight among Spider-Man, Batman, and Superman. As they argued, Antonio asked one of the girls, who were all in the back room—doing what exactly I had no clue—but when the first girl came out, I noticed she was one of the girls I saw dancing out in the rain that night. The girl asked me what I wanted, but I had no clue. It was not often that people asked me about anything, especially having to do with me. She then left, returning a short time later with a glass of orange juice. I was confused by that, so I sat there without drinking the juice. I said to myself, *Did she get a look at me and give me a regular glass instead of a plastic cup?* I was used to just cupping my hand to catch liquid and drink very quickly so I did not waste any of it, or I would go to the faucet and drink directly from it.

"Go ahead, drink, man. Bring this man some Cap'n Crunch cereal," Antonio instructed the girl.

As we waited, Antonio told all the guys in the room how I had saved him, and he said to put the word out that I was his little man so nobody was to ever mess with me. "I want all of you to look out for him like you would for me. You all hear that?" he screamed, and they answered in unison. Then he took out some money to give to me, and I put it in my pocket without counting it or even looking at it.

I went back to my seat, and that was when I saw a Nintendo. Immediately, I wanted to play it, but I did not want to step over my bounds. But when the girl returned with two boxes of cereals, one for me and one for Antonio, my eyes were so fixed on the Nintendo that the girl and Antonio took notice of my wanting to play the game. So they both asked if I wanted to play, and of course, I did.

I had been up in Antonio's apartment for a very long time, and it was now getting late. Antonio said he and his crew had some things to take care of, but before leaving the apartment, he handed me a brown bag to deliver to another apartment that was all the way on the other side of ours. I thought to myself, *Is this man nuts? He wants me to go all the way to the other side of these projects. He must be trying to get me killed.*

Well, whatever. Antonio must have been reading my mind or thinking the same thing because he immediately told me not to worry because no one would ever bother me again as long as he was around, but I was not about to stake my life, hopes, or dreams on that bunch of bullshit. Antonio handed over the bag again, telling me the word had already been put out that if anyone touched me, it was as if they touched him, and there would be hell to pay. *Didn't someone try to touch you? And if I had not warned you, you would not be standing here, so forgive me if I don't put a lot of confidence in your words.* That was what I was thinking but never told him.

"When you're done, come back here and wait for me."

I walked out of the apartment, heading toward my destination and my mission. I was walking very slowly because my stomach hurt so bad, but I soldiered on. I watched my steps closely while I walked. I reached our boundary and stepped over the line that ended the South Grove Posse territory or SGP, entering another section.

I saw a group of guys shooting craps on the corner for small change, and then one of the guys came up to me, asking if I had any money for him to bet, guaranteeing double my money if he won. So I handed him five dollars, which of course he lost. And then he came back to ask if I had any more money. "Yeah, I have more, but I am not giving it to your sorry ass, and I want my money back, asshole!" I yelled at him. Now I don't know if I was just mad that he had lost my money or that I just did not care about anything anymore. It could also be that I had lost my mind, but these guys would have killed me for what they thought was a disrespect. It's amazing how the people who don't even know about respect or how to go about getting it are the ones always yelling about giving them respect. People are full of shit.

The gentleman I was talking to turned around, leaping at me as he yelled, "Who the fuck are you talking to?" But he was restrained by two other guys, who told him to calm down, and then he completely calmed down, smiling at me. I took off running, and I'm not ashamed to say I almost peed on myself.

While I ran, I asked myself, *What the hell is wrong with you? Now those guys are going to come after you.*

All types of scenarios went through my mind, especially wondering what the other guy whispered to his friend to calm him down. He probably told him, "Don't worry, man, we'll get him later on his way home." Now I was truly afraid, so I had to take countermeasures. My mind never ran back on what Antonio had told me about no one hurting or bothering me. He was no god for me to put my trust in anything he said, no matter how cool I may have thought he was. I told myself that, on the way back to my house, I was going to take a different route that I took when I had followed my friend Shawn on many missions to spy on the enemy. I never saw it as dangerous because it was so damn amazing but fun at the same time.

I ran until I was sure that my pursuers were no longer behind, at which time I slowed down to catch my breath. I was surprised that I had ran so far and so fast that, when I looked up at the number of the apartment, I realized I had passed my destination and had to go back. Then I finally saw the correct number.

I walked up to a door that was different from all the other ones in the neighborhood and knocked. This door was an all-black metallic door that felt very heavy. I knocked on the door again, this time just a bit harder, and then stepped back, waiting for someone to open it. I finally heard the clicking of the locks before the door creaked open. There stood a very large black man with a beard and dark glasses. I told him Antonio sent me, and he then led me inside of this very dark building with all the windows painted over.

The smell inside this place was so unbelievable that I almost vomited. I was led deeper into this place that was a representation of hell. When my eyes had finally adjusted to the light, I saw that the floor was covered with people smoking what I came to know was crack. The people in the place looked like the living dead. Every time a little light passed over them, I could observe a sea of bodies reaching up their hand as if they were reaching to someone to pull them out of the sea they were drowning in. It was so horrible because these people did not look human anymore. I don't know if you guys have ever seen those horror movies where somebody looks normal, and then all of a sudden, that person changes into some kind of evil-looking spirit. Well, that was what they looked like every time the light was cast on them. It was almost as if they were not human and were allergic to the light.

"Follow me," the big man who had opened the door instructed. As I followed deeper and deeper down, it became hotter. The stench I smelled was made up of several different things. You could smell the stench of unwashed bodies, vomit, and what smelled like rotten meat, as well as feces. It was atrocious, but I kept my composure until we have finally reached a well-lit room that was a lot cooler.

This room was a far cry from the previous one. In this room was a large television, almost as big as the one Antonio had in his home. The big guy who had led me in through the maze of humans before we had finally reached this room sat in a chair that were all set up around a very nice table. The chairs totaled about twelve, just as they were in Antonio's apartment. The only difference was that they were all-black leather chairs with initials sewed into each of the headrests. There were also weapons on the table. If I did not just enter through a place of the living dead, I would have argued this was the office of a Fortune 500 company, not an empty office in the hood.

The big guy with the dark glasses on told me to place the brown paper bag I had, which I did. Then a girl walked over to me, handing me another bag to bring back to Antonio. After taking the bag, I was about exit the building the same way I had come in, but I was stopped by the big man. He told me I did not have to travel through the door behind him that led to the living room and back out where I had seen the guys shooting craps earlier. I can't even begin to tell you how extremely happy I was not having to go back through all those people who looked like the living dead. It was so nasty in there that I could still smell that stench all over me. I had been inside of the building for less than twenty minutes, but you would have thought I was living there, and no matter what I did, I could still smell that putrid odor.

I was so busy smelling myself that I never saw the guy I had a problem with earlier after he had lost my five dollars. They were right in front of me. I was looking around to see if maybe I stepped in or sat in something, and it was only after checking myself and being satisfied with everything that I looked up, bumping into the crowd of guys playing craps from earlier. I bounced back off the guys, who were a lot larger now than when I first saw them. I stood there stiffer than wood. I knew for a fact that I was going to get the crap kicked out of me, so I looked around to see my best plan of escape. Then I checked to see what was close that could be used as a weapon to protect myself. I saw a few metal pipes lying next to some nice-sized sticks. Before I had a chance to grab any of those weapons, the guy who lost my five dollars handed me a twenty-dollar bill, asking me why I had run from him when all he was trying to do was repay me. I didn't know where he got all of that nonsense from because I remembered it a whole lot differently, but I took the money. I was about to leave when he said, "If you ever need anything, little man, just let me know, okay? My name is Red."

I told him, "Okay, I would do that."

Then he said, "Tell Antonio Red said what's up," to which I told him okay. I turned away from him so I could get back to Antonio's place.

It was dark when I made it back to Antonio's apartment to see if he had arrived, but he had not, neither had my aunt and her kids, so I went back to Antonio's. One of the girls I had seen earlier let me upstairs in Antonio's apartment to wait on him. The girl then brought me something to drink. She also asked me if I wanted to place an order for something to eat because they were going to McDonald's for a bite to eat. I explained that I had no money. She then let me know that I did not need money. She kissed me, saying that they all had the payment needed. She called me handsome and left. I was not handsome. She was just making fun of how ugly I was. I sat down in Antonio's house waiting for him to return.

It was crazy how a guy with all of these nice things would leave his door unlocked and how people could come and go as they wished, especially since someone wanted him dead yesterday. And today he was walking around with a whole armada of people who could have very well been collaborators.

Sitting in the apartment alone playing video games, I felt safer than I had in a long time. I was allowed to do whatever I wanted. If I was hungry, I could go and look in the refrigerator, taking out whatever it was I wanted to eat and do so without fear of retribution. It was a great thing not to be restrained all the time, like I was back home. Around my aunt, I walked on eggshells; that way, she remained unaware of my presence. I would even hold my breath so she would not notice me. I mean, I would literally hold my breath as I tiptoed around the house. It was always so remarkable to see that it took my being over someone's house to realize something was wrong with the way I lived, but all of those ideas left my head as soon as I walked into my house with my aunt, who would slap all ideas of rebellion out of my head. I had not really wanted to be alone or liked being alone until today, which was the first time I had been by myself since Samuel's death, and I was not afraid as I played all the Nintendo games Antonio had, which was a lot. He had Double Dragon, Bad Dudes, and Bayou Billy. This kid had over a hundred games. I could have spent the rest of my life in his living room.

I had been playing with the Nintendo for such a long time that it was almost midnight when I got up to use the bathroom. Walking through the hallway, I looked in some of the rooms with doors halfway cracked. I saw nothing but hundred-, fifty-, and twenty-dollar bills sprawled all over the bed and on the floor. I could hardly believe it. I wanted to run in there, grab all the money I could carry, and bring it to my aunt. I guess it was to make her happy, hoping she would finally give me the love and acceptance that had eluded me for so long. But I thought better of it, deciding to just go do what I had originally wanted to do.

No matter what you're looking for, it always appears in the last place you look, and looking for the bathroom proved to be the same. It was the last door on my right. I entered the bathroom with a white and blue motif. The checkered floor matched the shower curtains. Even the towels and the little decorative soaps in the soap dish all matched, including the flowers, rugs, and even the paintings.

I walked back into the living room when I was done relieving myself and started playing my game again when one of Antonio's girls returned with the food from McDonald's and gave me mine. She asked me if I needed anything, and I told her, "No, I'm all right." She then told me that she was heading out and that Antonio would be coming back soon.

I said okay, returning to my game and food. When she was done, she left, and I looked inside my McDonald's bag to see what I had received. I pulled out a Big Mac with french fries and a beverage. I started to eat while playing the game.

Antonio and his entourage came in loud and laughing about something I did not know. I just wanted them to be quiet and close the door so I could return to my game. Antonio came to sit down on the floor with me to see if I was okay and if I needed anything. "No," I told him. "I'm okay. The girl brought me some food." I stopped playing my game to retrieve the brown paper bag, and I gave it to him. He took the bag from me and gave it to one of the other guys to bring it in the back room.

Antonio reached into his pocket, took out some money, and handed it to me. And once again, I put it in my pocket without looking at it. "This is what you will make each time you delivered this for me. And if you need anything at all, you can always stop by, even if I'm not here," Antonio told me, and with that, he left and went out.

I stayed playing games until it was almost two in the morning. I bolted out of Antonio's apartment when I saw what time it was, thinking my aunt had beat me home, but thank goodness she was not home. I went ahead and took my shower before my aunt and her kids came home and had to cut my shower short to serve them. I rarely ever had a situation of being home alone with no kids and my aunt, and I felt free.

After my shower, I got ready for bed, but I went to sit in the living room watching television, checking every few minutes, making sure my aunt did not sneak up on me while I watched. It would send her into a rage. For a minute, I did not care if I was caught in the living room. I guess this was payback for all the things my brother and I had to endure living with her. I was watching a porn movie and fell asleep doing so. I woke up around four in the morning, checking to see if anybody had made it back, but I soon realized that I was still alone because I was still in the living room watching a porn movie and had not been slapped or kicked by my aunt, so I knew that no one was in the house. My aunt had been away from home for a long amount of time before, but she had never slept outside the house and never with her children. For a while, I was concerned that once again I had driven some more people who cared about me away.

After seeing that no one was around, I decided to grab some food and take advantage of eating something before they came home. My uncle usually brought home an assortment of food, and my aunt would count every single one to make sure we did not touch anything. I did not really care right then. I was hungry. Opening the refrigerator, I was blown away with the amount of food in there. *Now I see why she's so fat*, I thought. There was Philly cheesesteak sandwiches, a pile of bacon, chicken wings, different types of sauces, and fried rice. There was enough food in there to feed half my neighborhood for years. I saw T-bone steaks, filet mignon, and I could go on and on.

There were dates and numbers written on each item on top of all this food. My uncle would bring home food every night, including really expensive meats. This did not include the regular groceries he bought for the house or the food he cooked at home. He brought home so much food that there was no need to go to the grocery store. My aunt and her children could not have eaten all this food alone, yet still we were not allowed to touch any of it. Then when it got spoiled, we had to eat it with her looking on, pretending she did not know it was bad, even though she labeled all of it beforehand. How much food could she and her children eat that we were not allowed to touch this abundance of food?

I remember one night after my big brother had died. My uncle came home from work late as usual, and he brought bags of food. My uncle turned on the light in the kitchen, which woke me up, not that I was even sleeping but pretended to be. I was still afraid to go to sleep because of my nightmares and daymares, if there is such a thing. Anyway, my uncle saw me lying there, not sleeping, and he asked if I had eaten. Before I was able to answer, my aunt interrupted, saying "Yeah, he already ate." Then my uncle rephrased the question, asking if I was still hungry. I was not hungry and had no appetite because I was still mourning, though I had not eaten in days.

My aunt was no help. She did not care if I ate or not. Most adults witnessing a child mourning and sick and not eating anything would encourage that child to eat to boost their energy so they did not get any sicker but not my aunt. She did not care one way or the other. Actually, I take that back; she did care one way, and that was for me not to touch her food on her refrigerator.

So that night, my uncle asked me if I wanted to eat something, which was his way of saying, "Are you okay? I'm sorry that you lost your brother," because he was not a very emotional guy, at least that was how I have seen it. I was not hungry when he asked, but I said yes, knowing that I would pay for that later. I think I mostly said yes as some type of payback for me and

Samuel for all the years of bullshit we went through. My uncle gave me one of his famous Philly cheesesteak sandwiches, and though I was not hungry, the great smell of this sandwich made my mouth water, so I started eating.

Out the corner of my eye, I saw my aunt staring me down with malicious intent and deep hate, but I kept eating with her looking on, not moving. It got so uncomfortable for me that my stomach started to hurt so bad that I could not digest my food. Then my aunt yelled, telling me to hurry and get to bed. My aunt turned to my uncle, asking him why he gave me something to eat this late. He just said, "It's lots of food. What difference does it make?" And they went off to bed. That was when I could eat in peace with no stomach pain and able to digest my food. Let me tell you, that was the best cheesesteak I had ever eaten, and I had not eaten anything at par ever since. My uncle was a tremendously great chef. I miss his cooking.

As I waited for my aunt and her kids to return, I realized that I had not looked at the money I was given earlier by Antonio, so I reached in my pocket, grabbing the money, and began counting it. When I was done counting my money, I was surprised to find that it totaled six hundred dollars. I just knew there had to be a mistake, so I counted it again, and I still came to the same total; it was still six hundred dollars. Then I thought Antonio may have accidentally given it to me, and since he told me I was welcome to go to his house anytime and I knew that he was awake, I decided to pay him a visit.

    I knocked on Antonio's door and waited for an answer but got no reply, so I knocked a bit harder, and this time, I got an answer. There stood Antonio, telling me to come on in. He then asked if I wanted something to eat or drink. "I'll take some juice," I told him as we walked upstairs into his apartment. He asked me why I knocked when he had told me his door was always open and that I was more than welcome to just go in even if he was not home. I told him okay, even though I did not believe him because, with all the nice and very expensive things in his house, why would he leave his door open? People could steal from him. Then again, he had a lot of money and could easily replace any of it.

    When we made it upstairs, I told him I needed to show him something, and he told me to go ahead. But there were a lot of people around, so I whispered to him that he had given me six hundred dollars without knowing it. Antonio laughed and told me there was no mistake and that, each time I made a delivery, he would pay me three hundred dollars. I could not believe that Antonio had given me all this money from a delivery. I knew that he had some money, but to be giving them all away, I thought, *This guy is the richest person I know.* It was mind-blowing. Here I was with six hundred dollars when I had not seen two pennies in the same place. I was ready to make more delivery right now.

    With my conversation over, I asked if I could play the Nintendo games, and he said, "Go ahead, little man." I eagerly went on to play. The first game I played was Duck Hunt and then Super Mario Brothers. I would stop playing the game only to check if my aunt had returned, but like before, she was not home. I was happy being home alone, and then came that dreaded feeling of abandonment, which I really hated. Then I remembered I had some money, and I would be okay on my own, but even still, I did not want to be alone again.

    While I was playing the games, Antonio came to me and said something that got my attention, making me stop the game and put the controller down. "Do you know who killed your brother?" And of course, I had no clue, but he said he thought he knew the parties responsible. Most of the drug crews had an understanding that they were not to shoot with women and children around, but some people did not follow that rule. He went to say he knew who was out there arguing, but only one guy was doing all the shootings. I could not believe what he was saying, and then he told me they were going to handle it for me. I wanted to kill the guys who killed my brother but did not know how, and now I was shown a way to do that. With all of this new information, I did not know what to do or say. I did not even want to play these games anymore.

Since his apartment was right next door to mine, I went home, and it was still open the way I left it. My aunt was still not home. It was almost five o'clock in the morning with no signs of my aunt, so I turned on the television and started watching and soon realized I did not want to be there. So once again, I went next door to Antonio's place; and just as he had said many times, the door was open. I just went in, sat down, and continued my game, which was still on the pause, almost as though I never left. After all, I was only gone for a few minutes.

Before the sun had begun to rise, Antonio told me he had to make a run and then gave me another package to deliver. This package was larger than the one he gave me. I took it and got ready to leave when he stopped me and handed me what I figured was a toy gun. Antonio asked if I knew how to use it. I told him that I indeed knew how to work it, and that was a lie. I think he knew I was lying, so he proceeded to give me a brief and impromptu lesson. I did not see anything wrong with me carrying a gun to do these deliveries because I thought he was taking care of me. I took the package. I had come to know and understand what was in there. This was the eighties, and people used cocaine to brush their teeth. It was everywhere, and people used it in clubs, and it was like ordering a drink.

Once again, I headed out to go make my delivery. Even if he did not give me any money, I would have gone out and did this anyway. While walking, I took out the gun to look at it, playing with it. Then I started to think of Samuel, wishing he was still here so we could both work for Antonio to make a lot of money, and then we would follow our plans to run away when we had enough to do so.

I reached the apartment number, but I was supposed to go down to the side of the building and knock three times. I saw the stairs that led down to the boilers, where I saw the same group of guys shooting craps, including the one person who lost my money and ended up giving me a twenty. I later found out that that guy worked for Antonio, and he did not know that Antonio had put out an order that no one should mess with me or else. So after losing my money and I was mad, he did not give me back my five dollars. Somebody told him that I was Antonio's little brother, so he gave me a twenty instead. I brushed past them.

Once again, I knocked on an all-black metallic door three times as I was instructed to do. I stepped back a bit when I heard the locks on the door being let loose. I did not understand exactly what these people were trying to protect, especially since there was nothing but a sea of zombies smoking in there all day, and they smoked like death. It made no sense to me, and this time, I was determined not to enter the building after seeing those people sitting around in the dark. Their faces would change every time light was flashed on them. I have never seen hell, and I hope I never will, but if someone was to ask me what my depiction of hell was, that would be how I would explain it. Just standing there gave me the creeps, which was why I stepped back when I heard the door being unlocked.

I started to smell the very distinct odor before the door was open. The door opened after a few minutes, and I handed the package to another big guy with a long beard, which was braided into two sections, and he had a bald head. He grabbed me and pulled me in the door. I stood still before I followed him because my eyes had not yet adjusted to the darkness, but just as I had seen in the other place I took the first package to, there was a sea of people in the dark, smoking and looking like the living dead. The smell of this place was worse than the first one because there were more people in here, and it was a bigger room.

The guy led me through the maze of people before we made it to another room that was lit up and nicely decorated without that horrific smell. I sat down at the table as I was told to, and then the big guy ordered a young girl to take the package I had brought and gave me one to bring back to Antonio. I then got up to leave when I heard a ruckus coming from the next room with some guy yelling he did not do anything, but that obviously meant nothing to whoever was beating or torturing him. I was very eager to get out of this building, but the big bald guy with the braided beard asked if I wanted to see something when a guy leaned over and whispered into his ears as he pointed at me. So you can only imagine my fear at this point, especially after I heard the noise of someone being beaten very badly. Even though Antonio had put the word out that I was his little brother and no one should mess with me, I did not believe it because he was not in the same places that I was, and he surely was not god. So how the hell was he going to protect me at all, especially in the one place I needed it more than anywhere else, which was my home?

The big bald guy now walked up to me and stood over me as I sat in my seat. He was looking down on me with his big belly inches from my face and asked me if I wanted to see something. It turned almost from him asking me to him telling me that I did want to see something. Before I answered, he grabbed me by my hand, leading me to the next room. I followed him behind, but I did not enter the room.

I stood in the doorway, where I saw about seven guys standing in a circle, with two guys tied down in a chair, and their faces were bloody. Both men had been stripped down to their underwear, and then I heard one of the seven guys standing around in a circle asking the two men in the chairs several questions. The first question he asked them was "Who paid you to do the hit on Antonio?" Then it hit me that I knew one of the guys because I remembered he was one of the guys who had fallen out of the car that night. I remembered him because of the braids in his hair. When the men in the chairs did not answer a question, they were beaten, or a nail would be hammered in their knees or private area. There were a lot of different tools being used to drive home their point. I saw guns, hammers, nails, heated metal pipes, lighting fluids, and the list went on.

Then another one of the seven guys asked where their other homeboys with them that night were, and even before they had a chance to answer, they would do something else to them. At that point, I figured that they were not looking for answers, and they just wanted to hurt someone. Watching all of this made me sick, and there were so much blood.

As I turned to leave, the big bald guy told me to wait. He took a light, held it close to the two guys being beaten, and asked them if they knew me, to which they said no. So the bald guy told them I was Antonio's little man, and I was the one who saved him that night. I had seen enough, and I was done with all of this.

I ran out of the room and back outside, where I could finally breathe, and I took off running, trying to escape what I had just seen, which was now haunting my mind. I reached Antonio's house in no time. I gave him the package; and as he had done before, he handed me money totaling three hundred dollars as he had promised. He must have seen the look of terror on my face, and he asked me what was wrong, so I told him I did not like going into the dark room with all the stinky people. He must have thought that was funny because he started laughing. I did not think there was anything funny about what I had just told him. Either that or I had missed out on the joke or the punch line. When he was done laughing, he told me, "Okay, you don't have to go through those doors anymore." He would let all the people involved know to take me through the regular apartment.

I walked downstairs after my conversation with Antonio to find that no one was home yet. Now that I was making a little money, I knew that I could purchase a lot of the essentials I really needed and the things I wanted, such as clothes, shoes, and different little accessories. However, I knew that one definite thing that was feasible to me was my ability to get something to eat but in small increments. There was no way I could have been able to purchase tennis shoes, clothes, or any variations of this, especially the kinds of shoes I wanted. I would have no way of explaining away those things because my wardrobe consisted of only two jeans and maybe three or four shirts—that and one extremely old and worn-out pair of tennis shoes that talked to me. So you see, there was not too much room to wiggle because my aunt knew what my wardrobe was made of. And if I had any new items on, she would ask where the hell I got it from, and I would not have had an excuse to explain myself to her.

I searched for a place to hide my money so no one would ever find it or even think of looking in there. I found the perfect place, which was under the sofa that served as my bed. Underneath the sofa, one of the legs would come out, so I made a little bigger hole, and then I put nine hundred dollars there. I could hardly believe that, within less than three days, I had made more money than some adults made in a month. What was I going to do with all this money? I had no clue. I had learned a lot of street skills, but I had not been put up on the finer things. I was like a country bumpkin who got money.

My aunt and her kids came home at around two o'clock in the afternoon, but they were only going to be home for an hour because they were going to have Thanksgiving dinner with some family members. I was caught off guard and dumbfounded because I had been mourning for my brother for so long and had been in a fog that I didn't realize it was already Thanksgiving.

The one thing I loved about the holiday was this stuffing my uncle made. It consisted of onions, sausage, shrimp, and some other ingredients I could not identify. Then he stuffed in Cornish hens before baking it, and we each got one because there were about eight or nine. My aunt got mad at my uncle because she did not want my brother and me to have our own. She said we should be given one to share, but my uncle gave us one each anyway, telling my aunt if she was still hungry, there were two more for her to have. Once again, as we ate, my aunt had that look of evil and hate, not regular hate but super-duper evil hate as if she just wanted to dive on us and shove that Cornish hen down our throats.

I learned that I was not invited to go with my aunt and her kids for the Thanksgiving dinner. I was going to be alone at the house with nothing to eat because my uncle had not made a Thanksgiving meal this year. Like everything else in my life, it hurt, but I told myself I would be okay. At least I was not going to be around her for a while. I watched as my aunt and her children got ready for their trip. Everyone was so happy, especially Juicy, my aunt's eldest child. And when they were ready, they walked outside to pack up the car before leaving.

When they were gone, my uncle told me to get ready to go with him to his job, so I did, but I was not excited about that because I knew I was going to be bored the whole day. Because of the holiday, he was going to be working overtime, which was over twelve hours. But having no choice in the matter, I got ready, and we left the house.

During the trip, my uncle was usually real quiet and would never talk to me, so I was afraid of him this day because my uncle was changing a lot lately from the nice guy I knew. Even though my uncle was not an emotional guy who would tell you he loved you, he would always find a way to show that you were okay with him. That guy was gone, and I had no clue who this guy I was with was. I was not sure what spell or voodoo curse my aunt had placed on him, but I was very sure of myself that something was wrong.

Usually, when my aunt would bring him in their bedroom, after an hour, he would return as angry as hell. Now I don't know about you guys, but anytime I ever went into a bedroom happy with a female, I would always leave that bedroom happy, and the female would have issues walking for a while. I think they were doing it wrong; it made no sense. You're supposed to go in angry and come out happy. Whatever they did, I knew he always came out angry. His anger only lasted a few minutes but not now. He was always angry, and his face was different, and I feared him, especially after cracking my brother's head.

We arrived at a fancy hotel where my uncle was a chef. I was very impressed that my uncle worked here as the head chef. We got out of the car, and he led me into the hotel. I had never been in a hotel before except for the time when our plane crashed, and my mother and I had to stay in it for the night. That hotel was very nice, but it was nothing like the one my uncle worked at. He walked me into a large room that I now know to be a bar. I had never seen a bar before, but I liked it. My uncle introduced me to the bartender, and he asked him to take care of me before he left to head over to the kitchen. "Okay, sir, what is your pleasure?" the bartender asked me.

"Huh?" I replied.

"What would you like?" he asked, rephrasing his question.

"I don't know," I informed him.

UNLOVABLE

So he told me, "Let's start with an ice cream sundae."

That was when my eyes and my stomach got really big. "You have all of that here?" I asked him.

"Of course," he told me. They had just about anything you could think of to eat. I was now even more impressed. I had only enjoyed a sundae in school because I had read more than thirty books in a competition our library was having to make students read more, and then you had to write a report on the book. I had always been a reader, and I decided to enter the reading competition. The only prize that we were told we would get was a certificate and the joy of reading, so a lot of students were not interested. So it was only ten of us in the competition, and when it was over, they made an announcement for all of us to proceed to the library for the certificates. When the other students heard it, they joked that we read all those books for nothing. But when we got to the library, it was fully decorated, and there were all kinds of ice cream, toppings, brownies, cookies, and whatever you wanted to make a sundae with. Some other foods were there, so we started eating. And when the bell rang at the end of the day, the other students saw us, and then came envy. "Why didn't they tell us about the sundaes before?" they complained. I can't tell you how much ice cream sundaes I had that day, but you can believe I was sick after.

I sat patiently as the bartender began making me a sundae. He used three different ice cream flavors and put a lot of caramel and a load of other items and toppings, and it was finally ready when he put a cherry on top. Of course, you know there were about five cherries, not one. He put the sundae in front of me, and I sat there looking at this concoction that was dripping with caramel and looking so good. I thought, *This day may not turn out to be as bad as I thought.*

I began eating my sundae and talking to my new friend, the bartender, whose name I don't remember. He told me what a good guy my uncle was and how much of a great friend my uncle had been to him for over twenty years, even helping him land the job he now had. Then the bartender revealed something to me that I had begun to acknowledge myself. He said that, even though he knew my uncle to be a strong man and to never show his feelings, he had begun to see chinks in his armor and that something was bothering my uncle for these last few months. The bartender tried to coax information about what may have been going on at home or whatever because he was worried about his friend.

I, however, was no fool. I had learned my lesson about discussing any problems with anyone, especially after the last time I told my teacher something, which got back to my aunt. Then not learning my lesson, I talked to a friend of mine named Cynthia, who was asking me if my aunt treated us well because of all the bruises she saw on me at school that I thought was covered up. I told her how badly we were treated and that my aunt did not love my brother and me and how differently we were treated from my aunt's children. I don't have to tell you that my aunt overheard me cry. I also don't have to tell you how badly I was beaten. I had marks all over me with blood in my wounds. I cried the whole night, and I was in so much pain. And for some reason, I thought she had broken my bone because I had deep bone pain. And not being able to withstand it anymore, I cried all night, with my brother doing his best to alleviate my pain and holding me all night as I cried.

What I did not know at the time was that because of the stress I had suffered, along with the several beatings, I started to develop a fever, which then brought about what I would later find out was a sickle cell crisis. I did not know it then because my aunt had never brought us to the hospital no matter how sick we were. One, she did not care; and two, it would not have been in her best interest at the time. I mean, think about it. If you were a child abuser and if the children you were abusing were to get sick, would you bring them to the hospital, knowing that the doctors would call the cops to have them check out the lack of care we were receiving, as well as the bruises? Then she would be in trouble.

The bartender and I talked a bit more. Well, actually, he talked, and I listened, not saying a word about what I had seen about my uncle and the change that I had noticed in him. My uncle looked as if something were possessing him. The life in his face was now gone. His eyes were all dark and scary. And when you talked to him, he would turn in your direction very slowly and deliberately as if he were an android under some remote control or something. Whatever my aunt had done to my uncle was notable, and although I was only nine at the time, I had a wise fifty-year-old man's view of the world. I noticed a lot that children my age and some adults older than I was could never foresee or understand.

The bartender continued to talk about his friend and the close relationship they had and how he now worried about him. It was then my uncle walked in the bar to check on me. "I see you started the party already. Oh boy," my uncle said, placing a steaming hot plate in front of me filled with rice and seafood. "Make sure you eat some real food. Oh boy, that sundae looks good." Then he left. The guy who had just brought me this food was the kind, understanding uncle I knew and loved, and I knew he was back because he kept saying his favorite word, which was *oh boy*. I think the fact he was away from my aunt for this length of time broke whatever spell she had on him, which meant she would have to start the process all over again. It would take some time to completely have him under her control.

As I have already told you, my aunt was a practitioner of voodoo, which she used to control my uncle for only a short time. That changed, however, when my aunt's mom came to stay, and they would train together. Well, it was more like teaching her daughter some new tricks, allowing her to control my uncle a lot more or longer. Even though I was only a kid, I was able to perceive a lot of things others were not capable of seeing, and it was not of my own doing. My God was merciful and gave me that skill. And what I did not see then I later saw as I got older, and that is the reason I am writing this book now. I can write it and know how to make it very informative.

As for me and my new friend, the bartender, we sat and talked—well, he talked, and I listened, ate, and gave an occasional nod or okay. Years of abuse made me very leery of adults, especially women, as well as men who had beards. I figured they were all wicked because I had suffered abuse at the hands of people with those characteristics.

As he talked, a crowd started to come into the bar, and my new friend gave me a bunch of tokens and told me there was an arcade I could go and play in. And if I ran out of tokens, he told me to come and get some more from him. But if I had not return by the time the crowd was gone, he would come and get me. I told him okay, and I took the food my uncle had prepared for me after finishing my sundae.

I walked in the arcade, surprised at how many games were in the place. I saw some of my favorites, like Bad Dudes, Double Dragon, and Super Mario Brothers. I also saw some games I had not seen before. I sat at one of the games, which was set up like a table; it was a World War II airplane game, and the objective was to destroy both air and ground targets. I sat down at the game and began to play. Before long, I was lost in my own world. I had forgotten about having to go home later and the trouble that waited on me when this day was over.

Even though I hated it and I was always terrified when my aunt was around, it still hurt me so bad when I heard my uncle trying to persuade her to take me, and she repeatedly turned down all his efforts. I mean, I knew no one wanted me, and everyone who had always said, "This poor kid, I wish I could help him," turned right around to make excuses on why they could do nothing for me, even though they always complimented my aunt and uncle on what a nice, respectful, smart young man I was as if they had anything to do with that aspect of my life. If there was one person whom I would give credit to for helping me have those characteristics, it was my grandmother, whom outside of God I owe everything to. She was the only person who can take credit for any of those things. Plus, she was the only one to love me unconditionally. I don't know about you, but if you heard people reject you your whole life, it would take a toll on you. And it is not just anyone. I'm talking about so-called family, and the strangest thing was they preferred my brother, even though he was the troublesome one. I don't want you to think I'm clamping on my brother because I'm not; it's just the truth. So as a child, after hearing my aunt tell me that no one was ever going to love me and that there was something wrong with me, I started to see that it was true, so I did believe it. And my aunt made sure I heard that at least once a day.

While I played my game, I thought of Samuel and how much he would have loved to be here right at that minute, playing with me. Just as I looked up, I saw my uncle leaving the door. I must have been deep in thought not to notice him there checking on me. My uncle was a different man when he was not around my aunt. The man who was checking on me now was totally different from the man who was just left the house with me and who had brought me to work with him. Between the time he was around his wife and now, there was a drastic change in him. This was the man I liked, the uncle who made me feel as if I was still a human being. This was the uncle

I had come to know when I first came to live with him and my aunt in New Jersey.

I had been in the arcade playing games for over two hours before I noticed that I was down to only a few game tokens, but I started to get hungry again, so I decided to go back in the bar for something to eat and hopefully some more game tokens. When I walked into the room, it was empty as it had been when I had first arrived with my uncle. "Where are all the customers who were just in here?" I asked the bartender. He told me that there had been a rush, but they were now gone, and he was not expecting another group to come in about thirty minutes to an hour.

"What can I get you, my friend? Would you like some more to eat and another sundae?" the bartender asked me. With a nod, I answered yes, wondering how he knew that I wanted all of those things, but he seemed to miss that I wanted some more of the game tokens, and I knew he was busy with other things, and he had been so nice to me that I did not want to bother him with trivial things.

When he handed me my meal, as well as the sundae, I took them from him, thanked him for everything, and turned around to head back toward the arcade so I could use the last few tokens. Then something told me to turn around again and ask him for the damn token. *It's not every day you get opportunities like this, stupid. Take advantage of it, you fool.* Now I was sure it was my brother's voice because I knew if he had been there, he would have found a way to get more tokens. I decided I was not going to bother this nice man who had been so good to me, causing me not to talk to him and ask for things, which I was deathly afraid of and had no skill of doing. *Turn around and ask for the damn tokens. I want to play some more.* Now I didn't know if that was my brother's voice or mine that time, but whoever he was, he had now become very selfish, talking about wanting to play some more. Hell, I wanted to play some more.

And just as I got the courage to ask for the game tokens, a group of men started to come in the bar, chasing my little courage away with their loudness. I started kicking myself for not taking the chance to ask for those game tokens before those men entered the bar. Now I was sure I would not get the chance to ask for them again as I was afraid of talking in front of a crowd, especially a strange one.

I continued walking toward the arcade when I heard the bartender call out to me. "Yo, I forgot to bring these earlier when your uncle came in to check on you. He gave some money so you could play the game, but I told him not to worry about it." I was so excited that I could not believe it, but I kept my composure, and I ran over to the bar nonchalantly, took a brown paper bag filled with tokens, and thanked him. I then turned around, heading to the game room once again.

Wow, I thought. *These tokens are going to last me forever.* It was that time I started thinking about Samuel and how he would have loved to be here with me. If Samuel had been here, he would have found a way to play all these games even if we did not have tokens. Thinking about my brother brought a smile to my face, followed by a stream of tears, knowing I would never see him again. It seemed writing this book brings tears to my eyes every time I write about my brother Samuel, making it hard to finish it because, each time I do think of him, it reopens old wounds. So I put the book on the shelf for a week or so before I'm able to write again, making this time not any different from the others.

When I was done, I had no appetite, so I started playing my games. Once again, the thought of my brother caused me to start tearing up. I guess I thought of my brother so often not only because I loved him so much and I always will but also because we had been through a lot, starting so early in our lives that we had no clue it was even an abusive relationship, especially with me thinking that this was my fault and something was wrong with me, causing me to strive to become a better person. But it seemed that I would never change because, no matter how many things I tried, nothing worked. For a long time and even now, I always thought that Samuel's death was my fault. Every time I needed my brother, he would always come through for me. And now that he was dead, it was making me think that I could have done something to help him when he needed me, and then he would be here with me. People had always told me not to blame myself because there was nothing I could have done and that, if had tried something, it would have been two funerals instead of one. I never paid any attention to those people, and I know you, my reader, are probably thinking the same. But what you need to know is when you have been through something so traumatic with someone and that person has always been there to protect you and find a way to feed you when you got hungry and then, all of a sudden, he is gone, you start thinking what you could have done differently to do for that person what he has always done for you.

While playing my games, Uncle Francis walked into the arcade to tell me to finish up with the game as it was time to go home. I had been playing for so long that time had kept up on me, but it seemed I had just sat down. I finished my food and returned to the bar to give the bartender the tokens he gave me. "I will keep them for you for the next time you are here," the bartender, who was my new best friend, told me. I smiled, thanking him, and my uncle and I left.

On the way home, we sat in complete silence for the first ten miles. Then my uncle apologized to me about my aunt not wanting me to go with her and her children. My uncle told me there was hardly any space in the car because it was packed with all of these things. I was not an idiot, and I knew that never was the case. I remember when our aunt took us with her anywhere so we could watch the kids while she did her thing, whatever that was. But even then, we would pack up in her Monte Carlo, and that was with my brother, making us tightly stacked on top of each other. She took us then, but now all of a sudden, there was no place for me. My uncle could have made a better sudden excuse than that one, so I accepted it without saying a word.

He was telling me she and her kids were going to spend the night at someone's house. There was no place for me, which was one of a million things I knew of myself. It became clear to me that no matter where I went, there would never be a place for me. I was never going to be someone who would or could ever be loved, just as my aunt had told me, and I believed her. Why wouldn't I? After all, I was seeing it play out just the way she said it was going to be. I felt so alone at that time, more so now than ever before. With Samuel's passing came a lot of dark, thick, cold feelings of being all alone. It became so physical that you could literally feel and smell it.

We continued driving as my uncle tried to still sell me wolf tickets about why my aunt did not take me with her. The more he talked, the worse my loneliness became, knowing and thinking that this was how my life would be forever until my dying day—alone with no one there to be by my side. Thinking of this brought tears to my eyes. I know that you guys reading this book are probably thinking, *Damn, this kid cries a lot*, but I was only nine or ten years old at the time. That was a major part of my childhood all the way through my teenage years and to my twenties. I cried because I was not capable of doing a lot to change my life, at least not at that particular time. Outside of that, so many other factors made it worse; that was pain, frustration, anger, and a myriad of other things. I could not even begin to describe it or how much it hurt to articulate my feelings properly then and now. My aunt had really done a great job in wearing me down, taking away what little joy I did have in me during these times of my life, yet still I wanted to please her so I could attain some kind of affection, which was not going to happen until hell froze over and the devil gave free sleigh rides. In other words, nothing was about to change for me.

Uncle Francis and I sat in complete silence for the remainder of our ride home. I think he stopped telling me that my aunt's not wanting to take me with her had nothing to do with me. It was something I was not going to believe unless the Lord came down from heaven to reassure me of what my uncle was saying, and I also think my uncle was not even buying his own stories. I believe he must have come to the realization that his excuses were full of crap. I also sensed that more of my aunt's spells were working their way out of him.

I sat there in my seat trying to wipe away my tears and not make any sobbing noise because I did not want my uncle to know I was crying; if he did, it would make me weak. I had a great day at work with my uncle, but all of a sudden, I felt deep sorrow and foreboding now that my day of happiness was over, and I was back to my miserable existence. And if my aunt found out what a great time I had that day, I would surely pay for it, especially since her leaving me behind was supposed to be some sort of punishment. After all, there was nothing left in the house for me to eat that day. So if my uncle had not brought me to work, I would have had to wait until she returned home, and even that would still not have been too beneficial for me because she and her children would have already eaten, and there would be no need for her to cook anything, especially since I would have been the only one who was hungry. Once again, I would still have to wait until my uncle came home, at which time I would have to make a decision when my uncle asked me if I was hungry. Now if I said yes and he fed me, I knew for a fact that my aunt would see to it that I would pay for that meal. Or I could turn down my uncle's offer and go to bed hungry.

I don't even think my aunt knew my uncle was going to bring me to work with him because, had she known, I would have gone with her. There was no way she would stand by to see me having fun and happy. I did not even understand why I even cared that my aunt had not taken me with her. After all, this was not the first I had been left out of their family functions. My brother and I were always on the outside looking in.

I remember one particular time when my uncle, my aunt, and their kids left my brother and me behind. They had kept us out of their plans. They first went to the park and then spent a day at a hotel. They had gone out and left Samuel and me at home because that summer's day was so hot, and all that we had to keep us cool were a couple of fans. Well, my aunt and her children were the only ones who sat in the living room in front of the fan as my brother and were in the dining room in the sweltering heat. When they could no longer stand the unbearable heat, they packed up some food and drinks and headed over to the local park and zoo but found that even that would not help. Most people with common sense would have known that if there was a statewide excessive heat alert that had already taken eight people's lives, then it made sense that going outside in the heat to hang out at the park was not a great idea. Anyway, after realizing their plans may not have been the best way to go, they packed up their things and went over to the hotel my uncle worked. They got a room and spent the day swimming and ordering room service, while my brother and I sat at home at home alone, hot, and hungry.

But we learned to appreciate any day my aunt was never at home. We learned that no matter what we came up against or what we went through, as long as we faced it together, we would always come out okay. So even that day was as hot as it was, my brother and I faced it by coming up with ways to keep cool. For example, we got some ice, making sure to refill the ice trays so my aunt would not find out that we had touched her refrigerator, and we turned on the fan. We sat in front of it and rubbed the ice all over our faces, trying to keep cool. It actually worked.

As for something to eat, it would prove to be a little trickier than keeping cool because my aunt kept and paid very close attention to every bit of food in the house, making it hard for us to take anything without her knowing. So we had to be careful with our selections, and we came up with some kind of choice. Rice and oatmeal were two foods we could eat without her knowing. The only thing was we had to eat them without cooking since we did not know when she would be home. So we soaked the rice for almost an hour until it softened, drained it, and added water and sugar. With the oatmeal, we ate it as it was. If we had cooked the rice or oatmeal, the smell would surely linger in the air, which my aunt would have definitely smelled; and besides, we had eaten these things so much that I started to enjoy it a whole lot.

My uncle was still trying to convince me that my aunt's leaving me behind had nothing to do with me. He did not want me to feel bad or unwanted, especially since my mom had abandoned me and saw how bad it hurt me. He saw that it bothered me a lot, even though I never spoke of it, and he wanted me to know that he and my aunt were never going to abandon me no matter what happened. My uncle's statement had not filled me with a whole bunch of confidence, especially when, not too long ago, my aunt wanted to put us in an orphanage, thereby handing us over to the state so we would be out of luck. I had heard both my aunt and uncle talking about this very same thing, and she said the only things and people she had any feelings for were her own and that she had no responsibilities for anyone else. So why did she even have to go through this with two useless kids, one unwanted by his parents?

We pulled into our projects, which were identifiable by those brown bricks. Fear and dread always overcame me every time I saw them, and this time was no different. My uncle parked the car and got out. I took a deep breath as I slowly opened the door and got out just as it started to rain, followed by a few claps of thunder. It was that very moment when I heard a car's horn from behind me. Then I was immediately blinded by a set of lights.

Then a pain in my stomach struck me so hard that it felt as if someone had hit me with a blunt object. I was literally moved back a few steps. Unbelievable, right? Anyway, the pain went from my belly all the way through my back and traveled up my spine and down again, followed by an icy chill. I could not understand where it came from. The feelings and pain that I felt at that very moment were very familiar, but the only difference was their intensity. Usually, when I had this pain, it was because the three o'clock bell had rung to finish the school day, and the pain would fester me on the walk home. When I saw those famous brown bricks, the intensity would automatically rise, knowing what waited for me behind those bricks, which I hated so and were the bane of my existence. However, the pain I usually had would always start mildly, increasing into this unbearable pain that would not quit, but it would stop at some point before the night was over.

The lights of the car that had blinded me had finally been cut off, now revealing the cause of this horrible pain, which of course was something I already knew. There was only one person who brought that reaction out of me, and that was my aunt. My uncle walked over to the car as my aunt got out of it. She immediately called my name, and I damn near passed out. I'm very serious. The sound of my name out of her mouth always told me exactly what her intentions were. I mean, after living with her for such a long time, I began to pick up on little things, like her habits or thoughts and way of thinking. What my aunt's words meant was she hated my guts, and that was nothing new, but the rage I was picking up on said I was going to get my ass handed to me when my uncle left to go to work in the morning. There was a lot of time.

I did not know where the aggravation in my abuse came from. What I already knew was she hated my brother and me, and she felt it was not her responsibility to care for us, which I absolutely agreed with. After all, she was not my mother. My aunt had always been mad at my uncle because she believed he was too nice, and that made him weak. She said my father had known that fact because they were brothers, so my father pawned my brother and me off on him, knowing my uncle would not refuse since he loved his little brother so much. My aunt believed my dad planned on pawning us off on both of them for a long time so he could go chasing women instead of being a parent taking care of his children.

Another thing that made my aunt take out her frustration on us was that they could not save any money or even have money in the first place because they were busy taking care of us. At this point, I don't want to sound unappreciative, but I really don't see how that was. The only clothes we had came from a flea market or yard sale, and I don't mean the good flea market with nice things but the garage type. Our tennis shoes were the free ones my uncle got from clothes bins. Yeah, I knew about clothes bins before they were put on every corner like they do today, though I did get some Nine West shoes that were in a dollar bin. And all the shoes we had for years had developed holes in the soles. The only other thing she could really claim as spending money on us would be the food we did eat, even though the refrigerator was off-limits to us. So I plan on paying her back with the money I make from the sale of this book, so you guys have to help me out.

We were up against the odds, my brother and I, especially when my aunt would bring my uncle back into their room, where she went over all the things she hated us for and said that they would never get there if my uncle did learn to say no to people asking for money. My uncle needed to also say no to the one person who had brought all of this about and whom she blamed for all their problems and woes. As you may already know, that person just happened to be my father; but since she was not able to reach him or was not able to punish him, my brother and I would have to suffice for the time being.

My aunt's abusing us by herself was not enough for her either, so she tried to incorporate my uncle into her madness. Big word, huh? Yeah, I said incorporated. Just kidding. Anyway, my aunt wanted my uncle to join her. It was the reason she would always bring him to their room for an hour, telling him whatever it was that could get him angry to the point of beating and abusing us as she often did. But she did not have the courage to just tell my uncle what it was she wanted him to do, which was what I did not understand and still don't even now. After their talks in their bedroom, it always seemed as if she had achieved her objective because my uncle came out of the room angry, something he was not before going in.

My aunt's plan was to corrupt my uncle and to get him to do her bidding. She wanted him to become just like her and see things her way. Outside of the daily abuse my brother and I were suffering, she wanted to give us up by turning us over to the child care services and tell them our parents had abandoned us and that she and my uncle took us in for a short amount of time until they were able to reach the right agencies. That way, they could give us to the proper authorities. They would say they had no knowledge of us or our parents but just happened to come across us standing out on the street in the middle of midday traffic, at which time they got really concerned and took us with them until they found a place for us to go. This was the story my aunt would tell my uncle, which she would also tell my brother and me but with more explicit words and tones. I heard this story so often that I was able to repeat it.

At first, I was seriously afraid of that happening to my brother and me because my aunt told us that those people, whoever they were, would treat us worse than she ever did. What she did to Samuel and me was only because she loved and cared for us since she was the only one who was willing to take care of us. No one else would step up to do so except her after we were abandoned by our so-called parents. "Not even that Uncle Richard you guys wanted to go to. See? Y'all are the most ungrateful asses. And you, Shawn, your own mother does not even want you, so you know already that no one will ever love you like I do. But you, you're just fucking useless and ungrateful. Don't fucking ever look at me when I'm talking to you, you damn asshole!" my aunt would say anytime she really got mad at us or whenever I looked her in the eyes when she was talking to us, and that took place almost weekly.

What caused my aunt to get even angrier than usual, not just at Samuel and me but at my uncle too, was the fact that he was just not like her. He was not a coldhearted witch. Even when she gave my uncle the one-hour talk, he definitely would get very upset, but his anger was temporary, and he was back to his usual kindhearted self, who would try to meet those needs of ours. He knew the kind of woman my aunt was, so he understood what we may have been going through, maybe not all of it, but he knew something was going on, even though he never said a word about it. I think my uncle's escape from his hell of a marriage was to stay away from it as much as he could, and that was to work a whole lot.

Chapter 8

MELVINA'S STORY

In the beginning, though, my aunt was not like that—at least that was what I was told by my dad, my uncle, and my brother Samuel. When my uncle was first pursuing her, she was an attractive petite young lady, but my uncle was also the handsome jock who was sought after by a chorus of women. My uncle was a tall muscular dark-skinned African man whose accent those women found irresistible, and even though he liked this girl named Melvina, he was also interested in another girl. My uncle actually preferred this other girl over Melvina Young, but since he was not exactly sure which one would make the better wife, he decided to ask my father because he was his favorite brother out of the nine other ones.

Since my dad was a ladies' man in his own right, he decided to make a trip to the country of Sierra Leone, where Melvina lived, since he was right next to her in another West African country called Liberia. My dad made the journey to meet Ms. Melvina, or should I say Ms. Young, and upon meeting her, my dad instantly liked her and her kind, humble demeanor. So he reported back to my uncle that she would be a great catch for him and that this was the one for him. My uncle accepted this glowing report of the woman who would soon become his wife.

Then my uncle asked my father to process the necessary papers needed to bring her to the United States.

When my dad brought my uncle's new wife to the United States, they became great friends and hung out a lot. Because of my uncle's work schedule, she had nobody else to talk to and no friends, so my father, having so much love for his big brother, stayed with them not only because his big brother asked him to but because he felt she really needed an ally. My aunt needed someone on her side because, after she and my uncle Francis had gotten married, their honeymoon phase was over rather quickly. My uncle had begun to see some women whom he was spending a lot of time with after work instead of coming come, and it just so happened that this other woman, who I would name Nancy, lived right in the same projects that they did. Go figure.

I have to say that this part of my uncle's life was stupid because everyone knows that's a no-no, especially when you're married or when your woman lives with you. Anyway, my uncle would go over to this other woman's house all the time right after his twelve- to sixteen-hour shift, and he did not always come home to his new bride. Now that I know my aunt and the kind of person she is, I don't blame him, but it's not right, especially since he married her. If he wanted to play the field, he should not have made that leap, saying he would be faithful and committed. So anyway, my uncle kept his affair going with Nancy and went over her place after work more frequently now. He also began to come home less and less. This woman Nancy, this home-wrecker, I think was the woman my uncle was in love with at the same time he was in love with my aunt Melvina, but he decided to go ahead and marry Melvina instead and was now regretting it.

One night after work, my uncle headed over Nancy's house to deliver some meat. Ha ha! I hope y'all caught that. Anyway, my uncle was a chef, and he did bring a lot of food home with him. My uncle got the food out of the car and prepared to enter the house of his lover, who was now married to a friend of my uncle, which was apparently not a problem for him because he was still delivering that nightly meat to her. Okay, y'all, I'm sorry. I know I'm stupid. That's going to be the last meat joke, I promise. Anyway, my uncle had his bundle in his arms, about enter the house, but there was a noise, and he turned to look. Seeing nothing, he turned back around to enter the house, but he still had the feeling that there someone was watching. However, he chose to ignore his instincts. After all, he was a very big muscular guy who was capable of defending himself. So once again, he started to enter the house. He should have paid more attention his instincts instead of brushing it aside because someone had been watching him this whole time. And before he knew it, he was coldcocked from behind, which caused him to drop his bags, along with all the other items in his arms. The first thought that entered my uncle's mind was that Nancy's husband had found out about the affair and had to settle it with him. Those thoughts soon left his mind when he saw his new wife staring down at him. She had decided she could take no more of his infidelity and that this was the night to confront both my uncle and the bitch my aunt called the home-wrecker. She had come to kick ass and chew bubblegum, and she was all out of bubblegum.

"What the fuck are you doing here? I knew you were doing something," my aunt hollered at her husband as she tried to kick him, but my uncle was able to block the kick with his hand before he was able to get up.

"This is a friend, and I'm just helping her because she is married to a friend of mine," my uncle replied, but my aunt was not hearing any of that bullshit as she put it. My uncle began picking up his things he had spilled all over the steps leading to the front of the door and onto the sidewalk, and that was when my aunt started hitting him with a flurry of punches and kicks. My uncle was now very angry, so he grabbed her by both arms before pushing her hand, causing her to fall on her bottom. Once again, he started picking up his belongings and had his back toward my aunt, so he never saw her get up and begin to slowly walk behind and attack him. Once again, he fought her off, and he was now more aggravated than he had been before.

"Go home, Melvina, before you really piss me the fuck off," my uncle told his wife, causing her to stop dead in her tracks as she was about to attack him again. My aunt saw the look in my uncle's eyes as he now stood in front of her with his fist tightly clenched. It must have been a look that scared her as she saw him swelling up. My aunt yelled all kinds of obscenities at him but remained standing in her spot, and when she was done, she decided to go home.

She saw the other woman looking through her window. My aunt started her ranting again, but this time, it was directed at the other woman, my uncle's side chick. "You fucking bitch! Yeah, you're a home-wrecker, and I'm going to see to it that your husband finds out you're messing around with my husband!" my aunt yelled, now picking up rocks, throwing them at the two people who were the center of her rage. Being pelted with rocks, my uncle quickly retreated in the apartment with his mistress, closing the window and shutting the curtains. When she was done attacking her husband and his bitch, my aunt started a slow, deliberate walk back home, crying all the way, but little did she know that her night was just beginning.

I don't know how my aunt even found out about the other woman except for the fact my uncle slept out of the house and would tell my aunt it was a work-related issue, but my aunt had a sinking feeling. Call it instinct or woman's intuition or whatever, but whatever it was, she was right. So one night, she decided to follow him or just wait until he left the house, and then she would walk around the neighborhood to see if she could find my uncle's car. After all, she knew that the woman my uncle was seeing lived in the same neighborhood; now I don't know how she found that out, but she did, and that was when all hell broke loose.

When she got home, my aunt completely fell apart, crying with so much pain and emotion that my dad heard her from his room. So he came out to see what the problem was. She broke down even more now, crying on my dad's shoulders, telling him how she had followed her husband, hid herself in some bushes, and watched him knock on the door of some woman who had opened it and kissed her husband before going into the house. When she saw that little bit of an exchange, she decided to come back the next night, only this time she was not just going to watch. So it was a little after midnight when once again she had hidden herself, waiting for Uncle Francis to enter the scene. And that was when she attacked him. When she had finished telling my dad the story, he could hardly believe it and promised his sister-in-law that he would definitely talk to his brother when he got home, and he did not have to wait too long.

It was almost three o'clock in the morning when my uncle entered the apartment and was past the point of being pissed the fuck off. Oh, no, he was at the point of "choke and punch a hoe." He had tunnel vision as he headed straight to his room, where my aunt lay sleeping, causing an immediate conflict and a war of words. They left the bedroom and got into the living room, where the argument got louder and angrier. Then it went from that level right to a hundred. That was when hands just started to fly, and before you knew it, objects started flying—I mean, all kinds of stuff, like plates, knives, dishes, and those ketchup bottles from back in the day. It was those damn bottles that took the ketchup forever to come out of no matter how hard you hit the bottom, the really hard ones. They threw anything they could get their hands on that was not bolted down, but with the hate, intensity, and passion they had, it was possible they could have thrown the house itself.

My dad and my brother were immediately awoken by the noise and the calamity in the house. Not knowing exactly what was taking place, my father headed out of his bedroom, with Samuel right behind, now grabbing our dad's hand until they were standing in the living room watching a horrific battle. A plate that was thrown almost hit Samuel's head, missing it by only a few inches. When my aunt and uncle saw how close they came to hurting their nephew, they stopped launching things at each other.

As soon as they had stopped, my aunt immediately started to assault my uncle with her fist and feet, and the fight was on. Grabbing my aunt by both arms, my uncle warned her that if she did not stop hitting him, she was going to truly regret her decision. But having heard anything he told her and having serious rage issues, as well as tunnel vision, she started to hit him again. He pushed himself away from her, and once again, she fell hard. My uncle warned her to not get up and attack him again, but she got up, attacking him again, but this time, he was hitting her.

Seeing how bad things had escalated in such a short period, my dad entered the fray, trying to put a stop to my uncle's hitting my aunt. He told my uncle if he hit his wife again, he would have to hit him as well. After hearing that, my uncle stopped attacking his wife. Instead, he left the apartment filled with anger. He got in his car and took off to parts unknown. No, I'm just bullshitting you guys and trying to sound intelligent talking about parts unknown. My uncle went back to the other woman.

Samuel was so terrified after witnessing what had just taken place, and when my dad and my aunt saw the fear on his face, they both tried to comfort him, telling him it was okay and not to worry. After doing that, my dad turned his attention to his sister-in-law and was now trying to comfort her as she was now crying very hard. My aunt was so bitter and angry and crying so hard that she could hardly get her words out, and my dad was not able to understand her clearly, so he told Samuel to go get her a glass of ice water.

Samuel returned with the glass of water and gave it to my aunt. She drank it very quickly and thanked Samuel. Now that she was refreshed and able to talk and be understood, she told my dad she could not believe this was the same guy she had first met in Sierra Leone when he was there visiting his mother. She made it clear that she was going to leave my uncle and return to Africa.

My dad told her that was not the thing to do and that he would help her and tell his brother to treat his wife with a lot more respect. He then told my aunt that he would never stand by when my uncle was hitting her. He explained how he hated any man who would put his hand on a woman, which was total bullshit because my dad was a hypocrite; he had hit my mother before. It just so happened that while he and my mother were living together and going to school in Detroit, Michigan, my dad had gotten a message that his mother had passed away. He became totally depressed because he could not afford to make it to the funeral. I mean, a round-trip ticket was at least two grand. Plus, whenever he decided to go back home, he would have to take something for everyone, as well as pass out some money because people back home really think everyone in America is fucking rich and that the streets are made of gold. So even if he had money for a round-trip ticket to Sierra Leone, he still did not have enough for gifts and other things. So one day my mother and father were driving from somewhere and heading home when they got into a heated verbal argument. My mom said something derogatory about my dad's mom, so he pulled over and started punching her. Then he got her out of the car by dragging her to continue his assault and was now starting to kick her. She was down, trying to get up. When she able to break free, she ran to a nearby house for help, now covered in blood.

I don't care what a woman does to any man, but there is no reason for a man to put his hands on any woman. And even after what my mom did to me, she did not deserve that kind of assault. Besides, only a punk ass or a coward puts his hands on a woman because he is not man enough. If they did that to another man, they would get their ass kicked and served to them on a silver platter.

So this was the same person who had the nerve to say no man should put his hands on a woman and that if he ever saw that taking place anyway, he would jump in and fight the guy who was beating her because he hated anyone who did so, and he would not just stand by and let it take place. Now you see the hypocrisy in this because they only assaulted women and children, so there was no way in hell they were about to jump into any fray with a guy. No matter what bullshit they told you, if it was not a child or a woman they had to fight, they would be quiet as a church mouse. It angered me when he had first told me the story because he said it as if it was a good thing; he was boasting about it.

My dad was comforting his sister-in-law, telling her not to worry because he would definitely come back home knowing that he loved his wife, who was pregnant and was due anytime now, making sure he did not miss the birth of his first child, which was a girl. They had already named her Jacye, after my uncle and my dad's younger sister. They did not have to wait too long before my uncle walked through the house not as angry as he had been the previous night. He just left work to come home and cook for his pregnant wife, who as soon as she found out she was pregnant put her feet up and stayed on that couch until she gave birth. Shit, even when she was not pregnant, she still did nothing at all.

My uncle loved his wife, and besides, the side chick he had been messing with already had four or five children, and my uncle was not ready for this kind of commitment, especially when he had a child of his own on the way and to be born any minute. One thing my uncle did was love and care for his family no matter how angry he may have been or how much he argued with his wife. He always made sure his family was taken care of that. So he would come home to cook and make sure all was well on the home front. When he was done fixing the meals for the week, he cleaned the house.

After the completion of his chores, my dad took him out to a bar for some drinks so they could discuss the drama that had been going on between my uncle and his wife. My dad told him that my aunt had no friends or family in this new country of hers and that the only people she had was them, so it was wrong of my uncle to put this poor girl through all the things he had done recently. Besides, my dad told him he did not want Samuel to witness the continuous violence and hard language used during these fights. "If it goes on, I will have to take my son and leave," my dad told his brother, who was now listening. My uncle reacted as if he had just had an epiphany, not knowing or realizing that Samuel was there and did see all of those things that were happening between his aunt and uncle. He told my dad how sorry he was about Samuel being around all of this nonsense and that he would make sure to never react in that way again.

A few months had passed without any incidents, and there was a new member of the family. My aunt had given birth to their daughter Jacye, and there was a calm in the house, even happiness. But all good things come to an end, while bad things last longer. Once again, my uncle stopped coming home night after night, so the fights started again, with my dad playing the peacemaker but taking the side of his sister-in-law.

My aunt and uncle's fights had gotten heated again with no signs of slowing down. My brother had already seen and heard all the fights, and it went on until I got there, but it was not as bad as anything I would witness. The fighting ended as quickly as it had happened. The end came when my aunt and uncle found and agreed on a common enemy, and that was our father. Little did I know then how much we were going to pay for those times, and I had gotten there just in time for this party of hate.

Chapter 9

BROTHERS' BONDS

Now I don't know where the breakdown among my dad, aunt, and uncle came from, but they claimed my father was the reason their money was gone because my dad used it to feed his needs instead of on the business that they had all agreed on. From what I had come to understand, since my uncle came to America, he had saved a lot of money to one day use to retire and build a house for all the Burlays in Africa. My uncle has also always wanted to open a family business. Since my dad was in the United States but had planned on returning to Liberia to continue the different types of businesses he had going, my uncle thought that my dad was the ideal candidate to use the savings he had to open a moneymaking family business. My dad and his brother decided the best business to open would be one that had a variety of services for the clients.

    The first thing they were going to open was a lounge that played American music videos and movies that also served food and liquor. In the daytime, the lounge would cater to not just adults but also to the whole family, which of course included children. At night, however, it would turn into a nightclub that played music and music videos, such as *Soul Train*, MTV, and BET videos from the United States. This part of the business would cater also to all types of budgets, but the other was for VIPs and executives and those who could afford a lot more.

The second business was on a large farm with these huge tents my dad had bought in England and shipped to Liberia. The tents were huge and held anywhere from four to ten people, and they were rented out to people who were executives or politicians or anyone with a lot of money to burn. The tents were all air-conditioned with intercom that connected them to an operator or to the kitchen to put in meal orders, and of course, the meals were delivered by attractive young women. The tents also had televisions in them and set up like a five-star hotel on the inside, with beds, desk, the whole nine yards. And some tents were suites. The menu at the farm was very diverse; it served barbecue chicken, roasted and baked chicken, and the regular African cuisine. And all the ingredients served were all raised right there on the farm.

I remember when my dad and his brother decided to start this family business because they were very excited, knowing that they would be very successful, especially since it seemed my dad had all kinds of business contacts, as well as very well-known in his country of Liberia. He even knew all the executives and all the politicians because he had worked with just about all of them. My dad had also run a very successful nightclub in Liberia that was frequented by a lot of those politicians and executives and was the talk of the town.

Every Saturday morning, we were allowed to sit in the living room with my aunt and her children because it was our job to record *Soul Train* and all videos with good songs, or sometimes we had a list of music videos that we were supposed to record. Heaven help us if we recorded any part of a commercial. We also recorded martial arts movies, mostly Bruce Lee's, that came on the Saturday karate matinee. Among the other movies we were instructed to record were the *Rocky* series and the James Bond series because, every year, there was a marathon featuring all the different Bond movies. *Rambo* was another one I recall having to record. If it was a hot movie during the eighties, we had it recorded. We recorded so much stuff that I remember the tapes filled up all the closets in the house.

I remember my dad traveling back and forth from Liberia to America and Europe, and he would buy these huge fryers, barbecue grills, commercial cooking equipment, televisions, and so on. He had set up the business, and it took off doing very well, with my dad coming to visit us almost every month to discuss business with his brother, telling him how rich they would soon be but that they needed to just be patient. It was around this time when my aunt began to treat my brother and I harshly as if she hated us, but when my dad came back, she was as nice as she could. We were so happy when he came to visit that we never mentioned the ill treatment we were going through, but the start of the abuse was really not too bad.

This new business the brothers had ventured in together had brought them even closer now than ever before, and every time my uncle had any conversation with his wife, it was always about how much he loved my dad and how smart he was. It was at this moment that the green-eyed old monster of jealousy started to turn its ugly head.

My aunt had always been jealous of the relationship between her husband and his brother, so she set out to put an end to that relationship. I guess my aunt figured she was not going to fight another person for the affection of her husband as she had done with Nancy, even if it was her husband's own brother. Somehow my aunt started to convince her husband that his brother was just there to use him so he could steal all the money he had worked so hard for, which totaled over seventy-five thousand from what I heard from my aunt. And for some reason or another, my uncle changed his feelings about his little brother, saying that my dad had indeed stolen his money and was living lavishly off this money that he had worked so hard for to save. Now the only thing that never made sense to me about that whole story was that my uncle had never confronted my dad about this stolen money, especially since my dad was always traveling back and forth to the United States and Africa, and he always slept in the house with us and stayed up all night, discussing all matters of the business. Back in those days, I loved my father and wanted to be around him all the time, so I would hang on his neck all night until I fell asleep, and he would then carry me off to bed, so I was present in all of those meetings.

The magic that my aunt was weaving on my uncle was so good that it started to work even on us. My aunt told us that my dad had also abandoned us, which I believed because he did not see us as much as he used to. As a matter of fact, years had gone by with no sight of him or even a letter from him. It was not too far-fetched for me to believe that another person had abandoned me because I was just unlovable. After all, I had already been unwanted, and I was reminded of it every day; my aunt saw to that. Samuel, on the other hand, did not believe it; he refused to accept it, telling me, "Daddy would not do that to us."

But I was just like, "Whatever, man. Believe that if you want, but just remember you have not heard from him in years either."

Chapter 10

HOME RUNNING

I had been making money from my little job with Antonio for a few months now, but even with all that cash, I was still a pauper, and I was still not able to buy those tennis shoes I wanted. But I almost slipped up one day when a friend of mine named Jason had bought himself a new pair of Reebok tennis shoes and somehow got the wrong size. Instead of just taking it back to the store and getting the right size, he decided to sell it to someone. But the problem was that most of his friends were all in the game like he was, and just like him, they all had an endless supply of shoes, and they did not want them. So one day after school, Jason set his sights on me because we had been friends for a while; and before I was making any money, he would give me some money here and there to buy little snacks and stuff like that.

I met him one day while he was out looking for his mother, like a lot of kids in the hood. Jason's father was gone, and his mom was a crack addict, who was more concerned about getting her fix than if the kids were hungry or how school went. Jason had two younger siblings, a sister who was eight going on forty because she was really mature beyond her years and a younger one who was six years old. Coming from that environment, he was an easy mark for the big-time dealers in the hood to lure into that life. Back in those days, kids like my friend and myself were sought after to do hits and sell drugs because the law did not prosecute kids as adults. So Jason started slanging rocks, and he was a natural because he was already very smart both academically and streetwise. Plus, he loved chemistry, and that was what crack was about—chemistry. He made money than anyone else and would always find new ways to bring in more, so he became a favorite of the headman. Jason was very charismatic, so it was easy to like him, and he was also very loyal to his friends and family members, and I was blessed to be one of those.

When Jason started his life in the game, the big man came to pick him up one day in his convertible Bimmer. He handed Jason a wad of money as soon as he got in the car, with Jason asking him what it was for. His boss told him it was a bonus for all his hard work and commitment. He then drove him around the other spots where he picked up his money and introduced Jason as the lieutenant, and afterward, he took him on a shopping spree, telling Jason that his new lieutenant had to dress the part. They ended the shopping with a stop at the jeweler, where he bought Jason a necklace with a medallion and pinky ring. Being a kid who has no male role model in his life and, all of a sudden, getting all this attention from someone, it was very euphoric for my friend, and it made him want to work even harder for his new father figure.

Now that he was making so much money and was always in the graces of his boss, Jason put his focus in making sure his siblings had a meal every night before bed. They ate snacks and lunches at home, and every morning, he made sure they went off to school. They were always nicely dressed, with their book bags on their backs and lunch boxes in their hands. The only problem was there was no one to do the same for him, and to also keep his mom at home and make his younger siblings have a mother, he would supply his mother with drugs to keep her off the streets.

I remember the first time he was making his brother and sister go to school and his sister got smart with him and said, "Why we got to go to school and you don't? I ain't going, and you can't make me because if you can stay home, I can too. You ain't my daddy!" Jason said she was going to school, but she refused, and he got a belt and whooped her behind. Oh my goodness, it was so funny, but after that day, she never said that again.

When he was done with his first dealing the first week, he made five hundred. I thought he was rich then, but he was not satisfied, and he said, "This ain't shit. I will make more."

I thought, *This guy is crazy. That's enough money for me.* But just like he had said, he doubled that money the next week, and then he tripled it and kept on going to the point he stopped coming to school. So one day after school, I saw him out on the corner, selling as was all the other guys. But the crazy thing about Jason was, even though he had been promoted and did not have to sell because he had people to handle that and he was supposed to just get the money in case his people were arrested, he would still be out there slanging rocks with everyone. He was just better when he took care of business because he knew nothing would go wrong, but I think he just did not want his profits to drop off.

When I saw him out there, of course, I asked why he had not been at school, which was a dumb-ass question, especially since I already knew the answer. "Because, man, I can't make this sitting in class." He pulled out two wads of cash that were so big he had a hard time pulling it out and putting it back in. After he did put it back, you could see the bulge in both pockets. When I saw that, I immediately wanted a piece of that pie, so I asked him to let me work with him, to which he answered, "Hell no. You're too smart to be out here, man. You belong in school, Shawn. Don't worry, you know I will always look out for you." He handed me some money as he had always done since he started earning, but I did not want a handout; I wanted a hand-up. After handing me the money, he left to go check on his other spots. Jason was five years or maybe a little less older than me, but he was very wise and never spoke as a kid.

As soon as he was out of sight, another guy who had overheard our conversation came up to me and asked how much money Jason had given me. Now I did not know the guy's motive for asking me a question like that, but I knew it was bad, so I did not answer until he said, "Look, I'm not trying to rob you. I'm just asking because if you're serious about money like your boy"—he pointed in the direction Jason had gone—"I can help you out." When I heard that, I got a little excited, so I immediately got out the money, and I counted it out. My mouth hung agape when I saw I had 150 dollars. In the past, when he had given me money, I would only get 20 dollars to 50 dollars, the latter being the norm. So for him to give me this much, I figured he must be making a lot more than I thought.

As I was about to hand over my money over to the guy whom I thought was about to change my life, I heard one of his friends warn him not to sell me anything because Jason would not like it; but in very colorful language, he turned around and said, "Man, fuck you. And Jay, man, he don't put no fear in my heart." Then he turned back to me, handing me some rocks in a little bottle, telling me to sell each one for twenty dollars, which meant if I sold each one, I would make three hundred dollars, doubling my money.

I put my book bag down and got to work, and before I knew it, I had made sixty bucks in about thirty minutes. Can you believe that? *If I stay out here for a few hours a day, I can still make a good amount of money for myself,* I said to myself.

It was at that moment when I heard an angry but very familiar voice, and I immediately recognized it as Jason's voice. "What the fuck do you think you're doing here?" he asked, walking on me and taking all my newly acquired wealth, along with my drugs. "Where did you get this? And who gave you this shit?"

Now fearful, my mind ran to the day when he had whooped his sister when she refused to go to school. It was at that moment when I saw his sister, her head shaking from side to side, saying, "Mmm, mmm, mmm, you gonna get it." My focus and daydreaming of his sister mocking my demise was broken when he asked me again where I had gotten the drugs, and without trying to rat him out, my eyes darted over to the guy who had sold it to me. But thankfully, Jason did not catch it, so he turned around to face his people, asking who did it. He knew it had to be one of his people who sold it to me because of the packaging of the drugs, as well as its stamping. Unlike me, the other guys wasted no time and pointed the finger at their friend only because they feared Jason's wrath on them. I was about to find out why they feared him so much.

Jason immediately turned his attention to the guy who sold me the drugs and asked him why he did it in the first place when he had told all of them that no one was to ever mess with me or ever try to recruit me or sell it to me at all. The guy did not say a word or even try to plead his case, so Jason asked him again. "Money is money," the guy replied and shrugged as if to say "fuck you."

"Oh really?" Jason said, and once again, the guy shrugged nonchalantly. That was when Jason two-pieced the guy. The hits came so fast that none of us ever saw the punches. After he was on the ground, Jason began to stomp on him. He was hitting the guy so hard that I was afraid he was going to kill him, so I called his name, hoping that would stop the assault, but he just kept on hitting the guy and yelling at him. "I'm tired of yo' ass, you fuckin' bitch! When I tell you something, muthafucka, you better hear me, kid!"

When he was through yelling his orders at the guy, he punched him one more time, letting him know he was fired. "And I don't want to see yo' bitch ass around here anymore! You hear me, nigga?" Jason said in a low growl. As the guy tried to get up, he stumbled and fell back down. It was at that point I saw how much blood was on his face and now flowing from his nose. His eye was bloodshot, and the right one was swollen shut now. He was finally able to get up and left.

I heard one of the other guys say, "I never liked his bitch ass." They all laughed, saying, "I know, right."

"Yo, Shawn, man, I don't want you out here doing none of this. Besides, you know yo' aunt will kick yo' ass if you ain't in the house when dem streetlights come on, and yo' too smart to be out here anyway."

After he said that, I wanted to say, "Look who's talking," but decided better of it not because I was afraid of him but because I respected him as a good friend or, better yet, a brother, especially the way he took care of me and protected me. It really reminded me of how Samuel used to do the same thing, and besides, after seeing the ass whooping he had just put on that guy, I was not in a fighting mood. Jason walked up close to me and took all the vials of crack I had left, paid me for it, and told me to go home.

I was actually glad later on after getting a chance to sit back and think about what just happened. I was very glad that my friend had gotten in the way, intervening to keep me out of that lifestyle. After I lost my brother, I was even more afraid that I would die next, and it scared me like you would not believe. I was so afraid that I hardly slept or ate, and I cried all the time both for my brother and because of fear, which led to anger, which then led to me not giving a fuck anymore. I decided not to be afraid any longer, and that was why I was out there trying to throw my life away, feeling I did not have too many choices. I was glad that Jason had stepped in because knowing myself and my willingness to prove myself and show that I was not weak, I would have turned myself into a monster, changing who I am today. But by the grace of the Almighty God, that never happened.

Jason helped me so many times. Little did I know it would soon be my turn to help him in the life he had warned me about staying out of. After saving Antonio's life, at least according to him, I got to be pretty well-known because I was now Antonio's gopher and delivery and pickup kid. And for the first time ever, I felt as if I was relevant, useful, and needed because all the drug dealers or anyone having to do with the drug game in our neighborhood, including the users, knew me. Most of them thought I was Antonio's little brother because that was what he would always refer to me as whether we were together or not, so after a while, everyone referred to me as his little brother, and the word was out that I was not to be messed with. Apart from the money I made with those deliveries, I would make money even if I was not doing it because people just handed me money in hopes of getting in good with Antonio or me telling him how nice they had been to me.

So now that I was making money, it got back to Jason who, of course, was part of that culture, but he never got mad or anything like that, which really surprised me. But the only thing that changed was he stopped giving me money, which I really did not need anyway. But it concerned me a bit because our friendship started to change, which I was not physically afraid of because of the protection I had newly acquired from my new relationship with Antonio, which gave me a sense of security. For the first time in my life, I felt safe except in my home. And only God could have helped me in that field. The change in my friendship with Jason really concerned me. After all, he had always been there for me even before he started his life in the game, and the change in our friendship began after I got in good with Antonio and even a little before that, at least I think so.

When Jason began his career—if you want to call it a career—he had never intended on staying very long unlike most of his peers who had entered with him. Jason wanted to make enough money to feed his family and get as much money as he thought he would need for college. That was his plan. He had always dreamed of owning his own businesses and working for himself, and he was really smart. His academic interest was in math and science, but he excelled in everything he did. Jason and I would sit and daydream about what we were going to be when we grew up and how much money we were going to make. We also made a promise that, no matter what, we would always be friends and whichever of us got rich first would help the other.

When he started doing his thing in the drug game, he—like all the other kids—started out on the bottom rung of the ladder, but with his ability to outthink the competition, it put him in favor with the top guys, especially when he came up with new ways to make more money and motivate the other kids to improve their sales. Having the top earner get a ride with the boss in his car was Jason's idea, at least that was what I heard. Either way, he was a favorite of all the young men; and as he got older, making all that money, he moved up the ladder of success very quickly. And the talk of college and owning his own businesses went right out the window. With the kind of money he was making out there, I thought he was already a millionaire. His rise to the top was halted when there was a change in the chain of command after the head guy of their organization, who really liked him and had taken him under his wing, helping him climb as fast as he had, was killed sitting his car in front of his girlfriend's house, and nobody knew how it happened or who did it.

After the death of his mentor and boss, things slowed down a bit for my friend, but the next guys in line started doing their thing. And even though they loved their boss, business had to keep on going. There was one who showed the most aptitude and the most promise, had the ability to lead, and was very charismatic. He was loved and respected by everyone, so he became the man and pulled up all his friends who had been loyal and had been with him since he had been on the corner doing what Jason had been. That guy just happened to be Antonio.

Now Jason was not doing as well as he had before. Having a new group of guys at the top whom he was not close with, he had to find a new way to get their attention because now he had more people to compete with. They were highly intelligent, street-smart, and older and had been doing this for a while. Plus, they were hustlers and had a million ways to make a dollar— something Jason was not. Even though he was academically smart, his street smarts and hustler mentality was not as strong as Antonio's and his crew, so he needed to come up with a new way to grab those guys' attention. Moneymaking was not going to do it because they were making more now than ever before, so what was he to do?

After he found out that I was in good with the people he was trying to get the attention of and that I was making money from them, I think that my friend became jealous of me because I think he saw that the dynamics of our friendship were about to seriously change. Maybe he thought that now that I was with Antonio and doing little things for him, making decent money, it would soon lead to me moving up to more things, especially the way I was being treated by everyone. He had always told I was smart, even smarter than he was, so for that very reason, he figured I was about to surpass him in something he had gotten in first, which bothered him a lot. If only Jason had known I had no intention of doing any more than what I was doing and that the amount of money I was getting paid for my little task was a lot of money too. I had no knowledge I was in the drug game, and I did not consider myself a dealer because I was not on the street selling anything, but because of that competitive nature, he thought I was in a race with him and that I was about to beat him—something he could not let happen at all because of that hard head of his and that competitive nature he has always been known for.

I remember a football game we had played against some kids from the neighborhood, who stayed a few buildings over from us, and we lost the game by a few points. One of the kids from the winning team had made a slick remark about us losing the game, and he started taunting us and making fun of my shoes and my clothes, which was something I was used to. I knew that they were not the best. Jason, however, was so angry not only for the boy making fun of me but also because we had lost. He began to beat the living daylights out of that boy. We all rushed over to pull him off the kid, but Jason was really strong, and he broke out of our grasp, and he kept on with his attack. A few adults saw what was taking place. They ran over and pulled them apart. Even the adults had a little difficulty in their attempts to stop the fray.

This was the nature of Jason's competitive ways, so instead of just coming to me and ask me to introduce him or put in a good word about him to Antonio, he could not because I guess he felt as though I would be taking care of him instead of him taking care of me as he had always done. I also feel that Jason also thought I was about to use my new connection to set myself up to one day become the main man.

Jason had come up with an idea to get what he wanted, and it would almost spill my secrets right in front of my aunt. It started when Jason had bought a pair of tennis shoes, and it just so happened that they were too small for his feet of size 9 and that they were my exact size, which was size 7.5. All the dope boys in our neighborhood were always competing with one another about who had the finest girls or the nicest cars or who was dressed the best. So it was no surprise that they had an endless supply of shoes because they bought them every day. Jason had bought these shoes for a very sinister reason. I had always admired his clothes and shoes, wishing I could also wear such nice things. But I knew pretty well that my aunt would never get me anything that nice, so I immediately put those ideas out of my mind, and I lived and wore those nice things through my friend.

Even after I started to make money, I was very aware that I could never get those shoes anyway because I would have to answer to my aunt about where I got them; and knowing her, no answer was going to suffice. Jason had always told me I was stupid for even caring what she thought. "Fuck that fat ass bitch, man, go get some gear. And if she asks, tell her I gave them to you. And if she tries to take a firm grip on you, leave," he would tell me. It was easy for him to say that. Of course, he was a lot more courageous than I was only because he did not have to deal with my aunt.

Jason knew very little about my life and what went on in my home, and that was because I was not really talkative, and I was ashamed. I knew everything about his life, however, because he talked about it, and he was very brash and boastful, constantly telling me how awesome he was. I think that was why I liked Jason and that was what had attracted me to his person, thus starting off our friendship. I kind of wished I were like that, having that kind of charisma and courage with that "do whatever, and whatever comes or happens, so be it" attitude. This was also what drew me to liking Antonio. He was a young man who answered to no adult, but they answered to him and feared him at the same time as they loved and respected him.

Originally, if they had ever had a time to get to know each other, I really think that Antonio and Jason would have been the best of friends. After all, they were the same people, basically kindred spirits. So in his attempt to get to know Antonio and get his attention at all cost, my friend approached me one morning with an offer that he knew I would be interested in and would tempt me. After all, he was my friend. "Yo, Shawn, man, I got an offer for you I know you will like," Jason said as I was on my way to school. I never really thought anything of it because, even though he no longer attended school, it was not out of the ordinary for him to walk with me to school so that none of the kids would make fun of my clothes and pick on me because they were scared of him. Knowing his temper, as well as his capabilities, they would immediately turn timid, not saying a word about me. Jason would still threaten them as they passed by, letting them know if any harm was done or any disrespectful word was said to me, they would love to regret that day they were born. I think he would do that because he was a bit of a bully himself and liked the power he held.

"What is it, Jay?" I asked him.

He pulled out a pair of blue and white Reebok sneakers, instantly grabbing my attention. "See these? Nobody has these. Do you want them?" he asked me as he raised his eyebrow in two quick moves, knowing I did want them.

"Why don't you want them?" I asked my friend. He had bought me a pair of Nike shoes for my birthday one year, but I could not take them not because I did not want them but because he had always been taking care of me, and I had never been able to do anything for him in return, and this was just too much. He, on the other hand, did not want anything. He was always just a good friend, wanting to take care of me now that he could. I also could not take the shoes because of my aunt; even if I told her it was a gift and the giver came with me to prove it to her, she would have still not let me keep it because, one, she did not believe I was good enough for anyone to spend any kind of money on me, and two, it was too good for me.

"They are too small, and I remember they are about your size from the last time I got you them other ones. Besides, you make money with your new friend, so give me thirty bucks for them," he said.

"That's it. Wow, man, for real?" I asked, hardly believing anything I just heard.

"Yeah, man. You, my boy, you know that. You know what, just give me fifteen and do me a favor," he said.

I knew those shoes had to be at least seventy dollars or more because Jason did not wear cheap shoes, so I asked him, "What favor?"

"Oh, nothing, just introduce me to your boy Antonio," he said nonchalantly.

Without thinking and wanting those shoes, I agreed to his terms without asking why. "Okay," I answered, and he handed me my new Reebok, the first nice shoes I had ever had.

"Okay, man, see you after school, all right?" Jason said as he turned to leave.

"Wait, don't you want your money?" I asked him as he continued to walk away from me.

"Don't worry about it right now. I'll see you after school, okay?" he yelled back to me as he started across the street.

I stopped in my tracks and took off my disgusting old no-name-brand shoes, but I was not stupid enough to throw them away. I knew very well I had to wear them back home. After all, my aunt knew my whole wardrobe. Shit, it was not hard to keep track of the same bullshit week in and week out. I slipped on my new shoes. They were the perfect size, and oh my, did they feel good! I started to wish my brother was alive to be part of that day. I know that someone who had never been through anything like this is probably reading this and wondering what the big deal is. Well, it's okay to take normal things for granted because it's your life, but putting those shoes on made me feel like I was a new person. I was cautious to only walk on the concrete and stay off the grass, or other children may make a mistake and step on my new shoes, which was a sure way to initiate a fistfight; it was not as though I had a ton of nice tennis shoes to spare.

Getting to school was more than just my regular escape from my house of horrors. Today was more than that. I was not invisible today, just wanting the world to pass me by, ignoring me as it had always did. No, today I was a regular student. Even though my shirt and pants were old and faded, I shone as if I were wearing all new things. Even the teacher who had embarrassed me multiple times by bringing attention to my clothing, asking me why I wore my shirt so much and if it was my favorite, to which I answered yes, would not ruin my day.

That day, I was the happiest kid in that school. No one was capable of ruining my beautiful day. I had even gotten the attention of two girls I had a very serious crush on, Diane Harper and Jennifer Maples, but I never had the confidence to approach either one of them. Why? Well, I noticed they only talked to the nicely dressed, cute boys with nice shoes, and these boys always had money to take these girls out and buy them whatever young girls at the ages of nine and thirteen wanted. These boys had all been just regular guys until they joined the drug gangs, becoming different overnight. *And look at me. I'm ugly. I don't have any money, and my clothes have holes in them*, I would tell myself. *You're just a useless human being whom no one loves or wants. Not even your own mother loves you, and you think that anyone will even like you, including these girls? Ha!* I was insulting myself even more now. When I did, it was usually while I was in the bathroom as I stared in the mirror, looking at myself and even punching at my very own reflection, which I hated.

When they spoke to me for the first time ever, both Diane and Jennifer complimented me on my shoes. It was as if I had been invisible forever, and for the first time, my invisibility had worn off, and I enjoyed it, wanting to show everyone I was right here. *Can you see me?* I wanted to shout out. *I'm here! Now look at my shoes and tell me how cool I am.* Yeah, it was euphoric and indescribable, an incredible feeling. My clothes did not even bother me. I thought all the kids were sitting there admiring my shoes, wishing that they had them. At least that was what I thought.

I was in such euphoria that I did not want to leave, but that old and very telling, horrible pain occurred in my stomach when that three o'clock bell was about to ring. I did not want the day to end, but I knew it would be without even looking at a clock or anyone telling me that the school day was almost at its conclusion. No, I knew because my stomach was telling me.

The stomach pains I had were so bad that they got worse as time moved. When my abdomen first began to bother me, I could go the whole day without bending over in pain, but nothing I tried to do eased the pain. Nothing was able to relieve any of it, so I tried to tough it out, but I could not take this anymore, and I knew I was going to have to put up with my problem through that whole night all the way until the morning. I would be up feeling every sharp, stabbing thrust, and that just lowered my spirits.

It was well past my thirty-minute curfew, and knowing what pain awaited me had me depressed. I did not want to go home but to just turn around and run in the opposite direction. *But how are you even going to do so when you could hardly move?*

That was when I heard a very familiar voice calling me from behind, so I turned around as fast as I could, which was still in slow motion anyway. "Yo, what's up, man? You awight?" Jason asked as he approached me after running across the street. He asked me why I was moving so slow. I looked at him and told him about this stomach pain that I had been experiencing for some years now. He told me I needed to see a doctor. I then smiled at his ignorance concerning my life; there was no way in hell my aunt was going to bring my black ass to the hospital even if I was spitting and coughing up blood on her feet or even if I was on my deathbed. I really doubted that she would come to my rescue by rushing me to the hospital; that would have just been Shawn's last day.

"So you awight? Are you still going to introduce me to your man? But if you can't, I understand. And oh, by the way, ain'tcha wearing the kicks I gave you earlier?" Jason asked as he pointed to my feet, where my old sneakers were now on instead of my new ones. Before school ended that day, I had changed my shoes in the boys' bathroom, even though I loved my new sneakers and wanted to never take them off. Another group of kids had made fun of my clothes and shoes after we lost a football game to them, but Jason, being the protective big brother, threatened them, including their families, with bodily harm. It made them stop their insults at that very minute. Even among his crew of dealers that he commanded and loved knew better than to go up against him because, once his fuse was lit, there was no stopping him except the Almighty God.

Jason had always looked out for me without ever wanting anything in return, not that I had anything to repay him with anyway. Now he had given me this great pair of shoes just so I could let him meet my new friend, Antonio. Knowing him got people being nice to me and giving me free stuff, such as with the candy lady and the ice cream man, who before had never said two words to me or had smiled at me, let alone give me all kinds of things. So for those of you reading this book asking yourself what in the world a candy lady is, well, I'm about to tell you. In just about all hoods, there was an older lady who ran a little store out of her house, selling candies, drinks, and other sweet treats and snacks to the neighborhood kids. This was also the same lady who sold liquor on Sunday when all liquor stores were closed. She sold liquor through the week, but she charged more money on those days. I guess back then I was ignorant of the power my friends wielded, making even a kid like me a bit powerful without knowing it at all.

Since he was so eager to meet Antonio, I decided to bring him over to Antonio's house to finally complete their introductions. I tried convincing myself I was going to overcome my pain so I would be a man of my word, even though I knew I would get another beating I could not bear and that my brother would not and could not save me. This time, I had only myself and God to rely on. God had already taken one huge punishment for me, so I dared not ask.

As I pondered what waited for me after my meeting, I gave Jason his shoes back. "What's this?" he asked, confused. "Why are you handing me your shoes? I don't want them." He pushed my hand with the shoes away. "I will let you meet Antonio, for you're my friend. You ain't got to pay me, so now you can take the shoes back to get your money," I said, still holding the shoes.

"I don't want them, man. They are yo's. Plus, I got too many shoes as it is, kid," Jason told me. I was so glad he had refused taking his shoes back— well, *my* shoes according to him—so I put the shoes back in my book bag.

We arrived at the corner Antonio usually hung out at, so I went there, hoping he was there instead of being at home because, had I had to go over to his house, I would have been discovered by my aunt since Antonio lived right next door to me. As soon as Antonio laid eyes on me and upon seeing me moving very slowly, he ran right over to me, asking if something had occurred resulting in my injury. His next three questions were the same, only he asked them in three different ways. He asked who had hurt me before saying how miserable that person was soon to be. All his people who had been standing next to Antonio came over to us when they heard him getting very angry, asking me the same thing again and again. I loved the attention he was now showering me with, and my pain started to disappear, along with my fear of even going to my house, knowing what awaited me there. As a matter of fact, all my fears were just leaving me alone one by one. No one had ever showed me this type of love and care except my grandmother, who would always be my heart.

When his crew walked over to see what was wrong with their boss, I instantly recognized the big man with a bald head and full facial hair who had those dark Ray-Ban sunglasses he wore on the first day we met when I was let in to that dark, dingy, and stinky room with all those people doing nothing except buying crack; they paid for it in one hole and received it in another one, and then they smoked it in a day. Seeing that big man scared me a little bit until he asked me what was wrong after Antonio asked me again. But I was not able to really talk. Well, I could, but the words were just hard to come by. Jason answered for me and told them all about my stomach pain.

"Is that true, my little man?" Antonio asked as he bent down, placing both of his arms on my shoulders, causing me to finally open my mouth before the words proceeded out.

"Yes, my stomach is hurting really bad, but it's a little better," I told Antonio. The big bald man—who scared me because he had a full beard and a mustache like David, my mother's husband, who was a horrible person, making me think all men with the same type of facial hair were bad people, and I had been right about it so far—asked if they should bring me to the hospital because he said I looked sick. Antonio agreed to that, but I was able to convince him that I was okay.

As we were still having our conversation, another one of the guys who were standing with Antonio came out of the crowd and said, "Man, who is this bigheaded kid, man? Can we get back to business?" That was the point the big guy turned around so fast that no one saw it. All we saw next was the feet of man who had just insulted me were dangling off the ground, held by the big guy. The big man must have been mutantly strong. The man he was holding was not a small man by any measure; he was also a big-sized man and was covered with muscles and tattoos.

Seeing how bad the offending man had made me feel, both Jason and Antonio jumped to my defense without any hesitation. "Yo, man, watch who the fuck yo' talking to, kid, you bitch ass nigga," Jason warned him.

Then Antonio turned around to face him and said, "What the hell did you say about my little brother, muthafucka?"

The man, now realizing that I was not just any of the other bigheaded kids in the neighborhood, started to apologize and backpedaled so fast that it was incredible. "Yo, man, I had no idea he was your brother. I'm sorry, Tonio," the man said as he was still in the air, with both feet still above ground.

"Don't apologize to me. Apologize to my little man, kid," Antonio said as he pointed at me, so the guy looked in my direction and did just that. "But you know, you've offended my whole family, and we need more than an apology on that one, especially him." Antonio once again pointed in my direction. "So exactly what are you going to do about that little bit of dilemma? What do you suggest?"

"Aww man, no problem. I got you." He then went deep into his pocket, pulling out two fistfuls of cash, which he offered to me. Not knowing what to do, I looked at Antonio for help, and all I got was a quick nod toward the man who was holding the cash. I quickly took it and stepped back before putting the money in my book bag. The big bald guy told the man he was still holding up that what he had just given me was not enough, and Antonio agreed. "Okay, I'll mark down my price for you since I offended your family. Is that cool?"

"Okay, man, we good," Antonio said. Little did I know that, right before Jason and I showed up, there was a drug deal in progress, and they reached an impasse on what the price of the product would be. When I showed up to see Antonio, I was insulted by the guy who could control the price of the cocaine. I think Antonio, being the slick businessman wanting to spend less to make more and was always thinking five steps ahead of everyone else, saw that moment to control the deal in his favor. See? I told you guys. Antonio was a very smart and shrewd businessman.

I was very excited about all the money I had made by being picked on. If it were a job earning that much, I would always be at work. Then all my excitement went right out the window when it hit me that Antonio may ask for the money back when we were done with our conversation.

Then I remembered I was not out there on the corner on a social visit but to make an introduction of Jason and Antonio. Jason has been so eager to meet him. For as long I've known Jason, he never got excited about anything, so his urgency to meet Antonio surprised me. Right as I was about to make my introductions, Antonio said, "Yo, who is this kid? He looks familiar to me."

"Yeah, I was just going to introduce him to you. This is my friend Jason," I said, pointing to him.

"Oh, okay," Antonio said. Jason stepped up to shake Antonio's hand before asking him if it was possible to have a word with him. And of course, Antonio told him all right because of me. As we started to walk, Antonio's people started coming after him, but he told them to wait for him. He then gave his undivided to Jason.

As we continued our walk, Jason began telling him about how he was close to the last head of state and that he had started and incorporated some of the things they did now, as well as bringing other smaller crews that were looking to make more money, and with more people came a lot more power, which rivals would think about before they did anything stupid. Jason also told Antonio how he felt he should be in a more prominent position. "After all, my people make more money every month than some of the others make in a year." Jason told Antonio about some of the new ideas he had, saying he had even more ideas than that. He said if he had more people and more guns on the street, he could make him more money than he could ever imagine.

When he was done, Antonio told Jason he had heard about him for a while because their former boss was a mentor as well to him; and even though he knew Jason from their mentor, he had no clue what he looked like. Jason had also heard of Antonio but just never knew what he looked like until that day. The funny thing Antonio had said to Jason was, even though he did not know what he looked like, he did know which crew he belonged to since he was now the boss and had gone to his crew to ask about him so he could make Jason a part of his cabinet. But he had been told that Jason was not part of them, so Antonio got another man, who was kind of the second choice. Jason could hardly believe it but put it out of his mind for the time being.

After I heard their conversation, it now was clear why he had been so excited and eager to meet Antonio, so I joined the conversation in support of my friend by telling Antonio all the great things Jason had done for me after becoming a drug dealer, especially how he would walk me to school and threaten any and all person who made fun of me, particularly after finding out about my brother's death. I think he did it because he felt sorry for me, but I did not care what his reason were; all I knew was that he was a friend, and I cherished my friends because I did not have many of them. I was an outcast because my clothes were shabby. I was under constant attack by kids who would ridicule me.

I remember one situation when we were in the lunchroom. One of the ladies who worked as a custodian started to make fun of me. As she talked, I hoped all the noise in the room would muffle what she had to say, but that was not the case; it got even quieter as the kids would get the attention of some of their friends so they could listen. And before I knew it, the whole place was silenced and now being filled with laughter at my expense. I was so embarrassed as the custodian spoke about how horrible my clothes were and how I looked.

Then one of my friends named Jay asked her to leave me alone, which did no good because she kept on talking, never relenting from her attack. I was starting to sweat and becoming really hot knowing all eyes were now on me. I wished I would disappear. So shortly after she had left, Jay told me to tell on her, seeing how hurt and ashamed I was, but I declined his offer, especially after what happened when I took his advice about telling a teacher about the abuse going on in my home. Needless to say, it did not go too well, so I was a little bit skeptical of this advice. Jay, however, would have none of it, so he called one of our teachers over to tell them about how I was just made fun of. The teacher asked me if it was true, and I unwittingly said yes. "Wait right here," she said as if we could go anywhere else.

A few minutes later, the teacher showed up with the custodian who had made fun of me and asked her she had made fun of me. To my surprise, she said she it was true, but it was a joke, and I had been laughing at the jokes too. "No, he wasn't. He was crying," James yelled out, embarrassing me even more because I was trying to hide my tears yet still someone else knew.

"Even if he was laughing or not, it's still is not professional for an adult to be in such a situation," the teacher explained to the custodian and made her apologize to me.

"I'm sorry. If I knew it had offended you, I would not have done nothing," the custodian said in broken English. I told her it was okay, and she turned around, leaving us sitting at our table. Then the teacher also apologized to me, hoping that had never happened.

Done with my tales of what a good friend Jason had been to me, Antonio told him that, since he knew me and had been such a great friend, he was promoting him to see what he could do. "I won't let you down, bruh," Jason said, so excited to finally get his chance. We said goodbye to Antonio and started toward my house, with my belly pain beginning all over again now that I was going home to face my fears.

For the very first time, I felt that I had finally done something for Jason after all of these years. And to tell you the truth, it felt great to help my friend, but I reminded him of something Antonio had said. Although I did not know what kinds of thoughts ran through his mind, I knew what ran around in mine, and I could not understand why one of his own people would say they did not know him when it was in their interest to help Jason because he would surely take them with him all the way to the top. He was just a loyal person, and being also a friend of his, I had to warn him and express my reservations about some of the people he hung with. Then I told him to just be careful.

Jason told me I worry too much because no matter what, he could control the situation, but he looked totally different from the confident words he had spoken. For the first time, I saw doubt and confusion in him, and some of the tough-guy confidence was gone and was now replaced by something a bit more than fear. It was as if he knew a dirty secret no one knew except him. I also knew that whatever Antonio had said triggered that look in his eyes. I insisted that he tell Antonio, since he was now working with him, about the guys in his crew so they would stay in their lane. Cocky and brash as he had always been, Jason put my advice on the shelf, telling me not to say a word about any of the things that we were just spoken. He then made me promise it to him, and of course, I did.

During his life in the drug game, Jason's smarts and charisma helped him rise very quickly, and that was doubled because the boss of their drug game liked him. Even some of the other top guys really liked him, and his rise to the top was a sure bet. There was no one who hated him, or at least they did not show it. But as it is with the game, jealousy and death are a sure thing. It was after the death of the boss that his haters began to show their true colors, and he found out later that some of those haters were people he used to call friends. So as you may have guessed, that brought about the end of their relationship.

We talked some more about these haters and what he should do, and he told me not to worry because he had it under control. I did not get a chance to hear the rest of his plans because of the pain in my stomach, which felt as if there were razor blades inside of me. It was then that I heard my name being called, and immediately, I knew who the voice belonged to only because it was the source of my belly pain and other pains in my life. It was my aunt, and I answered, "Yes, Auntie," in a low voice because it now seemed any move I made just caused me more pain. I did my best to answer without hurting, which did me no good. After all, I was sure to be in more aches and pains in a few minutes.

"Where the hell have you been? Now get your ass in this house!" she yelled. I picked up my pace, quickly heading toward her. It was right when I was by her that our eyes met. "Don't look at me, you dumb asshole!" It was followed by punches and kicks, knocking me down to the arm of her sofa, hitting my rib so hard that I could not catch my breath because the wind had been taken right out of my lungs. I thought my ribs were broken from the pain I felt radiating from there. My aunt slammed the door, and the real beating started. I was already on the floor in pain, but that did nothing to curb her appetite for my pain. She continued her savage beating, and I just knew she was going to surely kill me.

Leaving me sprawled out on the floor when she was done, I got up to take a shower, hoping the water would ease my pain. I washed away my shame and watched it swirl down the drain to wherever it was headed. After my shower, I sat down crying from pain. It was not physical pain but one I was unable to touch. The more I thought of it, the more I cried, but I was trying to muffle my cries so my aunt would not hear me. Standing there staring in the mirror, I insulted myself, spitting on and cursing my reflection. I was disgusted with myself and told my reflection how weak he was for crying and showing emotions in front of her. *You're a fucking useless piece of shit!* I yelled at my reflection in my mind. *Now I see why no one likes you or will ever love you because you ain't shit. That's why you don't have any friends. I bet Samuel would have not cried because he's strong, but your useless self is weak.* I kept abusing my reflection, yelling out at it, because I truly hated the person I was, the person who could not do anything right.

Then all of a sudden, the bathroom door flew open, and standing in front of me was my aunt, holding my new shoes in one hand and my book bag in the other. My heart stopped beating. At the same time, my knees felt like Jell-O, and I almost urinated on the bathroom floor, which would have surely meant another ass whooping. "Where the hell did you get these? Do you have money, huh? You have money, and I don't know!" My aunt's questions were coming so fast that I was unable to think, but I knew better than to just sit there dumbfounded.

"The shoes are my friend's, and I was carrying it for him so no one could rob him for it, and he was scared," I told my aunt, quickly coming up with that story.

"Okay, make sure you give to him. I don't want to see it on your feet. You know they're too good for you," my aunt told me.

"Yes, Auntie," I said with my head hanging low and eyes to the floor. I was just grateful she had not found the money I had balled up in my socks before I put it in the shoes. I was really about that because if she had seen me with that amount of money, she would surely know I had a source of it. I would have gotten my ass kicked until I revealed my connection. I was also glad she believed my story about the tennis shoes. After all, it was very well-known that kids had been robbed for shoes and Starter jackets. There had even been some deaths connected to those robberies, so it was not far from the truth that a kid would hide any of the articles the robbers were going after.

It was one o'clock in the morning when I decided to count the money I had received during the day. I was sure everyone was asleep, so I started counting. I quickly realized counting my money was not going to take as long as I had previously thought because all the bills were hundred-dollar bills. I got a great pace counting when, all of a sudden, I heard a sound, making me stop and hide my money. This kept happening for an hour, leaving me without a total, so I quieted my nerves to give myself a pep talk, telling myself all the noises were in my mind and that I should ignore them. But I should listen for footsteps of all the people in my house, and I knew everyone's footsteps. For example, my uncle's steps were deep, like he was trying to put his foot right through the floor. And my aunt's footsteps sounded like a pounding noise, and of course, my little cousin's footsteps were light, very identifiable from the adults.

When I finally calmed myself down, I started counting all of those beautiful one-hundred-dollar bills, telling myself I was rich. "I bet I have thirty thousand dollars. I can buy a car or a house," I thought out loud. I was so excited that I almost cried out of joy and happiness. When I finished with my count, I found out I had a bit over ninety-five hundred dollars. So now I had to hide it in a different place. In case my aunt found one spot, I would still have other hiding spots that held the rest of my money.

It had already been a day or so when Jason came running as happy as I had ever seen him. Most of the time, he was solemn. So to see the excitement in his eyes made me start smiling too, another thing I rarely did since I did not have much to smile about to begin with. "What's going on?" I asked, anxious to hear what this was all about.

"Man, thank you for hooking me up with your main man, Antonio. Man, we gonna make so much money, man. I'm gonna move my family and you out of here, man. We gonna be living in dem nice cribs those crackers be living in," Jason said, breathing hard and trying to catch his breath. I stood there excited for him and myself. He went on about the cars we would be driving and how all these girls would be on our jocks. For those of my readers who may not be street literate, *girls on our jocks* means we would have women all over us. Anyway, so Jason went on about the big mansions with butlers for everything and chefs to cook for us whatever we wanted to eat. He talked about living in a place with no roaches or rats, not having to hear gunshots all the time, and a home with no junkies shooting up and leaving needles around for kids to find them and play with them. Then he said he wanted to be in a place where the damn pizza man would deliver. "I like pizza. Can I get some fucking pizza?"

He then turned around and said, even though he did not like the police officers, he still wanted to live in a place where if he ever needed them, which he said he never would, he would have them there in less than five minutes, and they would also bring the fire department and the ambulance. Jason said something that I have always kept in my mind, and that was if he or I were to ever really need those services, we would surely be dead before they arrived. In our neighborhood, the cops would never respond to our call by themselves; they had to have at least five sets of police vehicles responding at the same time. So that meant if you were in dire straits, needing help—let's say someone was inside your house trying to kill you— and you called the cops, well, they would then wait for five cops to respond. In responding, some of them would ask the dispatcher what kind of call it was. And depending on the reply, they would agree to go or not. So now you were there in a life-and-death situation, where one minute seemed like an eternity, and the people paid to protect you were having a debate on whether your life and the lives of your loved ones were important enough for them to risk theirs. After the five cars have agreed to come, they all got there at the same time. When the ambulance personnel were sure the cops had arrived on the scene, then they would come; and by then, who knows? It may be too late.

I think that was why Public Enemy was one of Jason's favorite rap groups, especially when they made the song "911 Is a Joke." It was about real proud brothers and sisters gaining the knowledge of self, and even though Jason was a drug dealer, he was still very intelligent. As a matter of fact, most drug dealers, if they had the opportunity, could run a Fortune 500 company because many of them were smart.

Jason was very aware of his history, and he was proud to be black and an African, even though he had never been to Africa, which was another reason I think he liked me and would ask me all these questions on what Africa was really about. Back then, there was nothing but negative things on Africa like today except it is just a bit better. *Tarzan* used to come on television every weekend; it was a story of some white boy who could communicate with animals and saved this white band from the cannibals who were all black, and Tarzan would beat them all.

Yeah, whatever. And because of that, ignorant kids who had ignorant parents came to me asking if we lived in trees and all that bullshit. But Jason was the only person I knew, child or adult, who actually read a book and asked me intelligent questions. Even some parents and teachers asked me stupid questions like if I had lions in my backyard as pets. I would tell them Africa is a continent with many countries and that lions live in South Africa in a huge reserve or park and Serengeti. They would reply, "Oh, I know, but it must have been cool living with them." No. Actually, you don't know because, if you did, you would know better than to ask those stupid-ass questions you just asked me.

All day, I was thinking about the things Jason had told me about how he was going to take us out of this place. Up until then, I did not know it was possible to just pick one up and say, "I'm tired of this place. It's time to leave now." I had always thought people lived only in the places they were supposed to live in. I have always seen that white people lived in all the nice places, while black people stayed in those horrible dilapidated neighborhood, if you could even consider them neighborhood because no one living in those war zones were neighborly. Even though Jason was my friend and had always been a great friend, I never put 100 percent hope or expectation in his or anybody's word, except my brother's, who was now dead, and my grandmother's. There were not a lot of people whom I put any trust in. I came to find out that the people who mean the absolute most to you are the ones you have to be leery, of especially when it involves money.

Just recently, I have been hearing of married people who kill their partners for insurance money or kids who murder their parents for their inheritance. Those fucking bastards go to work for your sorry asses. How does a person who swears in front of God and their family and friends to protect and love someone go to do the opposite? That means they have no honor, especially when it comes to lying to God. So now with all of those going on as child, who do you trust and depend on when they who are supposed to take care of, feed, and protect you do not do those things?

I was happy for my friend because he was going to take his family out of this dump when he got rich. Honestly, I thought he was already rich. He made way more money than I was making, and I thought I was pretty rich, so I figured he must be rich beyond my imagination, but that was my idea of wealth. If you are only making a thousand dollars a month and then, out of the blue, someone gives you ten thousand dollars a month, you would think you are ballin' because, wherever it was that you spent that thousand, you could spend two and get more things with eight thousand dollars left over until the next month, when you get another ten thousand. Some who are a lot richer than you, like a millionaire, may laugh at you because they see you as a broke person trying to be rich, but you will always be rich until you try to compete with that millionaire—but not me; I was always rich. I just did not play in that arena. Not Jason though; he played in all arena.

As time went on, I saw Jason here and there; usually, he was behind the wheel of a new car, with the ladies hanging on him, and those guys he had been warned about were still around him. After the story Antonio had told us, I saw them as rats. I know you guys have seen the cartoons where a character runs off the edge of a mountain or something like that, and when they realize it, they will turn into a donkey or a lollipop with the word *sucker* on it. Well, that was how I saw those cheese-eating rats. It never made sense to me. If all those men were in the drug game, making a lot of money because I always saw them on the corners rain, sleet, or snow, why was it only Jason spending money? Well, I asked my friend that question one day, and he told me I was just jealous because he was not giving me money anymore. But he told me not to worry because he was always going to take care of me, especially when he moved us out of the hood. It was at that moment I understood we were not going to be friends too much longer.

What my good friend Jason had not realized or had forgotten was that we came from the same hood and that there was no such thing as a secret or privacy. If someone tells you it's a secret, then that means twenty people have heard it before you. I knew Jason had moved his family out of the hood a few months ago but had kept the place he had to keep certain things and to sleep when he was tired and did not want to drive the long way home. I found out the news that he moved from Antonio, when his mom came looking for him when his younger siblings had told her they had not seen him for a while. Since she was once a crack addict and knew the big drug dealers in the hood, she went to Antonio, now that he was the man, to see where Jason was. She found him in Antonio's house playing video games. When she asked him why he had not been home, especially since they had moved out, everyone in Antonio's was surprised, so I figured out that I was not the only one who did not know. The worst part was that, even after people found out, he was still telling me, "Any day now, man, we will be out of this place."

I never expected to go with him and his family because the one thing that was very clear during the early part of my life was that I was unwanted and that, everywhere I had been, people had always or would always find a way to get rid of me. That was just part of my life, which I was okay with. I was only hurt that he had told all the other folks and not me because, whether I went with him or not, I would have been the happiest and the proudest of him.

What Jason did not know was I had my own escape plan for getting out of my hellhole, even though I had been repeatedly reminded I would never amount to shit by my own family. Then society gave me only a few recourses, like all the black males within my age group and a bit older: (1) I would be killed by another black man; (2) I would spend my life in modern slavery, which was the prison system, which is so profitable that businesses with big names are getting involved, and because it's a business, no one sees it as slavery since there is just too much money to make; and (3) I was just a statistic. Oh, I forgot, I was also a natural-born killer. So no matter how hard I tried to escape any of those bad things, it would come back to me full circle; and I would have to choose if I would deal drugs, rob people, steal, or just be a cold-blooded killer. Yeah, I chose none of that bullshit. I am a child of the Most High that was why the devil took extra time to harass me and tell me I would never be shit.

One day as I was sitting out in front of my misery, which was my house —well, my aunt's house anyway—this guy whom I recognized as part of Jason's crew came to me, asking if I was mad that Jason had lied to me about taking me with him. "No, I'm not mad. He's my friend," I told him.

"Well, I am, bro. I been with mu'fucker for a while, man. He fed us that bull. He fed you by talking 'bout taking us with him and shit. Pssst, whatever yo," he said, pacing back and forth like some type of caged beast ready to launch at anything that came close enough to it. "I don't why you ain't mad 'cause if you never hooked him up with Tone, he wouldn't be shit. He'd be just like us. By the way, whatcha do to be so tight with Tone anyway? You saved his life and shit, right?" He smacked and chewed on gum he did not have in his mouth, now seriously starting to get on my last good nerve with his antics. "Man, if you wuz my boy and hooked me up with Tone like you did for Jay, man, ain't shit you want I won't get for you, like shoes, clothes, hoes, yo, whatever I got 'cause you saved Tone's life, right?" He was still smacking on his invisible gum.

"Nah, didn't save his life. They just saying that because he's always been nice to me," I told him.

"Oh, okay, but look, on the real, just hook me up with Tone like you did to Jay, man, and we both get paid, awight?" he said, moving in close to me and whispering like he had some highly important secret message. I just said okay so he could get the hell away from me with his stinky breath and clothes. It was as if somebody went to the cemetery and dug a month-old corpse, took the clothes off its body, and put it on him with the bodily fluids still saturated in the clothes for a month. "So don't forget, man. I think dude home, right? Oh yeah, my name is Li'l Red, awight? He home." He pointed at Antonio's door.

"Yeah, I'm not doing it right now 'cause someone may be watching and want me to do it for them too, so I'll wait until tomorrow and then do it all," I told him just so he would get the hell away from me.

"Oh, you right. Damn, you smart. Now I see why Jay liked you and was always bragging about you, but oh yeah, don't forget my name. It's Li'l Red, awight? Cool. Later," Li'l Red said before finally leaving. There was just something about that asshole I did not like, and it had nothing to do with his personal hygiene. Jason introduced us about a year ago, and the thing I could not stand about him was how he was always moving around and scratching himself, which I saw why now. It was probably because he never took a shower. He also would never look you in the eye. When most people have a conversation, they speak facing you and look in your eyes occasionally. But the simple moron would have a conversation with his back to you, and he could never answer a direct question; he would try to lead you in a whole different direction. I did not trust people like that. I may have been young at these times, but I had come to learn a lot of things, and one of those was how to read people, which meant knowing who to trust. I did not trust that motherfucker, and I had made my reasons and feelings known to Jason, but he never put too much trust in that.

When Jason started to do his thing in the drug game, he used to give his mother her drugs so she could stay home more; but as time went by, he saw that all he was doing was making the situation worse. Plus, it was getting expensive. If his mother were a customer, Jason would have probably been the highest earner in the game. As his brother and his sister were getting older, they began to understand what was going on with their mom. Jason realized it was setting a bad example, so he stopped supporting her habit by not giving her any more drugs. So once again, she was on the streets, doing whatever was necessary to get her drugs. This time, Jason could control the problem, even though it was no longer in his house, because he had the ear of the big man in the hood. So he was able to get the word out that no one— absolutely no one—was to sell a thing to Jason's mom, not even Tylenol, even if she was complaining of a headache. Everyone who was dealing respected that law, and when they saw her, they were always turning her away so she could do nothing.

Li'l Red was selling her stuff unbeknownst to Jason and everyone else, but as I have said previously, nothing in the hood stays a secret for long. A friend in common found out and informed Jason, who of course was angry as hell, resulting in a fistfight, where Jason beat the living daylights out of Li'l Red. There had even been rumors about Jason's mom sucking Li'l Red's dick for some crack, and I really hoped that this did not happen. Before getting on drugs, Jason's mom was like a mom to Li'l Red when he had no one he could count on, and he was like another one of her children.

After the rumors started flying, the next time I saw Li'l Red, he was in a really bad condition. His eyes were bloodshot, and the other one was swollen shut. He was covered in bruises, scratches, and scrapes; it looked like someone got deep in his ass. I had asked Jason what happened, but he told me he did not know, but he should know like anyone else in the hood. They were saying that Jason had gone after Red, along with a few of the other guys from his crew, to ask about the rumors. It finally came out, after a few times of Jason asking with his fist and feet, that Red had embellished those stories to get Jason's attention because he felt jealous that Jason had been making all these moves without him.

I had always felt something about Li'l Red but had respected Jason's relationship with him. Jealous people can be very dangerous. After all, it was not like they were father and son or whatever; they were both men. Instead of being jealous of your brother, be happy for his fortune and let that be your motivation to do the same or be better. And if you don't know how, then ask for help. But this nigga, Red, was more on some Cain-and-Abel shit.

Even though Jason and I had not seen each other in a while, I would always ask about him when I saw a few of the guys who were common associates of ours or when I saw Antonio. Even he was hard to catch up with these days, but he had left the bald guy in charge; he was whom I got my package and money from. Working with him proved me wrong in that he was a pretty nice guy, even more so than Antonio, but that was only for people he liked. After all, he was in the drug game, which called for violence, and I have seen him get medieval on a few people once, reminding me to never get on his bad side.

While getting my package one day, he brought me outside to the ice cream truck, and I told him I did not want anything from the truck and that I did not want to be anywhere near it. The last time I was by that damn truck, it had brought me so many nightmares that I hated ice cream, and I had not eaten any of it since. But the big bald guy begged me to go with him, saying he needed me to go just in case his girl saw him out there. He could blame me for him being there, telling his girl that I wanted ice cream and that I had begged him to get me one because I had no money. I was still really not interested in his offer, so he did something I had never seen him do before or since then. He got on one knee so we could be eye level, and he said, "I know what happened here before, but you're with me now, and ain't nothing like that is ever gonna happen to you again as long as I'm out here." And then he smiled at me, got up, and told me his name was Cue because he was good at playing pool. I thought it was for his bald head.

Standing by the ice cream truck, I was anxious. I was paranoid that, at any moment now, all hell was going to break loose with gunfire, but it stayed quiet and calm. We made our purchase, and Cue had grabbed a bunch of candies, twenty popsicles, and twenty bags of chips. I thought, *No wonder he's fat with a big belly, eating all of that.* But to my surprise, he passed all of them out to the kids who had no money for ice cream and did not keep a thing for himself. I was so shocked at his act of kindness that I offered him one of my strawberry shortcakes.

"For me?" he asked, and I nodded yes as I looked up at him with a smile on my face.

Then I heard a voice say, "I bet I will not see that in your mouth." I turned to see who the voice belonged to, and I was instantly smitten when I saw this beautiful lady standing there in an all-white short set from Cross Colours with white sandals. She had a beautiful caramel complexion with big hoop earrings that had her name spelled out in them. She also had a necklace with her name, Kiesha, written on them. Behind her were two more ladies, one with a chocolate complexion in a Red Cross color outfit and the other with a lighter skin who was Puerto Rican. All three of them looked as if they had just stepped out of a *Jet* photo shoot. I was speechless, not that I talked much.

"Nah, of course not, baby. My man here was just being nice, trying to share," Cue told his gal.

Kiesha looked at me and said, "So what's your name, cutie?" I was speechless and started blushing. After always being put down and cursed out, you won't know how to reply to compliments. "So you not talking to me. You don't think I'm pretty?" Kiesha asked, and I just shook my head. "So you do think I'm pretty?" I nodded yes.

"This is my man, Shawn, and we just out here chillin'. Do you need something?" Cue asked Kiesha.

"You know I do. Me and da girls want to go out, but we need to go shopping." Kiesha was now pouting and now all over Cue. With that, he went into his pocket and pulled out a stash of cash bigger than the one I had gotten from the guy Cue had up off the ground for insulting me. Cue handed her the money, and she kissed him. Then she came over to me and kissed me. Oh my god, I thought I could fly. I felt ten feet tall, and the smell of her perfume remained with me until today. "Bye, cutie. Oh, by the way, keep an eye on him for me, okay?" Kiesha told me as she walked away, winking at me.

When she was gone, I asked Cue, "That's your girlfriend? Man, she's fine." I could not believe that it was possible for a man who looked like Cue to have a girl that fine; it just did not match or make sense. When he first told me about his girlfriend, that was not what entered my mind. I pictured a big, bloated lady who ate all the time and was ugly. But now seeing that was not the case, it made me believe I could get any woman I chose, and Diane Harper was going to be mine.

"Yo, I saw you checking my girl out. If you try to take her, I'm gonna have to give you one of these. Here," Cue said, holding his fist to his eye, twisting it, and then pounding it in his other hand.

"And I'm gonna do this," I said, swinging upward with my fist and making a pow sound with my mouth.

Cue yelled, "Ooh, he got me!" I kept on hitting him, and he pretended as if I was really hurting him. I wrestled with him, and he picked me up, and for the first time, I heard him laugh, making him not as scary as I had thought. Now my view of him had changed dramatically, and I liked this guy Cue, who had given me the chance to really see his many dimensions.

After our wrestling match, Cue thanked me for going with him to get ice cream, so we walked back toward Antonio's apartment, where Cue had now been at since Antonio was wherever he was. When we reached the doorstep, he handed me a stack of hundreds. I never even looked at it twice. I quickly put in my pocket in case my aunt was somehow spying on me from a nearby window since we lived not too far from where we were now standing. I thanked Cue and turned to go home. I did not turn around again to see if he was still standing there, which I would normally do because I trusted no one, but I felt he was still there watching to make sure I got in my house safely. If only Cue had known that it was not the things and people outside that he should be concerned with. It was the elements inside my house that were now my concern as it had always been, and it would remain that way unless I made some changes.

I walked in the apartment with my stomach now turning. The pain hit so hard that I actually fell to the ground and then balled up. It was as if someone made me swallow razor blades and then made me drink. I had always been able to deal with the pain; today, however, was different, and I must have reached my breaking point. There was something different about this pain. No matter how bad my stomach was hurting, the one thing I knew

better than anything was I needed to get off my aunt's floor quick, or she would do it for me. I managed to get up on one knee, and that was when I heard the voice that brought true fear in my heart and made the blood in my veins ice cold. "What are you doing?" she asked me in a rather calm tone instead of the loud, angry, hate-filled one I had become accustomed to hearing.

"My stomach hurts, Auntie, and I fell down," I told her, staring at the ground so as to not make the mistake of looking her in the eyes.

"Well then, get up and go lie down in the dining room," my aunt said. I could not believe it. There was no slapping or hitting, not even a "get the fuck out of here, you dumb ass." This was not the usual response I would normally receive, but I was not the one to look a gift horse in the mouth.

I got up to go lie down on the couch in the dining room, which had served as my and my brother's bed for those years he was alive, but it was mine alone now. Even though my brother had passed away almost two years ago, it seemed like only yesterday, and being on that couch was creepy for me. On certain occasions at night, I would still cry myself to sleep for my brother as well as because of fear since I still saw the figures of skeletal people standing behind the thin, see-through curtains hanging in the dining room. I also cried because I still had the feeling that I would die like my brother had. I don't know the person who said that time heals all wounds, but my wound have still not healed, especially when I am thinking of Samuel; the floodgates open, and I still cry.

It was only after I saw my cousins sitting on the couch nicely dressed that I figured that they must be going somewhere. I was too scared to look in my aunt's direction to see if there was a reason for the outfit and to see if she was dressed too, but I thought she would be. I was surprised that she was not stretched out on her couch like she did every time she was pregnant, especially now when she was five months with child. I was not happy about this baby coming since I knew it was up to me to raise this child by myself, with Samuel not being here to help me anymore. Samuel and I raised the first one of our cousins, and before she was even two years old, the next one was born, which we started out raising together before he was killed, leaving me to do it alone. I hardly had any sleep. During the nights, I had to boil water to warm up the bottles I had made up previously. The baby woke up three to four times a night, and this did not include diaper changes. My aunt used to leave us at home alone with these babies almost as soon as my uncle left for work, which was just about every night. We had no idea how in the hell to take care of any babies. Shit, we were babies ourselves. Now I was about to go through this process all over again alone.

As I pondered what was about to take place with my aunt and her children, wondering where they may be going, my uncle burst in through the door, with sweat dripping from his forehead from the summer heat. He asked my aunt if she was ready to go, and with an answer of yes, she ordered me to get the hell up, grab the bags, and put them in the car. With those few words, my brief seconds of convalescence from my stomach pain were over, and her voice and words seemed to go straight through my stomach like a knife, causing my pain to increase to a thousand brought on by fear. Just her presence was able to weaken my body, causing trembling and my knees to become Jell-O. I was just weak with fear. This is the only way I can really describe it at best, but the real way it felt could never be described and a trillion times worse.

I quickly got off the couch, still in terrible pain, and carried out my aunt's bags to the work car my uncle had brought home. I was pleasantly surprised to see a Porsche 944. As I put the bags in the car, two kids I went to school with saw me and were impressed that I was getting in this dream car. "Wow, is that yours?" they asked, astonished. The shabbily dressed kid who went to school with them and never spoke to anyone, the same kid they had made fun of from time to time was now right here getting in a Porsche.

"Yeah," I told them, shaking my head.

"Cool, man. See you at school, okay?" they said, waving and running. I waited until they were out of sight before I started smiling from ear to ear, giving me renewed strength to go back in the house to bring out my cousins to the car.

My uncle asked my aunt if she had cooked something or left some food for me while they were gone, and of course, she had not, making my uncle very upset, asking her why when she knew they were going to be gone all day. "What do you want him to do for food?" He was so angry that he went in the kitchen and began to cook.

The familiar voice of my aunt came out, the voice and tone that usually sent the fear in me and started the issues in my abdomen. Just that was enough to make me start to feel sick. Even her footsteps were enough to give me jitters. It was a horrible existence being scared all the time. It was like trying to walk on eggshells without breaking one.

"What are you doing? We have to leave," my aunt told my uncle now angry.

"This would not have to be if you had done this already. What do you expect the boy would eat while we're gone?" my uncle asked his wife. "Besides, this won't take long." He finished the seafood gravy he was cooking. My uncle was a great cook. There was nothing he had ever made that we did not like. I guess that was why my aunt was so healthy (wink, wink).

When he was done, he went in the refrigerator to point to the famous, one-of-a-kind Philly cheesesteaks he had made the night before.

He had brought seven of them, but there were only three left because my aunt had inhaled four of them already. I told you she was healthy. My uncle told me I could have them, which was a rare treat for me. When she heard that, my aunt came in to tell my uncle that I did not need all of that for just one day. "We're gonna be gone for a while. Besides, if he does not finish it, then he does not finish it. Who cares? Now let's go," my uncle told her. She lingered by the refrigerator, picked up the cheesesteaks like she was going to take them with her, and quickly replaced them when he approached to retrieve her. As they left, the look she gave me was enough to stop my heart from beating.

I escorted them outside. I still had to carry both of my cousins to the car and put them inside. I was nothing but a personal servant to my aunt and her children, but at least they still had me and had not gotten rid of me yet, so that was better than nothing. I stood out there waving like an idiot until they were out of sight. Finally, I could breathe a sigh of relief, knowing I was going to be free for a whole day with no worries or hassles.

I walked back to the house and lie on one of the couches in the living room, something I would not do under any other circumstances unless I wanted to shorten my existence on this planet. I turned on the television and started watching a movie called *Hank*, which my brother had woken me up to watch one night. Samuel was daring like that. Whenever he was sure everyone was dead asleep, he would turn the television for a few minutes or so. To make sure no one heard it, he put it on a very low volume. Then he would wake me up, or I would wake up on my own. When we did things

like that, we would watch things we knew we were not supposed to watch, like the Playboy channel. I guess that was our way of fighting back and a way of maintaining a bit of our childhood we never had. I think I'm starting to know how Michael Jackson felt, but I'm not buying any monkeys.

Around midnight, I kept running to the window, checking the parking lot to see if my aunt and uncle had arrived. And every time I heard a noise, I freaked out and turned off the TV, running to the window to see if it was them, but it never was. My senses were so sharp those days that it was ridiculous. It had to be because God helped me. If my aunt was to call and got no answer, you would pay with your ass.

It was now two o'clock in the morning, and I was sure that my aunt and uncle were not going to be home until the next day because they had done it before. And even though they never informed where they were going or when they would return, I was sure they gone to the hotel my uncle worked at, like they had done the last time. It was so hot that there had been a citywide warning for everyone to stay inside. There were even mobile pools that come through the poor neighborhoods for a set amount of time. They also had a truck to pass out water to the poor and unfortunate, which I was, and so they stopped by, but I did not go outside. However, I did hear kids out hollering and screaming.

Now that I was sure I was going to be home alone, I felt at ease a little bit, and I was able to finally eat something now that my stomach had stopped doing flips. The meal my uncle had prepared for me was out of this world; it was so unbelievable that I told myself I was going to eat the whole thing, including the cheesesteaks, just to piss my aunt off and see the look on her face when she returned from her little vacation. I knew I would pay for it one way or another, but it was not like I got a bunch of these at any other time, so come what may, I was going to enjoy it. I went to the refrigerator, which was a first in almost forever, and grabbed one of my uncle's famous Philly cheesesteaks to warm it up. I had only had one of these before, and I remember it being so good that my mouth began to salivate in anticipation of tasting that wonderful sandwich. Now the smell of it warming up filled the air, and then it was finally time for me to bite in.

Suddenly, the night was filled with arguing, yelling, and then gunshots, causing me to hit the floor, taking my sandwich with me. I saw that living in any hood would prepare anyone for military service. I slowly got off the floor, heading to the kitchen window in the back of the apartment, facing the parking lot, where the shots had come from and where the arguing was still heard. When I got to the window, I saw a group of young men arguing. Then all of a sudden, they started with three of the other guys who were just standing with them before they took off running, being pursued by the other guys. Before I knew it, there were gunshots again. I tried to see if they were any of the guys I knew—like Jason, Cue, or Antonio—hoping that it was not any of them. As the group ran, I dashed to the front windows in the living room to try to catch a glimpse of them so I could rule out that it was not any of my people, but all I saw were their backs, not able to identify any one of them. I wanted to open my door after a few minutes had gone by, and I started to hear people starting to gather outside, inquiring what had just taken place, but I decided not to, especially after hearing those gunshots.

Since it was late and I was enjoying my night alone, I decided to be nosy. One night when my uncle had arrived home, he came over to where I was lying down, making absolutely sure I was asleep, which I was not because I was never that comfortable in that house to fall into a deep sleep. Besides, like I said before, my senses have always been tip-top. Anyway, after he made sure I was asleep, I opened one eye, and I saw him place something inside this old record player, so I decided to see what it might be.

I ran to the kitchen window once again to check the parking lot for my uncle's car. Because of my paranoia, I did several rechecks. My heart was pounding out of my chest, feeling scared for some reason. I climbed the footstool to get the record player to retrieve whatever it was my uncle had placed up there, afraid that I would be caught. I know you guys are reading this and asking yourself why I was scared to do this if everyone was gone. Well, that was my life living in constant fear. If you have never experienced it, it was like going to war or something. I could never really explain it enough for you. So I climbed up the footstool and lifted the record player, and there was a letter from my father addressed to me. As a matter of fact, there were a few of them. Some of them were addressed to both my brother and me, and some were addressed to us individually. I brought them down to sit down and begin reading, reminding me of a scene out of the movie *The Color Purple* when Celie found letters from her sister.

I had read through some of the letters with my father saying how he was and that he could talk to us but could not. He also said that he had not sent us any money because, if he did, he would have to convert it from Liberian money to the American dollar. That made no sense to me because Liberia was just a smaller version of the United States, only in Africa, and they used the dollar. Then he talked about my brother's death, which I did not fully read because I would start hurting and the tears would come pouring, reopening my wound, which had not healed at all yet. In the other letters, he talked about the Liberian war and how he and his girlfriend had to walk forever to try to escape the senseless killings going on. Innocent people were tortured and killed right in front of the American Embassy as the U.S. Marines did beer runs. After all, these were not human beings, just savage niggers killing one another and destroying their own home, which of course they could never rebuild again, so there was no need for the international community to do anything unless white people were dying.

The letters my dad had written was from years earlier to the present, so they covered a wide variety of issues. My dad even wrote a letter to my uncle about how he was now ready to take care of his responsibilities, which I guess was me. I guess I was supposed to be put up on a shelf, not growing or anything. He saw himself fit to reclaim me. Hooray for me. He then said how his elder brother had wanted him to stay in Nigeria to do some type of business that would have made him a lot of money, but he could not because of me since I was his only child with no guardian; the other kids at least had their mothers there for them. My father then ended his letter by saying he was in Atlanta, Georgia, and would be coming down to New Jersey to reclaim me, I guess. I put the letters back in that record player, making sure it was done exactly the way it was, ensuring that I did not even move any dust.

The letters made me feel a lot of different emotions. Even if he had been writing us, it did not matter to me because my brother was dead, which was not anybody's fault, but he did leave us in that hellhole. After all, he had children in the United States to take care of, and gathering us once in a blue moon for a week or so was not being a parent. I was still angry at my dad.

One thing in that letter reminded me to count the money Cue had given me, so I went to my secret stash to begin counting my money, and for the first time, I got the idea to just take the money I had and run. After all, I thought I was rich. So I went to grab my book bag and started putting in my few things, especially all the awards and scholastic paperwork I had been keeping for all those years, which my aunt did not care about. When I was finished packing up, which did not take a lot of time since I did not have much, I sat down to think all things over. I decided I would wait for a while, make some more money, and then leave. So I put back all my money in the hiding places, making sure I hid it better this time. I made a rip in the bottom of my couch in the dining room, which was really my bed, and hid all my money inside, and then I sewed it back up. I knew very well that no one was going to move that because it has been there over three years. The legs on it were broken, and nobody had ever attempted to fix it or do anything with it, especially since it was only a place that my brother and I used.

When I was done with replacing my money in a different place, I went back to my sandwich and my movie, but it was hard for me to concentrate on anything except the letters I had just read. The words my father wrote made me angry because they were nothing but excuses on why he could not do something about us and why it was not possible. I don't know about you guys, but I would be where my children are no matter what, and God forbid the day if I had a child who was living with someone else. I would make sure to see my child every day so that he would know me and I would know him.

The next morning, I woke up to find out I was still on my own, something I enjoyed. It was and would always be part of my life, and I think I had already made peace with it, so I was and would be fine with it. I then I got up to get ready for school. Since my aunt was not home, I decided to wear the Reebok that Jason had given me. I was supposed to give it back to him when my aunt found it. It looked as if it might rain, so I grabbed my old sneakers just in case I needed to change.

The last time my aunt and uncle had gone on their little vacation, they were gone for almost two days, so I figured and hoped they would do the same this time as well. My stomach had not hurt the whole time since she left that night. I started to associate my abdominal pains with her presence until I had a really bad episode this morning. Then I knew there was an even worse thing going on.

When I was dressed and ready for school, I stepped into a dark morning because of all the rain clouds, and wind was blowing so hard that it pushed me back a few feet. I was so happy for this type of weather because this was my favorite. Stepping out again after being blown back a few steps, I noticed two of my classmates waiting for me, which was a first. I immediately noticed that they were the two who saw me putting the bags in my uncle's Porsche and had asked me if the car was mine, to which I told them yes. "You want to walk?" one of the boys asked me. I nodded yes as I walked down to meet them.

"Man, those are some nice shoes, Shawn," the other boy said.

"Thank you," I said, looking down at my shoes. I felt so good that I had my shoes on and that they were not making fun of them or my clothes. I had made two more friends all because of a car.

"Where did you get those shoes?" the boy asked again, and I told him Foot Locker, not wanting them to know someone had given it to me. I continued walking with the two boys as they asked me questions about the Porsche. I even told them that my uncle had given me a key to it, telling me when I was old enough to drive, he would give me the car. Then I pulled out some car key I had found a long time ago and told them that was the Porsche key, and they were so impressed. I never worried about them knowing it was some other key because, like me, they lived in the projects, and that was probably their first time seeing a Porsche.

Another one of my new friends with one more kid they knew joined us, and they started to tell him I was the kid with the Porsche. They told him the same bullshit I had told them about my uncle giving me the car when I was old enough to drive or learned how to drive. They even had me show they key to my soon-to-be Porsche. The new kid was also impressed, asking if I would give them rides to go to the mall, chasing and fucking girls who would want us because no one else in the hood would have a car like us. *Us? There ain't no us, muthafucka*, I thought. Until a few days ago, I did not even know the car I was putting the bags in was even a Porsche. And not too long ago, these guys were making fun of me, and now we were buddies. *Yo ain't riding in fuckin' car.* I was now lying to myself, believing my own stories.

We were almost at school when the new kid who had just joined us said something sobering. It took me out of my car daydream. "You know the kid Jason, right?" he said, now gaining my full attention, knowing that there had been a shooting and other different types of riots going on. "I heard that he got smoked last night on that corner." He pointed in the direction that there was a shooting. It was at that moment it became really hard to breathe. I felt light-headed and those horrible feelings that surfaced with my brother's passing. I did not want to believe that my brother Jason was taken away from me. Who else did I know would be leaving my life? I had already lost my best friend and brother, Samuel, who was the world for me, and now Jason. I did not want the others to see me cry, so I convinced the other guys that he was still alive and that I saw him the night before when he came over to watch a movie. I knew I was lying, but it was a coping mechanism to keep from crying, something I did regularly. News traveled fast in the hood, and that was nothing to play about.

"How do we know?" I asked to see if he was lying to us, and I hoped and wanted him to be lying. But when he said that after the shooting he ran into Antonio to give him his money because he also, like Jason, was working for him, that was when I started believing him, still wanting him to be wrong.

"Yo, if you don't believe me, then ask your boy," he told me, pointing to Antonio, who was driving down. I told myself I would stop him and ask, but I did not want to find out that he was truly deceased, so I just let him drive by us. He waved to us as he drove by. I had not seen him in a while. I did not know whether he was the one in the car that had just went by because it was not one of his, and this one was a Land Rover.

That whole day, I was depressed as more of the kids started to talk about the incident. These kids lived in my neighborhood, and as I have told you already, nothing stays a secret for long in the hood. As the day went on, I had more of a feeling that it was really true that my friend had passed over something very stupid. The fact that not one person had made fun of me did not matter to me right then. I was trying to find out from Antonio or Cue. I knew, out of all the gossip, they would know what happened and where.

At three o'clock on the dot, I darted out of the classroom when our teacher dismissed us for the day. Usually, I was the last person out of the class because I hated being in my home with my aunt. Today, however, I wanted to leave to go see if my friend and brother was really dead, something I was hoping did not happen. I started to have my stomach pains again when those brown brick buildings were in sight. I began looking for my uncle's car, hoping that it was not there, but I also knew just because the car was not around did not mean that my aunt was not home. My uncle could have just dropped them off and left.

I now hurried up to take a peek around the corner to see if my aunt was home without her seeing me. If she was to put her eyes on me, I would have been ordered to get in the house. I ran around the back of the apartments, making sure my aunt did not see me if she was at home. When I got around the front of my house, I quickly hid in some bushes to see if the door was open, which was something my aunt did on very hot days, including turning the fan on, which was only pointed toward her and her kids, to stay cool because we did not have an air conditioner. I saw the door was closed, so I got up to put down my book bag where she could see it so when they came home without me, I could tell her I was in the bathroom the whole time, and she would not check anyway.

After putting down my book bag to go over to Antonio's house and stepping outside, once again, I saw more rain clouds that were very dark, like at any minute now they would burst open, pouring out their water. I went over to Antonio's house, and I knocked. I heard music and inaudible voices coming from his apartment that was getting even louder while I sat outside waiting for someone to answer. I knocked once more, telling myself it would not be long before the door was open. I heard footsteps, and then someone was heard releasing the main locks and chains that were put to stop any intruder. Now that was a pile of bullshit because I have seen the same locks, dead bolts, and other protective measures being pulled apart by a thief or a hoodlum desperate to get in the house.

When the door opened, it was Cue at the door. "Get in here quick," he said, breathing hard. I entered to see Antonio and some of the kids working for him. I asked him if it was it true that Jason was really dead, hoping Jason would soon show up. Without looking at me, Antonio nodded yes, and I began to cry. "What happened? Where is he?" I asked Antonio, mad that my friend was gone. I left his house. After all, if it had not been for Antonio, Jason would not have become a big-time drug dealer so he could take care of his family. He also wanted to be like Antonio, making all that money.

After composing myself, I went to Antonio to see what happened and how he was killed. Antonio told me that they were up in his house to get out of the heat. "All I know is what they told me," he said. Antonio explained that Jason and his crew were in Jason's house to escape the scorching heat. While in the house, they ate some ice cream, pizza, and more ice cream. While inside, they started to play a card game for money. While playing, one of the crew members accused another of cheating, so they began to argue over the game because there was a lot of money to be won. Before long, fists started to fly. Jason was angry with both of the guys fighting but even angrier at the accuser. It turned out that the crew member who started the fight was the same one whom I did not trust.

Later that evening, after the sun went down, Jason's crew came over to hang out on their corner and do their thing, which included making a lot of money, telling stories, and talking to girls. It seemed the two crew members who had fought earlier were now friends, playing another game called craps, where they rolled a dice to see if they could repeat the certain number or match them to their opponents' numbers, when another argument arose. The same guy Jason had beaten up for saying Jason's mom had sucked his dick for crack, who was Li'l Red, had once again said he was cheated by the same crew member. Angry and tired of all the accusations, fists started to fly, but Jason put an end to the fight, turned around, and punched his friend for starting this fight. When he was done beating him, Jason told him to never come back again.

Later that night, Li'l Red showed up at Jason's door to apologize for his behavior, assuring that nothing like that would ever happen again. He also told Jason he had no place to go and got on his knees, begging Jason to forgive him, telling him that Jason was the only family he had. So once again, Jason let him back into the fold. That was the kind of person Jason was; he had a big heart. If he loved you, there was nothing he would not do for you; but if he hated you, watch out.

Jason letting his friend back into his crew came with a bunch of stipulations, which included Li'l Red getting on drugs, something he thought Jason did not know; he was told to sell it but not use it. According to Jason, that guy became his own best customer. Another stipulation was he had to apologize to Jason's family for lying about Jason's mom sucking his dick. The third order was he had to show that he could stand on his own before moving in with Jason's family. The last thing he had to do was to pay back the fifty thousand dollars he had borrowed from Jason.

It came out that Jason's friend was an addict, selling the substance he was hooked on, and had run up a pretty hefty tab he owed to his supplier. If he did not pay it, his light would be put out permanently. To save his friend, Jason paid the bill off on condition that Li'l Red pay him back, and all the parties involved agreed, but that was over two years before. I never understood how a drug dealer like him never had money, and he would never offer to pay for anything. Li'l Red was the last person you would depend on, but Jason still kept him as his friend.

There was one secret Li'l Red did not want anybody to find out, especially Jason. It came out that Li'l Red's drug addiction was so serious that he owed other rival drug crews so much money that they put the word out for his head. Instead of asking Jason for help, he instead went and got a kilo of cocaine to settle his debt but only paid back half the money. His degree of drug use had gotten so bad that he had used a great deal of his product. This guy just kept on digging his own grave; it was getting deeper and deeper by then, trying to make the money back by gambling. That was the reason why he started a fight, accusing the other guys of cheating. Antonio had to kick him out of his house.

Li'l Red was seen walking the neighborhood, talking to himself. Then he went to Antonio's house to hang out because this guy did not really have a place of his own. With all the money he had, Li'l Red did not even have a car but have new shoes and clothes and thick new gold necklace. But every time Jason asked for his money, he always came up with a story of why he did not have any. The tensions between Li'l Red and Jason became so thick that you could feel the static in the air. The two friends got into an all-out brawl while at the mall, adding more shoes to their collection. That was just unbelievable. They had some shoes you could not find anywhere; that was how expensive they were, and they had so many shoes that some of them were forgotten and left in their individual boxes.

While at the mall one day, Jason happened to buy shoes for Li'l Red on condition that he pay him back; instead Li'l Red was always crying broke. If he really was, Jason would have bought those shoes for free, but Jason was well aware that Li'l Red had money because he was his boss who knew how much made. He wanted to see how far Li'l Red would take this lie, knowing he owed him money. So their friendship came to a head one day when Li'l Red was spotted in the mall spending a grand at a time on his girl and her friend. Then Jason's crew member called him from one of their car phones, telling him to come down to the mall, and they went back to keep an eye on Li'l Red. Jason arrived in no time, since he was on his way to the mall anyway, and went to where the rest of his crew were spying on Li'l Red. As soon as they took him to see for himself, there was Li'l Red spending a lot of money on some tricks instead of paying his debt. When he had seen enough, he left the mall without being noticed.

The next day when they met up, Jason once again asked for his money and got nothing in return but more excuses, so Jason played his ace card, revealing that he had seen Li'l Red at the mall spending all his money. Li'l Red had an excuse ready for that too; he denied ever being at the mall and then changed his story. He said his brother was at the mall, and he must have been who they saw. Now it was true he did have a brother, who was also a drug dealer and on the same crew, but he was nothing like him. Besides looking alike, they had nothing in common. And it just so happened that it was his brother who had called Jason and reported on him, leaving him without an escape route. Li'l Red finally told Jason, "You're making all this dough, and you ain't sharing, bruh."

"Man, what the fuck? Out of everyone here, you've had the most chances to succeed, but you too busy getting high," Jason told Li'l Red in an angry voice as he moved closer with his fist now clenched, looking as though he was about to knock him into the following week.

Before all the animosity, money, and women, Li'l Red used to be a true hustler in making money, dreaming that one day he and Jason would be the top men in this business. But when Jason started to climb faster than him, jealousy started. The more money Jason made, the more others felt that he was obligated to them, but Li'l Red felt he should do more for him. The one thing that everyone liked about his crew was they made money and that there was more to go around. But the more money Li'l Red made, the more he got deeper into his addiction, partying, and women.

"Man, where the fuck is my money?" Jason asked again without getting a reply. "I'm going to count to three, and when I'm done, I better have money in my hand." Jason held out his hand as he started to count, and when he finished counting, he asked for his money again but go nothing because he was not being taken seriously, which was a big mistake. The next thing we saw was Li'l Red falling back, with Jason right on top of him. Jason's hands were so fast that we never saw him throwing punches. The fight lasted a few minutes only, and since Li'l Red's brother did get along with him, he never tried to stop Jason. Li'l Red had always been a bully to his younger brother and anyone who was weaker than him. It became a little bit of a payback. While still on the ground, Jason removed all his jewelry and money as interest, but Li'l Red owed eighty-five thousand.

The night after being kicked out of Jason's house for accusing others of cheating, Li'l Red lost the rest of the money on craps. He thought about robbing everyone at the crap game, as well as the card game. It would have been more than enough to settle all his debt, but he knew if Jason was around, he would try to put a stop to it. Then he would have to kill him because if he was left alive, Li'l Red would have to be on the run, constantly checking over his shoulders, so he decided to wait. That whole night, he was seen walking the neighborhood, pacing and talking to himself.

Li'l Red's opportunity came when he saw a guy win the card and craps game. Li'l Red figured he would have the money on him on the way to his house. Plus, he would definitely be alone, giving him the upper hand in surprise attacks. His plan soon fell apart when he saw Jason, Antonio, and Cue all come out of the house together, heading over to Antonio's house, where they hung out for a few more hours. At around two, Li'l Red was now freezing as he waited in the cold, his teeth chattering uncontrollably. Right when he was about to quit, he thought what would happen to him if he did not get the money he owed; he would become permanently frozen.

Then finally, at about three o'clock in the morning, his target came but ran back in the house. That was when Li'l Red got really paranoid, and the drugs just enhanced his paranoia, with him now thinking, *Did I get seen? Did he smell me? I bet he could hear me talking.* Not knowing what to do next, Li'l Red ran around the corner just in case they came looking for him in the hiding spot he was just in. If he was not drugged up and paranoid and without voices talking to him, Li'l Red might have heard Jason call the guy he was out to rob, and he would have been there to see that Jason was so drunk that he had to be put on the passenger side of the car of Li'l Red's target, whom I would name Mark.

Ten minutes later, Li'l Red returned to see Mark's car and him sitting in it, but he did not see Jason, who had the passenger's seat, lying flat on his back. Seizing his chance to act, Li'l Red opened fire with a submachine gun, instantly killing Jason. Because the shooting came from the passenger side, the bullet hit him in his head, throwing blood, brain matter, and skull on the scene, which was disgusting. Knowing that no cops were coming for about thirty minutes or so, he took his time, being very deliberate. That was when the driver's door opened, instantly getting Li'l Red's attention, so he walked over to Mark and started removing money, jewelry, and drugs. Then he turned to look in the car for money. He did find more but did not see Jason lying there until he turned on the interior lights. Li'l Red started yelling, crying that his friend was gone, asking him to come back, and saying he was so sorry. That still did not stop him from taking all of Jason's money.

Upon hearing the shots, Antonio, Cue, and the others in the house went out to investigate the shooting and saw someone by the car that belonged to Mark, and the fight was after they saw Mark's hand on the ground. Li'l Red took off running, so Antonio ordered his people to go after him, not knowing it was him in the first place. Antonio and Cue went over to the car, where Mark was barely hanging on, and Antonio told him to hold on. Cue went to search the car after not seeing Jason around, but he knew that he was with Mark. That was when he saw him lying down in the car. "Shit!" Cue yelled out, now arousing Antonio's attention.

"What is it?" Antonio asked. Cue finally informed him Jason was dead. Not believing what he was just told, Antonio asked his question but got no response in return, so he got up to take a look at whatever it was Cue was looking at. That was when he saw Jason's lifeless body. Cue and Antonio decided to get him out of the car. They walked around to the passenger side of the car to open the door, and Jason's skull rolled out, leaving blood and brain on the sidewalk. When they were certain Jason was dead, they put Mark back in the car, heading to the closest hospital because waiting for an ambulance would mean two people dying instead of one.

The other crew members, including his brother, had caught up with Li'l Red, who was now acting out and crying. He was cornered by his pursuers, and that was the time I heard people outside my window arguing. Then when I looked out the window, the brawl started, followed by the foot chase, with his own crew now shooting at him. Now was unclear on what happened after the shooting. I heard that Li'l Red was beaten up and kicked out of the crew for good. That was when I heard that Li'l Red was crying, ranting and raving, saying that he was going to kill himself.

The next day, Li'l Red was still trying to cope with what he had done, as well as trying to get back in the crew, but all he got was a fuck-you and an ass kicking. A week after that, his body was found with several bullet holes in the back of his head; and when anyone spoke of Li'l Red, they called him the bowling ball.

Almost eight months later, Jason's family moved back into their apartment in the hood because, without him, they could not afford that expensive house, especially after his mother went into depression and back to her addiction. Even Antonio, Cue, I, and a few other crew members gave them money to help out, it did not do any good because their mom just smoked it up. So not having a lot of choices, something happened that Jason was trying to prevent. Jason's little brother took his place in the crew, and he proved himself to be a smarter and better dealer than Jason was. He started his rise by doing something Jason had told him a long time ago, and that was to have ten different moneymaking ideas. And if only four were profitable, then you would have money in four ways to rely on.

My depression had gotten so bad. I was only thirteen, and I was already a very capable parent, now raising three kids because my aunt had delivered her last baby, a boy named Mel. I had seen more deaths than most people, and I had lost two close people whom I loved more than words could tell. My stomach pain had gotten worse as well. I did not have a lot of resources, so I did not know what I could do for it. I had to endure it, but I just could not. Even at night when all was quiet and peaceful, I was up in pain or up from nightmares about Samuel and Jason, and it was really wearing me down. The fear of my aunt, along with the abuse, wore me down even faster, so I decided it was time for me to leave and maybe find my father. This was something that needed planning. Even though I knew my aunt was not going to put out an all-points bulletin about my disappearance, that was for sure, I wanted to be absolute certain I had a good head start.

After seeing Antonio and Cue that day, I wanted to tell them goodbye, but I did not want them telling on me. So I made my final drop, collected my last pay, and went home, where my aunt was in one of her foul-ass moods. I would pay dearly for it, but the only difference in this situation was that I knew—or at least I thought I knew—why she was upset at me, and once again, it dealt with food.

The incident took place a day after they returned from their merry vacation. My uncle was about to fix me something to eat because they were going out again without me. I know you are asking why my aunt and uncle were going out so much and leaving me behind. Well, you see, my aunt told my uncle that they should only worry about their families and that I was not part of it. As a matter of fact, that was made clear to me when they had a family portrait made without me.

So as my uncle was about to make me something to eat, which was the only thing my aunt could not get him to stop doing, she had warmed up some stew that had been in the refrigerator for a long while and was now spoiled. I was told to eat, so I started eating it, afraid of what the consequences were going to be if I did not. As I was eating, my uncle came to ask me if that was going to be enough food to last me until they returned. Seeing it as my only escape, I told him that I did not like the stew because it had a weird taste. He tasted it, and sure enough, he spit it out, saying it was spoiled. He threw it away to start making me something else to eat, which pissed off my aunt, which was something awful. I did not have to turn around and look at her to know she was staring at me with an evil look, and if she could, I would be hurt badly. I could feel her stare burning hot in the back of my head, and I knew it was going to bite me in the ass.

My aunt was heavy in witchcraft, and she was able to get my uncle do things he himself was not aware of, but the only good thing was she could not bring him all the way down to her level. So this was the reason my aunt found motivation to punish me. I forgot the reason she gave for my punishment, but I just did not care anymore. I was just ready to get it over with.

That night, the beating I had received made me angry instead of scared, so I sat out on the windowsill while it was raining, and I really loved the rain and how it felt when it hit my wounds. I looked down at my arms and the cuts in them. When I saw the rest of my body, I got angrier. I made sure everyone was now asleep, so I started coughing really loud. Then I turned the television on really loud and turned it off, but nothing happened.

Being sure that everyone was asleep, I grabbed my book bag, which was already packed up; the only thing I had to do was retrieve my money. I went back and sat on the windowsill, trying to persuade myself to run before my aunt found me. Then I heard movement in the back room, and I jumped out on the window. I hit the ground, running like a madman. I did not want to turn around because I could feel my aunt on my heels, and I had to escape.

I made it to the hill that lowered into our parking lot. The rain had stopped, but there were puddles everywhere, and it was a foggy, dark night. The streetlamps did very little to fix that. Now breathing hard, I had made it to the street at last but did not feel at ease, so I decided to run down the street where I could catch a cab, and it would be easier then. I saw a set of headlights, thinking it may be my aunt. Because of my paranoia, I decided to hide in some bushes by the road. But when I saw a sign on the roof, I thought it was a pizza delivery guy. Then I remembered pizza was never delivered here, so I knew it could be a taxi. I stood up from where I was crouching and waved down the taxi. I quickly jumped into the cab.

"Where to kid?" the cabdriver asked in a very deep voice, and without thinking, I told him to bring me to the Amtrak station. The cabdriver was an overweight guy, probably in his mid to late fifties. We did not talk much on the way to my destination. I slouched down in my seat, thinking my aunt may be driving by and spotted me. Everything seemed to have happened so fast that I thought I forgot something mainly my money, so I continuously checked, but it was always there.

When I saw the Amtrak station, I was a bit relieved, but I knew that I was not out of the woods yet, so I ran over to the next available ticket agent to purchase a ticket for the next train, which cost about four hundred dollars. I purchased the ticket and rushed to the train because I only had a few minutes before the door would be closing. I made it and found my seat, and I slouched in my seat, which was very big. Unlike the others on the train, I had no seats in front of me, and mine reclined with an extension for the feet; since they were for adults, I had more than enough room. Room was not my main concern. I was doing backflips in my mind, telling the conductor, *Let's go before she catches me.* I felt as if I were going to explode.

Finally, we were moving, and our tickets were being inspected to make sure everyone on the train was supposed to be there. I was next to get my ticket checked, and it was done rather quickly. "Traveling alone, sir? Where ya headed?" My heart stopped when the conductor started asking me questions. I thought he knew my secret and was about to pull me off the train to be brought back to my aunt, something I refused to let happen, so I calmed myself down and told him I was going to see my father in Atlanta, and it was kind of the truth. "Okay," he said and then told me to just ask him if I needed anything.

We had been traveling for over an hour, and I had a conversation in my head with Samuel. For the first time, I was happy and excited instead of afraid, something I had been my whole life. But now I knew what peace felt like, so I turned to Samuel and Jason to tell them, *We're free, fellas. We are free. My brothers, we are truly free.* I said that over and over again as the train sped on.

To Be Continued

I hope all persons who will read this first book will enjoy it and will be anticipating the release of the second. Because my story is so long, spanning over thirty some years, I decided—well, my friend told me—to make it into two books. Thank you for buying my book.

www.ingramcontent.com/pod-product-compliance
Lightning Source LLC
LaVergne TN
LVHW041907070526
838199LV00051BA/2532